DIASPORA WITHOUT DISPLACEMENT

DIASPORA WITHOUT DISPLACEMENT

CELINA DE SÁ

The Coloniality and Promise of Capoeira in Senegal

DUKE UNIVERSITY PRESS *Durham and London* 2025

Project Editor: Michael Trudeau
Designed by Matthew Tauch
Typeset in Arno Pro and Anybody
by Westchester Publishing Services

Library of Congress Cataloging-in-Publication Data
Names: Sá, Celina de, [date] author.
Title: Diaspora without displacement : the coloniality and promise
of capoeira in Senegal / Celina de Sá.
Other titles: Coloniality and promise of capoeira in Senegal
Description: Durham : Duke University Press, 2025. |
Includes bibliographical references and index.
Identifiers: LCCN 2024057238 (print)
LCCN 2024057239 (ebook)
ISBN 9781478031970 (paperback)
ISBN 9781478028741 (hardcover)
ISBN 9781478060932 (ebook)
Subjects: LCSH: Capoeira (Dance)—Social aspects—Senegal. |
African diaspora. | Race awareness—Senegal. | Black people—
Senegal—Social life and customs. | Ethnology—Senegal.
Classification: LCC GV1796.C145 S225 2025 (print) | LCC
GV1796 .C145 (ebook) | DDC 793.3/19663—dc23/eng/20250210
LC record available at https://lccn.loc.gov/2024057238
LC ebook record available at https://lccn.loc.gov/2024057239

Cover art: Photo by A. Ibrahim Traoré.

To Dona Celina, our past,
and Selah and Yael, our future

As culture becomes less a synonym for performance than its field of work, and as performance complicates our understanding of cultural practice so that we recognize the rehearsed and produced and creative nature of everyday life, perhaps we may be excused for wondering who the artists are, who the ethnographer, the dupe, the closet colonist. Who, ultimately, pulls the theatrical strings? Who is positioned where in this most uncanny, post-modern drama of cultural encounters?
—DIANA TAYLOR, *The Archive and the Repertoire*

All of us are suffering coloniality, it's just that the significant presence of white bodies in South Africa and the United States make it easier to visualize.
—PANASHE CHIGUMADZI, "Why I'm No Longer Talking to Nigerians About Race"

CONTENTS

PREFACE

Capoeira—a combat game developed by enslaved West Central Africans first documented in the late eighteenth century in Brazil—is now an Afro-Brazilian symbol of national pride. It is a multifaceted practice that involves instrumentation, song, community interaction, and a distinctive aesthetic often misunderstood as "dance-fighting."[1] Scholarship about capoeira notes Senegal as the first place where the Afro-Brazilian combat game, developed mostly in the diaspora, actually returned to Africa (Varela 2017), referring to the legendary occasion when Mestre Pastinha (Vicente Ferreira Pastinha) performed with a small crew of students at the First World Festival of Negro Arts (FESMAN) in Dakar in 1966. That is where the story of capoeira in Senegal ended. This book picks up where that story left off, when another visionary, Moctar Ndiaye, saw a little Senegalese boy (who had been adopted by a French woman) throwing his legs in the air on the historic Gorée Island beach. The boy and his mother were on their own personal origins journey, reconnecting him to his roots since he had left Senegal to live with her in France. He had struggled as a racialized child in French society, and his mother was advised by the adoption agency to ground him in his place of origins. He became Moctar's first teacher, and Moctar spent the next two decades of his life spreading the gospel of capoeira, which is widely understood by practitioners to be the quintessential practice of Black liberation.

Moments of diasporic return are imbued with the weight of what they do or do not accomplish. While some have investigated the rupture of the Middle Passage, others have looked to the Atlantic gap less as of a rupture than as a channel that links regions by oceans rather than divides them (Ferreira 2012; Gilroy 1993; Hartman 2006; Wright 2015). Whether existentially rewarding or disappointing for returnees, the African side of return is equally complex and filled with expectation, disappointment, and aspiration that comes to bear on how returns play out. Diasporic connections with the Americas are rich with potential for West Africans without any actual return.

I unpack events such as capoeira roots tourism trips that are widely recognized as diasporic return when Brazilian capoeiristas (and others) visit the African continent. I also move beyond those moments to reveal how West Africans have already been carrying out the mundane work of return over several decades through a process that is nonlinear, fraught, and unpredictable. Almost thirty years after Mestre Pastinha and his students performed a demonstration of capoeira in Dakar, Moctar and the first cohort of Senegalese capoeiristas, who formed a group called Les Messagers du Vent (the Messengers of the Wind) that later became Africa Capoeira–Ilha de Gorée (which they nicknamed Afreecapoeira), visited Brazil early in their passion to learn. Moctar would spend the next two decades building up Senegal as a symbolic home of capoeira open to everyone. He also had to defend it in the face of Brazilian and European neglect, empty promises of support, and even attempts to claim capoeira in Senegal without having invested anything in it. The leaders and active membership also presented unexpected twists, going from predominantly Senegalese participation to almost no Senegalese and an influx of West African non-nationals and white Europeans. The copresence of coloniality and promise at the heart of this community is the subject of the stories in this book.

In a way, this book is also the story of my own return. My father, Mestre Beiçola (Ronaldo de Sá) was among the cohort of the first Brazilians to bring capoeira to California in the late 1980s. In fact, my parents met through capoeira, when my mother was training in Berkeley and my father taught a workshop at her academy. My siblings and I were raised in a capoeira household, and as kids we took samba and Afro-Brazilian dance classes, paraded in the San Francisco *Carnaval* every year, and learned to play a range of instruments, all with my father as our teacher.

But I was a reluctant student. Capoeira's spinning moves often made me dizzy. I dreaded the intimidating moment of approaching the *bateria* (orchestra for capoeira) to play in the *roda* in front of so many staring eyes and to face the unpredictability of my opponent's attacks. I also struggled with my connection to the idea of Brazil, a place that was integrated into my daily reality but that I visited only every other year. I was also a heritage speaker of Brazilian Portuguese, which often shook my confidence of my transnational belonging. Growing up with a capoeira legend also meant having other (mostly Black) Brazilian *mestres* around, along with countless (mostly white) Americans who were dance, music, and capoeira students passionate about "Brazilian culture." I vehemently rejected capoeira training for many years, aspiring to be a normative American teenager who played volleyball.[2] Still, my background had always made me curious about racial identity and the possibilities and limitations of performance.

I grew up always wanting to visit "Africa," knowing that my grandmother, Dona Celina (to whom I owe my name), knew her grandmother, Christina, who we believe had been captured from her home in Angola and enslaved in Brazil. When I first encountered Afreecapoeira during a semester abroad in Senegal, I felt a flood of familiarity, of knowing how to greet people and how to move in the space. I joined them in singing the same songs I had sung at capoeira *rodas* all my life. Moctar and I came to the conclusion that we might have been in Rio de Janeiro at the same time back in 1998, when he and a few of his early students took a trip there funded by the Brazilian Embassy of Senegal. He even visited the house of my father's capoeira *mestre*, Mestre Touro, which we also likely visited when my family moved briefly to Brazil when I was nine years old. Training with the people from Africa Capoeira made me fall in love with capoeira for the first time, an ocean away from the world that introduced me to it. When the prospect of my earning a belt came up, the association leaders told me I would have to decide whether I would stay in the tradition of my father's school (where I had received my last belt at twelve) or leave my lineage to join them. I was honored to be welcomed, and I earned two belts from Afreecapoeira over my time studying with the group. I still proudly claim my training from Dakar but, of course, acknowledge the deep foundation of my training from my father.

Toward the end of my fieldwork, my father visited me in Dakar, and he was greeted at the airport by a boisterous group of my friends in Afreecapoeira who played pandeiro (a Brazilian tambourine) and sang his welcome to the continent for the first time (figure P.1). They were eager to have him teach a workshop over the course of his stay. Conversations about the history and goals of Afreecapoeira culminated in a kind of informal meeting at one of the top student's house, about how best to build a collaboration between my father's US- and Brazil-based networks, on one hand, and Afreecapoeira, on the other. After a long discussion, my father came to his own conclusion, which he formulated as advice: "Don't wait for anyone else or ask permission. Protect what you have and just keep doing what you're doing." Ibrahim (*apelido* Propheta), the student at whose house they met, later told me he was grateful for this perspective and that it inspired him to preserve Afreecapoeira's autonomy. My father now tells the

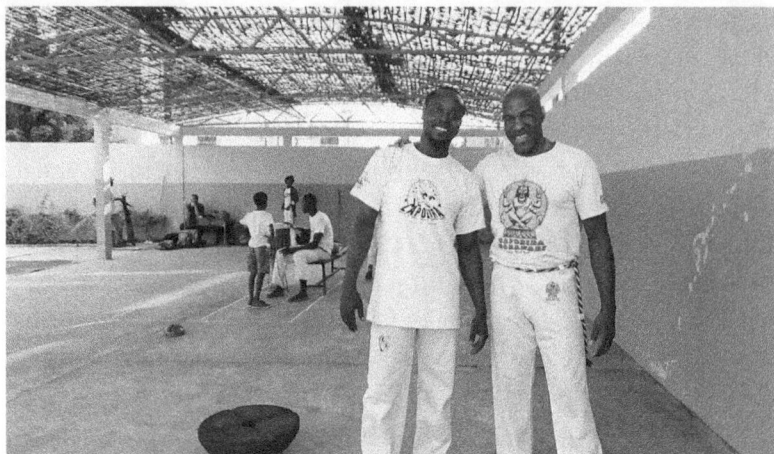

P.1 Propheta (*left*) posing with Mestre Beiçola (Ronaldo de Sá, the author's father) in the Afreecapoeira training space in Dakar in 2016 during Mestre Beiçola's first trip to the African continent. Photograph by the author.

stories of his time in Senegal proudly, sharing how much he learned from connecting with Afreecapoeira's motivated capoeiristas.

Today, West African capoeiristas in Senegal are forging new connections with the Black Atlantic. They enact (or reenact) historical ties through an imaginary of Black kinship, even as so many historical links among West Africa (Senegal), West Central Africa (Angola), and South America (Brazil) remain difficult to trace in the Black boxes of Atlantic history. Those Atlantic gaps make up the space that embodies coloniality's investment in erasure. That inaccessible past is also a space of imagination and potential.

MOVING ORIGINS

A group of twenty-something martial artists arrived at the Port Autonome de Dakar to take the ferry to Gorée Island, as they had done dozens of times before. This morning was special. We awaited the *batizado* (baptism) graduation ceremony, where we would each earn a new, higher-level belt in the Afro-Brazilian martial art capoeira. Two members of our group, Africa Capoeira–Ilha de Gorée (Afreecapoeira), which is based in Dakar, called to say they were on their way, hoping to catch the same noontime boat ride. Kassoum, whose capoeira *apelido* (nickname) is Gavião (Hawk), a Senegalese-Ivorian capoeirista who grew up playing capoeira between Dakar and New York, shared an update about Elena, *apelido* Lagoa (Lake), a Burkinabé woman who had moved to Dakar to complete medical school. Her phone had stopped working after she dropped it in the ocean during our women's acrobatics training, a group we playfully called "Les Amazones." The capoeiristas who had arrived early gathered at the dock, sipping from Dixie cups of Nescafé and launching roasted peanuts at one another. In anticipation that we would need our white uniforms to be clean for the ceremony, I showed up that morning in a T-shirt, shorts, and sneakers. The rest of the group chose to look more polished. The men sported Dutch wax print button-ups, while Ashael, *apelido* Encantador (Enchanter) went a step farther, rocking fitted jeans stylishly torn at the knees and patched with brightly colored fabric. Bigue was fully dolled up: Her teal eyeshadow matched her tank top and headscarf, and her orange sandals echoed her equally bejeweled orange handbag. Her peers affectionately referred to her as "Iemanja" (the Brazilian goddess of the sea) for the regal way she carried herself. While we were waiting, she became the target of a flying peanut, which broke her serious demeanor and caused her to burst into laughter.

Aboard the ferry that day, members of Afreecapoeira took the opportunity to once again disregard the sign that read, "Tam Tam Interdit" (Drums Forbidden). We slapped and rattled pandeiros (tambourines);

strummed the bowlike berimbau; clapped in unison; and sang boisterously, to the delight of locals and tourists who filmed our spontaneous jam session with their smartphones. Upon landing at Gorée Island, we made our way through the cobblestone alleyways softened with bougainvillea-flower-covered walls to arrive at a school courtyard. We slowly took over the space, pulling instruments out of our backpacks, taking off our shoes, and piling up our bags. After a family-style meal of yassa poulet (grilled chicken in onion sauce) and chilled bissap (hibiscus juice), some stretched out on mats to rest while others tapped a 6/8 beat on the pandeiro to accompany the Afropop blaring from a cell phone. We stretched our wrists, shook out our calves, and practiced handstands, warming up for the intense workout to come.

Next, it was time to get changed. In just a few minutes, we were all in white—loose elastic pants for maximum flexibility and matching white T-shirts emblazoned with the school's logo, made especially for the event. Those who had received belts the year before fastened the braided yarn around their waists for the last time. Bags of newly braided belts in combinations of yellow, white, and blue rested patiently on the staircase as Gabrielle the tough love "mama of the group," sorted the colors by level. Gorée Island—the site of a historical slave port and centuries of trade networks—is now the headquarters for West African martial artists continuing a legacy of play, combat, and musical expression created by Africans taken in Angola and brought to plantations across Brazil.

Moctar Ndiaye is a native Goréean who has taught capoeira on Gorée for almost thirty years to the children of the island and a diverse group of young adults living in Dakar. His students call him by his capoeira nickname, "Lion," which refers to his Wolof last name, Ndiaye (of the lion clan). Lions are also a symbol of the Senegalese nation-state, and a performative practice of the false lion (the Simb) is danced across ethnic groups in the country. At the castle on the peak of the island and in the plaza on the island's dock, capoeira gatherings have long burst forth in the open air, free-flowing movements now saturating the historical site of containment. The Mariama Bâ girls' boarding school that occupies an old army barracks is where Moctar teaches the local children the diasporic art of combat and liberation. The Boubacar Joseph Ndiaye Cultural Center—dedicated to one of the country's most renowned historical preservation activists, who renovated the island's main "attraction," the Maison des Esclaves (House of Slaves) in 1962 and created its accompanying museum—is where Afreecapoeira inducts generations of new recruits into the tradition through annual *batizados*.

The pink wash of the Maison des Esclaves holding chamber, at once both swollen and hollow, has become the ritual site where hundreds of African martial artists have "played" capoeira to pay homage to those who once awaited a tragic voyage to plantations in the Americas.[1] "Parana ué," as capoeira is colloquially known in West Africa after a popular Brazilian song, is a phrase with which many Goréeans are familiar, as this Afro-Brazilian martial art has seeped into the social landscape of the historical island. Along with an anthropologist and fellow capoeiristas who went to greet her own potential ancestors, West African capoeiristas made a pilgrimage to the island as proof of a new trajectory of this improvisational art of liberation. They gathered in a circle while our teacher, Moctar Ndiaye, began to sing:

Gorée
me chamou pra jogar
Capoeira na roda
Mas um dia eu chego lá
Eu chego lá
Se Deus quiser
Eu chego lá camará
Eu tenho fé

Gorée
called me to play
capoeira in the roda
but one day I'll arrive there
I'll arrive there
God willing
I'll arrive there, comrade
I have faith

In capoeira, singing provides a narrating voice to comment on the events occurring inside the *roda*—the circle of peers in which two capo-eiristas "play" one another—and to provide thematic context related to capoeira. In this adapted capoeira song, the Senegalese capoeira vanguard from Gorée Island—who replaced "the sea" (read, Africa in general) with "Gorée" specifically—performed a yearning for return to homeland, despite that homeland being the place he had lived all his life. What the song calls our attention to, then, is not the longing itself—a classic trope in the affec-tive repertoire of diasporic subjectivity—but the adaptation of "the sea" as a referent for Africa to Gorée Island in particular. This performative musical utterance pins the origins of Afro-Brazilian capoeira's trope of exile to a longing for the singer's own West African home(land). The performance is made successful by his embodying a diasporic exile who is crying out for Senegal.

It is well known that Africa often represents a heritage for Black people in the diaspora. Blackness, however, is also a heritage for Africans. This book is organized by a set of misrecognitions at the heart of the tension among race, origins, and diaspora. Xavier Livermon (2020, 32) argues that "(mis)recognition as diaspora inhabits the space of 'friction' that may exist between Black people in Afro-diasporic spaces while also insisting that such friction can be productive spaces of affinity." Analyzing misrecognition illuminates the insidious nature of diaspora as an unlikely source of coloniality. While ordinary young people train to become martial artists, the cultivation of these new selves as "capoeiristas" reveals at once the limitations and the possibilities of subjectivity in postcolonial, urban West Africa—a space of former French colonial rule and intervention by American and European nongovernmental organizations (NGOs) and militaries; an exoticized cosmopolitanism; a Western tourist playground; and a romanticized diasporic Motherland.

Brazil holds a strong presence in the imaginary of many West Africans, as it does for most of the world, for its well-known soccer legends, eroticized images of women on pristine beaches, and being the land of samba and Carnaval, one of the most famous festivities in the world. But Brazil also captures the attention of many practicing capoeiristas in West Africa because of its successful portrayal of itself as a racial paradise (Smith 2016a), a place that overcame slavery and transitioned to a society where all racial groups have long mixed freely. Indeed, this portrayal is the basis of Brazil's claim to racial democracy, a claim that has been debunked as mythology (Hanchard 1999b; Smith 2016a). While some West Africans romanticize Brazil's racial democracy, Afro-Brazilians and Europeans similarly romanticize Africa as a site of historical richness and Black symbolism, the site of origins for much of what Brazil prides itself on as a national culture influenced by Africa, but, ultimately, a unique, creolized national culture. At times, these urban postcolonial artistic communities draw on diasporic histories and perform diasporic bodily forms of liberation *at the expense* of contending with their own historical contexts and at the expense of confronting social hierarchies specific to West Africa, some of which are racial hierarchies from transnational circulations and from local histories of colonial categorization.

Senegal is not a place of capoeira's historical origins, which can be traced predominantly to Angola. Senegal is, however, the origin point of capoeira's "return" to the African continent. Capoeira was one of the iterations of Black performance that contributed to the ways Senegal was imagined and constituted not only as a new nation-state but also as a Pan-African "homeland" for the diaspora. In 1966, Senegal's first president, Leopold Sedar Senghor—one of the founders of the Négritude movement—held the First World Festival of Negro Arts (FESMAN) as the country was emerging from decades of French colonial rule. During the colonial period, Dakar was the administrative headquarters for French West Africa. Performers in the festival hailed from all over the world, and among the array of acts was a small troupe of Brazilians who performed capoeira to inaugurate Senegalese sovereignty. State-sponsored celebrations of regionalism and Blackness also mask regional and intranational hierarchies. State-sponsored Pan-African events in West Africa such as FESMAN, held in Dakar in 1966, and the Second World Black and African Festival of Arts and Culture (FESTAC), held in Lagos, Nigeria, in 1977, have had the effect that "ethnic difference and class formation were subsumed by the inclusive horizons of blackness" (Apter 2005, 9).

West Africa holds particular appeal for the consumption of performance, creating a circulation through "African dance" classes transnationally that route interested dance students from abroad to the region (Sawyer 2006). Performance was key to the French approach to colonial rule. The federation of French West Africa involved colonial administrators who were also ethnographers, theater programs, and colonial schools in Senegal attended by a range of West Africans. These multifaceted ethnographic, educational, and performative strategies of rule left a legacy of using the stage and other cultural spheres as a mechanism of politics, ethnic-cultural discourse, and experimentation with political formations (Izzo 2019; Kringelbach 2013; Valente-Quinn 2021). In other parts of West Africa, performance becomes a way of "mimic[king] the trappings of power as exhibited by the privileged power class and, paradoxically, also inhabits the space of the marginalized to push for more power," such as the case of Pentacostal expressive practices in contemporary Nigeria theorized by Abimbola Adelakun (Adelakun 2021, 20). Performance has been and continues to be a vital battleground of social and political power in West Africa from the colonial state to the postcolonial state, and from elites seeking control to grassroots movements vying for sovereignty.

With capoeira, we see another example in which Black performance becomes a space of exoticization and consumption of the African body in motion and in music and of how industries develop to supply visitors with dance experience and experiences in African settings. Dakar in particular is a regional hub of cosmopolitanism and a symbol of the legacy of the French West Africa's colonial headquarters. Wolof society in the peanut basin of Senegal became relatively privileged under French colonial rule (Barry 1997; Diouf 1998; Wilder 2005). Senegal's "special" standing as a postcolonial nation-state is rooted in its colonial position as a model for proto-citizens under a rubric of French civil and cultural standards. This reputation of intimacy with France obscures the history of Senegalese religious and political leaders who resisted complete domination by the French, such as Lat Dior, the ruler of the Cayor empire, and the Sufi saint Cheikh Amadou Bamba. They became icons of Black African liberation and sovereignty (Morales-Libove 2005).[2] In the era of independence, and again at the start of the twenty-first century, Senegal sits in ambivalence as a vanguard of cultural expression of Black liberation and as a kind friend of empire that chose a path of negotiation of political relationships with the metropole rather than a full break.[3]

The first time the combat game is known to have been performed in Africa, when capoeira was performed at FESMAN, is a story unique to Senegal. Yet there and across West Africa, almost all who become capoeiristas cite the film *Only the Strong* (1993) as their first contact with the art. This TV film, which became a cult classic, depicts a white solider who learns capoeira while he is stationed in Bahia and then returns to civilian life in the United States as an inner-city high school teacher. He uses capoeira to show the rowdy and wayward young men (including greasy-haired skateboarders) how to have discipline and stay off the streets. The film's popularity spread among what Donal Cruise O'Brien (1996) calls the "lost generation" of disenfranchised youth in West Africa—and in Senegal, in particular—who came of age in the 1980s and 1990s. Moctar Ndiaye, a native of Gorée Island, founded Afreecapoeira, Senegal's first capoeira school, where he has been teaching children and adults for more than twenty years. Despite the small scale of this initiative within Senegal's expressive cultural landscape, Afreecapoeira has had a wide impact. Moctar has instructed students in rural communities outside Dakar, as well as children of the upper echelon of the country, such as those of the world-renowned artist Youssou N'Dour and of former president Macky Sall. I once went to pay an overdue electricity bill and the cashier was a former student of Moctar's.

I show how West Africa historically has been—and, perhaps more important, continues to be—a site that is key to understanding race, embodiment, cultural innovation, the legacy of the slave trade, and what young people find politically salient in the twenty-first century. Victoria Collis-Buthelezi makes the case for a contemporaneity that South Africa once maintained with the imperial world that gave way to a West African–oriented freezing of "Africa" as relevant only in terms of Black ancestry (and not Black modernities). In the nineteenth century, the South African Cape was a site of global Black modernity and Black radical aspiration with West African, Black American, and other Black immigration circulations. This collapsed with the creation of the Union of South Africa under the British Crown in the early twentieth century:

> The loss of the Cape/Cape Town precipitated the calcification of Africa as a site of origin for those in the diaspora. Under this schema West Africa—from which transatlantic slaves came—became the key point of reference for New World blacks. . . . Whereas diasporic Africans could look to West Africa as a source of origins, the Cape was almost only ever conceived of as a place of coeval black modernity. Its loss precipitated the loss of a kind of coeval, global black modernity. From the diaspora, Africa became *only* the ancestral home. (Collis-Buthelezi 2021, 128)

West Africa, then, carries a legacy of representing ancestry and origins for the Black world at large, which is both a sacred position of grounding and a burden of being cemented. With a specific focus on Dakar, Senegal, I show how postcolonial urban sites in West Africa must be understood within the broader dynamics of regionalism and global transnationalism. West African regionalism emerges as the antidote to diaspora's failed promises. West African capoeiristas reimagine their own kinds of homelands in Dakar, Banjul, Cotonou, and Abidjan, alongside diasporic sites such as Salvador, Bahia, Brazil. They take new and old African spaces and symbols as homelands to be discovered.

Coloniality and the Promise of West African Capoeira

Although capoeira now exists across the African continent, it is most established in West Africa, in the Francophone coastal cities that are also key sites of the transatlantic slave trade. Without a strong presence of

Brazilians, West African capoeira practitioners collaborate with one another through local, regional, and international networks by regularly communicating on social media, hosting workshops, and attending annual events. These efforts were initiated by a few visionaries, mostly young men in the 1990s who, in their respective contexts, discovered capoeira and saw it as their calling. Collectively, they created an artistic network among the schools founded and developed by West Africans, including Afreecapoeira in Dakar; the Capoeira Association of the Gambia in Banjul; Ogun Eru in Cotonou, Benin; and Nukunu in Lomé, Togo.[4] Their efforts to advance these artistic social projects through training sessions, performances, and institution building pose key questions about the place of diaspora, its starting point, and the implications of the people and ideas that circulate within it. The boundaries of these capoeiristas' transnational communities are constructed through online interactions (i.e., learning Brazilian cultural habits from YouTube videos or emailing masters in Brazil, France, and the United States), and in quotidian actions of self-improvement (i.e., gaining mastery over one's internal world through physical training to advance skills for inclusion in global capoeira standards).

For many of the founders of this network, their historical and geographic positionality living in sites significant to the transatlantic slave trade is central to their mission to disseminate capoeira as a practice of Black liberation. Through their research online and from books acquired from passing visitors, some West Africans discovered the art form's history, along with the African cultural traditions that are embedded within that history. As a result, many have made claims to the capoeira tradition as decidedly African, alongside Brazil's material claim to the art's origin. They connect certain instruments or movements to specific ethnic groups, concluding that capoeira is, by definition, quintessentially an African and a Black form of combat. The reconstruction of African social categories in Brazil, the Atlantic dialogues, and the different ways racial hierarchies took shape in various African and Brazilian contexts are such that sometimes Blackness is seen as a continuity from Africanness through a process of racial formation, while *African* and *Black* are sometimes evoked as synonyms. This book attends to what those two concepts mean from the vantage point of urban life and performance in West Africa. It is an investigation of a Black diasporic perspective from African contexts outward that is also colored by internal migratory diasporas and their cultural manifestations. The concept of African origins is remade by West Africans themselves through their own diasporic imaginaries, opening up new possibilities for origins to be understood as flexible and mobile.

The artistic social network of capoeira schools in West Africa brings awareness to innovative acts of racial self-making in African contexts. Race is not only relevant in interactions between Africans and non-Africans (Europeans and Brazilians), but it also plays a role in the formation of social categories within West African regionalism, albeit in different ways. There, Blackness and whiteness are complexly tied to transnational circulations and global structures of race and entangled with other markers of difference in various scales (e.g., caste, class, religion, ethnicity, urbanity, and nationality). As the capital of the colonial region, "Dakar was a place designed by the French to meet the needs of European governance and life" (Keller 2018, 12). The colonial legacy is one of absorbing complexity, and constructed colonial categories, "such as *French, African, citizen, subject,*" "remained fragile" as Lebanese, Syrian, Vietnamese, Moroccan, and many other people circulated in Dakar, producing global connections and political solidarities that were criminalized by interwar French colonial authorities who treated these new residents with suspicion (Keller 2018, 5–6). The examples I explore in this book provide insight into how this capoeira community helps us reimagine what it means to be African for a diverse group of West Africans living in twenty-first-century Dakar, not as a category confined to ethnicity or its entrenchment in autochthony but, rather, as a political positionality that gathers multiple places, sometimes even playing with imaginative time travel. Through these reimaginings, West Africans challenge categories of diaspora, nationality, and ethnicity in part by foregrounding Blackness—rooted in both diaspora and home— as a central aspect of their identity.

Coloniality and promise are in tension at the heart of Black performance. Promise signals an entitlement to global Black heritage and an expectation of what embodied liberatory joy—of play fighting with friends and joining a global movement community—could do. Coloniality also shapes the heart of what draws people to that community of Black expressive joy. In holding both realities through each chapter, I argue that diverse groups of young people in urban West Africa are mobilizing performance, history, and symbolism to write themselves back into the diaspora, not just as the embodiment of origins, but as equal participants in diasporic exploration of heritage and innovation. In doing so, they also renew a practice of West African regionalism that always was, and continues to be, in dialogue not only with the colonial logics that tie them together but also with regional solidarities that insulate against colonial legacies. Urban African contexts are built from layers of regional migration that produce local concepts of intra-Black mixture and difference.[5] In pursuit of understanding how performance and artistic communities emerge from and simultaneously conceptualize race, class, and regional circulation, Livermon (2020, 69) advises that we should "think equally about the relations between differently classed Black people as much as (or perhaps more so) than the presence of whites and Black in the same space." By virtue of my focus on West African performance communities that draw on Afro-Brazilian cultural practices, this book speaks within the fields of African studies, South Atlantic studies, and Black Atlantic studies and the anthropology of diaspora, race, expressive culture, urban youth social movements, and migration to reexamine where and how we locate the practices and conditions of diaspora.[6]

The capoeira network I discuss in these pages raises issues related not only to West African processes of state formation and nationalisms but also to broader relationships among race, diaspora, and citizenship. Racial discourses of self-identification with Blackness are complexly hidden and silenced in contemporary urban West Africa, leading to a prevailing myth that race is irrelevant to the African public consciousness, particularly in countries understood as all Black or Black by default (Araujo 2010; Hartman 2006; Holsey 2008; Ochonu 2019; Pierre 2012; Wright 2016). What are the political and artistic dynamics for West Africans who identify with a transnational Black community? Because racial discourses of self-identification with Blackness are complexly hidden in contemporary urban West Africa, this type of artistic coalition building and the recognition of a shared history with African descendants in Brazil is significant. The diversity of capoeiristas in Dakar from across West Africa take on a Black sense of self as core to why they play, identifying as racial subjects practicing a fundamentally Black martial art created out of the conditions of enslavement.

Diaspora without displacement figures into how the construction of an Afro-Brazilian capoeira-based community brings out hypermasculine norms from global capoeira visual culture, as well as gendered expectations that confront young West African women in Dakar. Female capoeiristas in Dakar often have a difficult time moving away from the margins of the *roda* and into positions of capoeira leadership. Many describe the mastery of instruments and physically challenging acrobatic movements as a barrier that keeps women from advancing at the same rate as men.[7] While some women take the masculine energy of the capoeira space as an exciting challenge to prove equal capability, others find it to be an excuse men use to act in excessive and distasteful ways. White female capoeiristas also pose a challenge that, like racial dynamics more generally in Senegal, is not always explicit. During a routine *roda*, several white female visitors showed up to play. One of the few Senegalese women left in Afreecapoeira stepped up to play them, even though she normally would wait for others to play first. She burst into the game with explosive speed and energy, throwing relentless *queixada* kicks, forcing her opponent into a defensive stance until the orchestra broke into the song "Devagar! Devagar!" which is used to slow down heated games. Afreecapoeira does not adopt the common capoeira practice of being tough on visiting capoeiristas during the *roda*, which occurs regularly at other capoeira schools. Her frustration spoke to discomfort with a shift in energy from the space when the European guests arrived that could not be expressed out loud. Interactions inside the *roda* can therefore be a way of resolving tensions or making a larger statement about the dynamics of different social positions through the one-on-one confrontation space.

Roda interactions are not, however, the only ways that West African capoeiristas, and women in particular, approach sociopolitical issues. Many draw on diasporic symbols of feminine power to make social interventions in support of their local communities. Although they are not represented as often in the high ranks of capoeira groups, West African female capoeiristas enact diaspora without displacement by seeking out a Black "elsewhere" through cultural practice and finding female African role models in the process. I learned this when I returned to Dakar in 2022 and found a new cohort of motivated Afreecapoeira members. I met a new capoeirista, Oulimata, and was eager to hear her thoughts as a Senegalese woman in the group. Oulimata wears a hijab, is pursuing an ambitious career path, and trained as the only Black person in a capoeira group while living in South Africa, which gave her an interesting comparative perspective. Coming back to Afreecapoeira and seeing other Senegalese women excel deepened her pride as a capoeirista. She said:

> Gender is a big deal. Especially in capoeira, right? Because you want to be represented as women. And there are few women who come to train regularly. Almost all of them were part of this friend group, and I naturally felt drawn to them, and they were my people for a while. [They were] Italian, French, Burkinabé. There were a lot more Senegalese men than women. There was only one Senegalese woman, Bigue. When I see her, I'm just, like. "Ah!" How she moves is so amazing. And one more

with a beautiful voice [Paullele]. I didn't think that would mean so much to see other people that looked like me.

Oulimata explained that the gendered representation spoke more to her experience than racial lines. Yet seeing Senegalese women in particular master music, movement, and confidence seemed to touch her most profoundly. The racial geographies in her circulations among African urban sites such as Johannesburg and Dakar exemplify how race and other social categories—as well as differing legacies of racial and colonial history and contemporary migration—affect young West Africans' sense of self and belonging. As a Senegalese foreigner in Johannesburg in the predominantly white leisure space of the capoeira school, Oulimata's Blackness came to matter more. When she returned home to Dakar, the overwhelmingly male-dominated capoeira school there inspired her to embrace the diverse clique of women. She also gained appreciation for the few Senegalese women making room for themselves and those they inspire.

The Origins Debate and Its Afterlife in Capoeira Scholarship

Present-day Angola is the site from which the vast majority of African captives who landed in Brazil were taken at the height of the transatlantic slave trade; Angola remains one of the strongest cultural influences in capoeira's making. So when I describe my investigation into capoeira's uptake in Francophone West Africa, people often ask: "Why not study Angola?" At the crux of my argument is showing how postcolonial African orientations toward diasporic inspiration on one end also approach Africanness, origins, and heritage expansively and with great imaginative reach. The historical backdrop also supports a more complex and interwoven story that disrupts neat linear confines of Anglophone, Francophone, and Lusophone worlds as they are often understood today.

Since the mid-eighteenth century there have been many migrations of free and manumitted "repatriated" people from Brazil to Africa, to both Anglophone and Francophone sites, including Nigeria, Togo, Benin, and Ghana (Castillo 2016; Essien 2016; Matory 1999, 2005; Zeleza 2005). From the mid-eighteenth century through the late nineteenth century, waves of Afro-Brazilians (mostly formerly enslaved people) migrated to modern-day Togo, Benin, and Nigeria. These migrations and the alternative modernities they inscribed are a testament to how communities in the African diaspora have always creatively reconstructed place and the past (Matory 2005; Scott 1991). These innovations are often attributed to New World Black communities while we primarily look at continental African subjects to either confirm or deny their legitimacy.

As for capoeira in particular, the question of its origins has inspired fierce debates. T. J. Desch-Obi, for instance, laid out more than three pages in a single endnote on the debate over capoeira's origins, calling Matthias Assunção's analysis a "Eurocentric version of this denial" of the form's African origins (2008, 289). The two main sides of the debate concern whether capoeira is "African," with a progenitor in Angola (making Brazilian capoeira a kind of African continuity) or "Creole" and "Brazilian"—a nationalist argument that suggests capoeira would only exist through a hybridization of Afro-Brazilian, European Brazilian, and Indigenous Brazilian cultural influence. Capoeiristas were predominantly West Central Africans enslaved in Brazil (various Bantu from Angola) until the 1840s and 1850s, when Brazilian-born *crioulos* (creoles), *pardos* (mixed-race people), and freemen started becoming capoeiristas in increasing numbers (Talmon-Chvaicer 2008). Once capoeira is no longer disparaged as a scourge on society and instead valued as folklore, the question of whether or not it is African or Brazilian emerges, with most arguing that it is Brazilian (*crioulo*) rather than a purely African (*negro*) import. In other words, the concern over whether capoeira is African or Creole arises only in the context of Brazilian modernization as an explicit state project. The ambiguity of capoeira's origins is a lesson in how binaristic debates can perpetuate coloniality: when Black performance is not limited to Black performing bodies, diverse participation becomes a justification for erasing both Black epistemologies of movement and the credit African innovators are due. Racial binary making itself is therefore more telling of anxiety about Black performance than any resolution empirical evidence might bring.

If, as I suggest here, we move away from the assumption that capoeira is a singular, discrete object, we gain a deeper understanding of how African cultural innovation unfolds and intersects, proliferating in a diverse range of spaces, borrowing from and innovating on itself and its changing context. The dynamism of this innovation is evident with a clear origin, as in the case of Ifá, a Yoruba spiritual system that is foundational to African-based religions such as Cuban Santería and Haitian Vodou (Apter 2017; Castor 2017), or without fixed origins, as with Garifuna self-identification and religious practices (Johnson 2007). Rather than approach Africa as a black box holding the mysteries of origins to be uncovered, I instead pursue the question of what is at stake with knowing or not knowing capoeira's origins.

What is unique about capoeira's diasporic return is the fact that the object that we imagine to be capoeira today likely never existed anywhere in Africa. Although it is imagined as, and widely agreed on by practitioners to be, a returned art form that is growing in contemporary Africa, capoeira is arriving there for the first time.[8] Recentering African origins and contemporary African contexts does not necessarily re-essentialize the idea of Africa.[9] In fact, it can lead to a deeper understanding of the complexity of African embodied "traditions" that in fact reveals the essentialism inherent in European notions of the word (Apter 2017; Matory 2005). Underlying the debate over capoeira's origins is an *epistemological* and *methodological* concern: Can the structure of contemporary expressive practices (and comparing them across geographies) tell us about what these forms were like in the past and therefore show where they originated? Performance and dance studies scholars would say not only that they can but that we *must* turn to embodied knowledge for marginalized groups that did not have access to self-representation and self-historicization and to the written word that constitutes the (colonial) archive (Covington-Ward 2015; Daniel 2005; Taylor 2003). But the origins debate is also an *ontological* one: Is there something we can separate as "capoeira" prior to (and even during) its existence in Brazil?

Origins are historiographically contingent.[10] Capoeira's history was created somewhat retroactively. West Africans and Brazilians both participate in discursive formations of its origins in the present to connect its somewhat ambiguous and diverse traditions to specific locations and traditions on the African continent today. While Brazilians have speculated about the specific origins of capoeira's African elements, and built accompanying mythologies, West Africans today also participate in discursive formations of its origins to situate the art form's diverse traditions in specific locations on the continent. One of the major consequences of these debates is that Africa as a concept came to be synonymous with the idea of origins.

West African capoeira ethnography demonstrates how both origins and diaspora are being simultaneously constructed "here" and "there."[11] Dominant popular and scholarly narratives of the African diaspora are often structured in a way that not only imbues the space of diaspora with complex histories and social processes but also simultaneously marginalizes and homogenizes Africa in the present. In this way, African subjects come to signify and embody the past, preventing continental Africans and diasporic Black people from being considered contemporaries. However, ethnographic treatments of contemporary urban West African social and cultural phenomena often contribute to the idea of African contexts as linked to parallel global processes, but they rarely engage the centrality of racial subjectivity as an element foundational to West African's conceptions of global connectivity (Pierre 2012; Thomas and Clarke 2013). Based on Livermon's (2020, 31) idea that Africa is a diasporic space, with "diaspora as processual, circulatory, and polyphonic," this book turns our attention to how, despite the erasure of their contemporaneity, West African artistic projects serve equally as a mechanism of defining African people and their sense of belonging as they are projects of contemporaneity with diaspora and with "the global."[12] African young people are reimagining their social worlds to be transnational in ways that challenge the limitations of postcolonial nationalism and neoliberal marginalization. Precisely by taking African perspectives as a starting point, we see new possibilities for diaspora as an intellectual and lived framework.

New Life of the Origins Debate in Global Capoeira Scholarship

In scholarship on what I call global capoeira, the origins debate reemerges in ways that reproduce unproductive binaries. Research on capoeira outside Brazil focuses on the "authenticity" of capoeira practiced outside Brazil and how it is called into question (de Campos Rosario et al. 2010). It looks at the "capoeira diaspora" or "diasporic capoeira," centering the question of capoeira's "Brazilian-ness" in relation to the new sites of practice (Delamont et al. 2017).[13] Brazil (often homogenized) is the site of origins while other nation-states are the battleground of authenticity debates. The binary that reemerges becomes one of Brazilian versus foreigner, obscuring the distinct but intersecting racial landscapes that are at play in these kinds of performance spaces, even as they engage the historical reality of race for capoeira in Brazil. Furthermore, scholars nominally bring up whiteness as a factor in capoeira in places such as Russia and the United Kingdom, or the scholars' own whiteness, while arguing for diverse (white, non-Brazilian) participation in capoeira serves as a sign of capoeira's success as a cultural form (de Campos Rosario et al. 2010; Downey et al. 2015; Lipiäinen 2015; Wesolowski 2020).

The revived creolization paradigm has a new face as an inclusivity framework.[14] Practices rooted in pursuits among enslaved people of bodily, psychological, and epistemological liberation come up for grabs as a decontextualized object that, as Assunção put it, is "no longer linked to a specific class or group but rather to the feeling of encompassing resistance against oppression" (Assunção 2005, 191). Capoeira becomes detached from its trajectory as a Black form that Blackness survives with—and, perhaps, in spite of—diverse participation, which Tatjana Lipiäinen and others misread as essentialism. In this defense of freedom, playfulness, and openness, capoeira also becomes a way to borrow a loose notion of "freedom" that bypasses the contemporary racial contexts in which it operates, demonstrating a common example of the process of the coloniality of Black performance. This free-floating idea of freedom emerges from the link between "openness" and distance from African origins. Without the racially charged implications of capoeira's Black/African origins (even in Brazil with "Bahia"), scholars become free to ignore the racially charged implications of the practice today. The coloniality of Black performance here manifests as a triumphalist Creole paradigm in which participation by white people means that African cultural forms and knowledge have succeeded. In pursuit of defending inclusivity, these scholars critique the internal power structure of capoeira, unpacking hierarchy and authority from teacher to student while naming race within that structure but not directly seeing the racial dynamics as their own structured relation of power (e.g., Downey et al. 2015; Lipiäinen 2015). The stance by scholars and capoeiristas that slavery and Black resistance is at the base of capoeira, but that contemporary racial inequality is irrelevant in the practice, is often justified by perpetuating capoeira's reputation as "nonhegemonic," as an inclusive art form that, for scholars and capoeiristas, seems to transcend social barriers such as race, gender, and nationality.

While one vein of global capoeira studies celebrates capoeira's potential for inclusivity but rarely deals with its global power structures of race, another starts from an analysis of race, nation, and social hierarchies. These studies—which might be read as continuing from earlier generations of "Afrocentric militants"—investigate racial subjectivity as it interacts with the practice of capoeira as a globalized Afro-Brazilian combat game (Gibson 2014; Humphrey 2020; Joseph 2012). In some contexts, capoeira becomes a tool to address racial politics of the nation-state and the social landscapes of power in different contexts (Gibson 2014; Joseph 2012). The bifurcation of the literature into these two groups demonstrates how capoeira continues to elicit panic about cultural purity and origins as it circulates, even as the diasporic horizon keeps advancing to new sites (Aula 2017; Johnson 2007).

African and other Black capoeiristas' experiences illustrate that marginalizing Blackness and centering whiteness occurs regularly in global capoeira (Humphrey 2020). What's more, those engaged in critical race studies of capoeira mostly look at the binary of Westerners (implied white) and Brazilians (implied racialized), but do not touch the underinvestigated subject of Brazilian whiteness, especially in the role of the expert master and disseminator of capoeira around the world. Recent work looks at capoeiristas in contexts that rely on a foundational assumption of material historical connections. For example, Angolans are drawn to and claim capoeira because of the art form's significant Angolan roots (Wesolowski 2020), while Cubans look to capoeira to revive and value existing Black practices suppressed in a society that does not always value Afro-Cuban contributions (Gibson 2014).

West African capoeiristas both acknowledge that capoeira is new to West Africa and lay claim to capoeira as their heritage by virtue of its having been created by Africans and Afro-Brazilians. Given capoeira's overwhelmingly Central African influence, they sometimes make connections to a specific ethnic heritage while also taking on histories that are not empirically their own. The questions of which histories, which practices, when they occurred, and who can claim them are decidedly unwieldy and imaginative in a way that reinforces the idea of African Blackness as a constant becoming, as well as an ongoing construction of origins/roots/heritage and the imagining of a decolonial, racially empowered future. This intersection of imagined origins, racial self-making, and global Blackness reveals that the complexity of West African capoeira goes beyond a presumed "Afrocentric bias" that is rooted in origins essentialism. West Africans, in many ways, live in one of the most marginal regions in the capoeira world; they are further making a statement about unequal access to this African-based New World practice due to the privileged position of other global capoeiristas who have access to Brazilian economic migrants and their ability to make pilgrimages to Brazil (Griffith 2016; Joseph 2008).

Although it is the site where capoeira was first imagined to have "returned to Africa" when Vicente Ferreira Pastinha (known in the capoeira world as Mestre Pastinha) visited Dakar in 1966, West Africa has been marginalized in the hierarchy of the global capoeira network. In the hierarchy of this world, rather than being embraced for their own innovations,

African capoeiristas' value today is bound up in their ability to perform and embody origins. They are also expected to embrace an expansive definition of who can embody diaspora, including white European and white Brazilian capoeiristas who visit Africa, often as experts with status linked to the legitimating structures of Brazilian capoeira schools. Because they often choose to operate autonomously, West African capoeira schools often are not recognized for their own work and expertise.[15] The baggage of Africa as origin makes it hard to see the real story of continual, and multisited, African innovation.

Moving Through Origins: West Africans Reshaping Diasporic Return

The space of a capoeira *roda* is ephemeral and improvisational. The *roda* is also a repeated and predictably structured event whose actors participate in the symbolic reenactment of a pastime of enslaved people. Capoeira temporality both speaks to *the time of enslavement* through formerly criminalized movements and sounds and acts as a metadiscursive performance *reflecting on enslavement* through lyrics, new contexts, and resignification. As Diana Taylor (2003, 143) has argued, "Performance makes visible (for an instant, live, now) that which is always already there: the ghosts, the tropes, the scenarios that structure our individual and collective life." West African capoeiristas play a dual role within this collective life: They are at once the imagined origins bearers and contemporary diasporic subjects navigating the tropes of narrated enslavement and exile. For almost thirty years, they have trained and performed this act of bringing about a sense of closure at Gorée Island's slave fort, but a closure that is regularly enacted. At a *roda*, one witnesses joy, friendly competition, and displays of physical determination. West African performances of capoeira on Gorée Island are thus also reenacting the scenario of captivity to bring about a kind of resolution that is often repeated. Diaspora without displacement shows how Africans perform the resolution of diasporic return as a regular practice rather than as an event. West African capoeiristas' practice therefore holds brutality and levity simultaneously in a way that both hails and enacts diaspora.

Diasporic return is relevant to continental Africans, whether they migrate away from the continent or circulate within it, as a process of claiming Africanness as capacious against the limited subjectivities available from postcolonial nation-states entangled in coloniality (Coly 2019;

Ekotto 2020). Following Livermon, Tina Campt, Brent Hayes Edwards, and others, I see diaspora as an embodied and contested process, a modality through which Africans and Afro-descendants come to see themselves as both subjugated and empowered by racialization, as well as by gender and sexuality, while they negotiate shared and different histories. In the context of postcolonial urban sites in Africa I draw on the work of scholars such as Jordanna Matlon (2022) and Jemima Pierre (2012) and, specifically, Livermon's concept of "Afrodiasporic Space" (2020). These works are particularly crucial in foregrounding the long, rich history and dynamic processes of Africans borrowing, rejecting, and remastering Black performance and performativity. I work from the space of continental Africans' experiences of return through performance, both as a concept and as an act that attends to what it means to be African within the context of incomplete postcoloniality.[16]

French Atlantic and Lusophone Atlantic circulations during and after empire offer complex contributions to the discussions of racial categories and how they influence and are influenced by performance (Ekotto 2011; Ferreira 2012; Izzo 2019). West African capoeira provides an iteration of some of the grassroots—rather than state-driven—initiatives by actors that define themselves through a *racial* history, in part because their involvement in the practice leads to physical and intellectual knowledge about the slave trade as a corrective to public silence about race (Araujo 2010; Hartman 2006; Holsey 2008; Pierre 2012). Their engagement with diasporic art forms is indicative of a search for answers about their own experiences as racialized subjects who face a lack of open dialogue about historical processes. It also demonstrates how they attempt to work through their own experiences as migrated populations in urban African centers, where they are sometimes marginalized politically, economically, and socially. Urban West African martial artists are not just trying to write themselves into modern Blackness from the margins; they are also actively contributing to the construction of it (Pierre 2012). Their cultural "work" speaks to the aspirations of young people to enact Black Atlantic performances, serving to discredit the myth of race as irrelevant to the African public consciousness (Ochonu 2019).

Can diaspora be embodied as a condition of longing for, of seeking origins of, a desire to reunite a scattering and build community—all *without* the foundational event of displacement? Capoeira in West Africa does not fit neatly into other, more common formulations of "return." In contrast to what is common in relation to Ifá and Africana religions in the Americas, for example, West Africans rarely claim to be authorities in relation to their knowledge of the capoeira form. This is evident in the way many capoeiristas hesitate when they are asked about their knowledge of capoeira and its history, and suggest they are a separated by a few degrees from the "facts" by saying, "I was told . . ." or "I heard . . ." The issue of origins within the context of capoeira is not a specific claim to the past but, instead, a question of inclusion in the present and future of the form based on a generalized African foundation.

Afro-descendant Brazilians, Black Americans, and other Black capoeiristas from the historical diaspora have also worked to link their practice symbolically and materially with contemporary Africa. Many of them have built strong ties and lasting relationships that center and support West African capoeira institutions. Profesora Amazonas, for instance, is a Black woman whose capoeira school is based in New Jersey. She has made visiting Senegal and the Gambia to teach workshops and interact with Afreecapoeira a regular part of her life. However, the majority of non-African capoeiristas who engage with Francophone West African capoeira groups are white Europeans, predominantly French. Rather than focusing on the intra-Black diasporic exchange, which merits its own investigation, I shed light throughout this book on the more mundane reality of capoeira in West Africa. Not only does capoeira "return" to an origin that is other than the site of its historical roots, but the motors of this return are equally unexpected: initiatives by West Africans themselves, who are left to their own devices to develop the form with little contact with diasporic "experts," and frequent trips by white European capoeiristas who make up the majority of non-Africans with capoeira expertise and high status who visit, interact, and exchange knowledge with West African capoeira schools. Many of those white foreigners also have expertise and close links to the capoeira structures rooted in Brazil; they therefore arrive in West Africa with a privileged position derived from the valued cultural knowledge they have at their disposal. This reality has much more to do with the complexities of West African regionalism and the global effects of whiteness than a narrow view of origins and diaspora would make visible.

Diasporic Chauvinism

One of the effects of positioning Africa as origin is the creation of forms of what I call diasporic chauvinism. This is a formulation of Black cultural production in which incorporating "African cultural elements" in a diasporic tradition simultaneously requires a framework of Africa as both source of origin and pastness. This, then, translates to a complex relationship with contemporary artists on the African continent who continue to learn and innovate the same cultural form. Diasporic chauvinism is a monopoly on expertise by Black *and* non-Black experts founded on coloniality in interactions with African cultural producers. As a result, contemporary African artists seeking collaboration with the diaspora are often remarginalized.

For instance, Steven Feld and Robin D. G. Kelley's mutual interlocutor, Ghanaba—a famous Ghanaian jazz musician—called out "American jazz musicians" as perpetuating "racism" for the way they interact with Africans (Feld 2012; Kelley 2012). Referring predominantly to African Americans, Ghanaba characterizes "racism" as an iteration of what I call diasporic chauvinism. He describes how his Africanness did not fit neatly into a framework designed for the legibility of Black diasporic cultural production in the United States; he felt he was viewed as "too African" and, at the same time, "not African enough" because his musical sensibilities drew from a multitude of national and ethnic contexts in West Africa. His lack of discrete, recognizable, singular ethnic purity (the example he cites is Yoruba) made his contribution to jazz music in a diasporic context ill-fitting. Ghanaba's frustration comes from the kind of renewed regionalism—the eclectic resources of West Africa put in artistic dialogue with diasporic expressive forms—that is emerging but illegible under our current frameworks of Africa and diaspora.

What I call *diasporic chauvinism* is an intentionally paradoxical term that illuminates a consequence of triumphant moments of return in which nationalistic assertions of expertise foreclose collaboration with African artists. This assertion of expertise pertains to the knowledge inherent in the capoeira form itself, as well as to the narrative authority over its historical significance. I employ the term *chauvinism* to signal a kind of superiority that is not linked to structural inequality characteristic of white supremacist racism in ways that are more easily identifiable (Ebron 1999; Weitzberg 2017).[17] This is partly because these are social networks developed on the premises of a shared passion for Black cultural production. The gatekeeping practices of this form of cultural chauvinism are enacted by Brazilians, even those of African descent, who exercise ownership over cultural practices in ways that exclude Africans or marginalize their innovations. *Chauvinism* also speaks to the dynamics of masculine expertise. African female capoeiristas specifically bear the brunt of this structure of diasporic hierarchy (de Sá 2024). Ultimately, the national identity of the practice as belonging to an imaginary of a Brazilian nation has the contradictory effect of marginalizing diverse African participation and thus separating origins from contemporary claims to the practice itself.

The question that diasporic chauvinism raises in part is that of what counts as diaspora. Who embodies it, and who is therefore viewed as "returning" or taking diasporic performance "back" to Africa? The capoeira world—today a by-product of Brazil's campaign to mythologize racial harmony through a narrative of intermixture and cultural unity—epitomizes the space between Black performance and those designated as having cultural expertise in Black forms. Being a capoeirista and being Black diasporic kin become conflated, most evidently in the context of collaboration with African capoeiristas when non-Black Brazilians, and even white non-Brazilians, position themselves through capoeira roots tourism to Africa as diasporic returnees. What I call the *coloniality of Black performance* is the broader context within which dynamics such as diasporic chauvinism occur. It offers a lens through the contradictory ways that Black performance can rarely escape its own racial baggage of demands on Black performativity. Those who admire Black performance can also perpetuate coloniality through that admiration in two ways. The first is through consumption, and even taking ownership, of Black positionality through diasporic performance (by non-Black subjects, whether they are Brazilian, European, or others) that manifests as diasporic chauvinism.[18] The second is through racialization: Black performance always carries the possibility of racialization, which manifests in addition to and alongside other schemas of social difference in African contexts.

Diasporic chauvinism is not simply a claim of cultural authority and expertise. It signals a phenomenon intimately connected to white privilege. The phenomenon is an iteration of the incomplete process of the postcolony and an expression of a complex global commodification and "universalization" of Black cultural forms—the privilege and coloniality of tourism combined with the reality of late twentieth- and twenty-first-century migrations. Diasporic chauvinism involves a certain structured narrative of the imagined geographies of the diaspora and how these imagined geographies are embodied, emphasized, or invisibilized. Brazilians are no exception to this phenomenon, which can be found in capoeira schools in Western countries in which Brazilians are both the authorities and subject to being exoticized, fetishized, and objectified (Robitaille 2014). Afro-Brazilians who practice capoeira are thus in a position not only to continue the legacy of the tradition but also, as racialized subjects, to harvest greater significance from a return to the African continent from which they are descended. Still, the racial makeup of Brazilian *mestres* (capoeira masters) is not always so easy to define. White Brazilian capoeira experts sit at the nexus between diasporic chauvinism and the coloniality of Black performance.

Mbokk Capoeira: Innovating Through Origins and Renewing West African Regionalism

Capoeira also becomes expansively African in the present through West African discovery and innovation. African continental capoeiristas in the present, from Gabon to Senegal, lay claim both to the *origins* of capoeira's instrumentation (Alexandre 1974), movements, and symbolism and to *innovation*—namely, the freedom to invent new ways of doing and using the form. But innovation is just that—new and unexpected—so it doesn't unfold in predictable ways. Unlike ways that young artists are revising and inventing new approaches to other movement traditions, such as dance in Guinea-Conakry, innovation in capoeira in Senegal does not mean that the movements themselves look any different from how they would look elsewhere (Cohen 2021). The capoeira itself is not more or less "African." In fact, it's disappointingly recognizable as capoeira from anywhere for those looking to exoticize Africans' reclaiming of an Afro-diasporic form. Afreecapoeira is committed to a faithful training of Afro-Brazilian capoeira styles and to learning all genres.

Innovation emerges from sincere efforts to reproduce the original, but from the context of urban West Africa, and from the ambiguous positionality of West African capoeiristas' embodying both origins and diaspora. Attachment to both origins and innovation is rooted in contemporary West African practitioners' belief that they possess a significant and special relationship to the diasporic practice. Innovation, then, does not emerge from the sanctioned culture bearers shifting ritual through modifications over time, as is the case with Yoruba ritual (Apter 2017; Drewal 1992). It also does not progress in a linear trajectory of vernacularizing capoeira until, for example, it takes on the personality of "Senegalese" capoeira. In certain moments, the original songs that emerge from the group and directly comment on capoeira in Senegal are prominent in *rodas*. Then new capoeira songs emerging in Brazil and elsewhere become more popular for the group. Performance that is ritualized through repetition is not static but always building on what came before it, and is "by its very nature intertextual by virtue of the embodied practices of the performers" (Drewal 1992, 3).

Improvisation is not a tool of just the highly skilled and extensively trained to express virtuosic achievement. Neither is it strictly for the performers. Next to play, improvisation is the mode of learning when onlookers are inspired to take what they see into their own bodies. Improvisation is also the mode of recall, when a former active member draws on the energy of the moment and their past training. For instance, members of Afreecapoeira and the Capoeira Association of the Gambia met during an *encontro*, a gathering of various capoeira groups, on Gorée Island, where we all wore blue event T-shirts. As the *roda*, capoeira circle, progressed, a Senegalese woman in her thirties wearing loose black pants and a light-pink T-shirt and dreadlocks down to her waist joined us. She had been a member of Afreecapoeira years earlier and came to reconnect with her capoeira community for an afternoon. She tried to keep her dreadlocks wrapped up in a long scarf, but as she spun in a *queixada-armada* kick sequence, leaped to the side in a joyous *ginga*, and dipped down to kick Souvenir in a *chapa* from the ground, her hair and scarf were set loose to swing with her flow. The men outnumbered us that day, and the woman made sure to cut in to "buy" the game with each of the women present throughout the *roda*. By the time she played a third, more instructive game with Seinabou, a beginner-level Gambian capoeirista, two little Senegalese girls who had been watching and clapping with us during the event started their own *roda* next to ours. They peeked over every few seconds to copy what they saw, and kicked, escaped, and cartwheeled with impressive accuracy. The taller girl added her own twist: a diagonal disco finger dance celebration between each step of her brand new *ginga*. Her tiny opponent whipped her beaded braids around, turning and dodging. We then brought the two girls in to show off their new embodied skill, only thirty minutes old at this point, and join us at the center of our gathering.

My interest in destabilizing origins and problematizing returns emerges from attending to the relationships that African capoeiristas had with those concepts through their personal intimacy with capoeira. The *berimbau*, for example, is considered one of the central distinguishing characteristics of capoeira and likely originates in West Central Africa. It is found among Bantu and Fang groups and is related to a bowlike instrument among the Fang called the mvet.[19] I first learned about the mvet from a Gabonese capoeirista living in Dakar, who told me that his training had inspired him to do research on the Fang people from back home. "I'm not sure, but I think the berimbau comes from Gabon," he shared with me in a spirit of collaborative discovery and openness (rather than a reclamation of origins). While capoeira scholarship continues to debate the "Brazilianness" or distinct region or ethnic group of capoeira's "Africanness"—in this case, from which region of West Central Africa the berimbau comes—African capoeiristas are undergoing an invisible but incredible phenomenon of discovery, recovery, and conjecture. Often from their displaced site of migration in Dakar, they ask: Could *this* be connected to *that* back home?

African capoeiristas imagine, connect, and speculate about their cultural histories' links to those developed across the Atlantic not as specialists steeped in the tradition but as curious minds open to the journey of discovery. Nasser, an Afreecapoeira member I interviewed in 2010, saw aesthetic similarities between capoeira and other cultural practices from his home country of the Comoros Islands off the coast of Madagascar. The founder of the first capoeira school in Benin, Contra Mestre Fassassi, teaches not only capoeira and Afro-Brazilian folkloric dances, such as maculelê (in which pairs of people dance with wooden sticks); he also teaches morengue as a creative exercise for people to think about other African movement traditions. As he tells it, "Morengue is a folkoric dance like capoeira that is practiced in all of the Indian Ocean, most especially in the Island of Reunion." Fassassi is from Agoue, what he called "one of the most historic cities in Benin," and through becoming a capoeirista he has built a repertoire of African diasporic folklore rooted in the slave trade that imaginatively stretches from Brazil to the Indian Ocean.

Enock, a capoeirista from Benin who came to Dakar for higher education, learned about his family's connection to Afro-Brazilian repatriates to West Africa in the nineteenth century as a result of going down the path to becoming a capoeirista. After diving deeply into capoeira training, he showed his mother YouTube videos to give her a sense of his new hobby. To his surprise, she responded, "That is our ceremony." He discovered in that moment that his heritage included the members of Benin's Aguda community of Afro-Brazilian returnee descendants. So while he started practicing capoeira for the aesthetics and friendship, and because it was a window into the fascinating world of Brazil, his own Afro-Brazilian heritage was revealed to him in the process.

Only a year into Enock's training, a sense of duty to the future of capoeira in Africa set in. For the twentieth-anniversary event, most spent the week sleeping in shared quarters on Gorée Island for a full bonding and immersive experience (and to avoid having to pay the expensive daily fees to take the ferry back and forth from Dakar). When he discovered that Kassoum (from Senegal, Ivory Coast, and the United States), Dieudonné (from Senegal and Guinea-Bissau), Bigue (from Senegal), and I (from the United States and Brazil) would not be joining the others for the overnight stays on the island, he pled with us to stay with the rest of the capoeiristas on Gorée during the event. "We [the newest recruits] thought the event would be a good time to learn about how the group was before, and learn from you guys," he said. "We were hoping to benefit from your experience and spending time with you, and most of you are staying over with us on the island." His appeal to our regional West African and African diasporic group demonstrated that the legacy is something that belongs to all of us who shared the experience of keeping Afreecapoeira alive.

Liberation is not just about the transatlantic slave trade. It serves as a modality through which to navigate life in contemporary Dakar. Despite how central African enslavement and Black pride is for many West African capoeiristas, most do not hold history at the forefront of their minds in the day to day of training. The healing of community building and embodied expression in the present is what keeps so many dedicated to capoeira in Dakar. Coumba, a Senegalese member of Afreecapoeira, told me about capoeira's healing potency for her, saying, "When I play capoeira, I feel good. When I'm a little upset and I come and sing, I feel better. I forget my worries. It's not to become pro, but to be well. It's kind of spiritual. When I play I don't think of roots, I just think of playing. It's a freedom. You forget everything else. The movements make you forget everything else. You only think of succeeding in the movements."

West African regionalism is most evident in capoeira through the community's playfulness in and outside of the *roda*. Play is a quality of improvisation that opens up space for commentary, parody, and critique. In short, "Improvisation is rhetorical play" (Drewal 1992, 5). No one exemplified this playful wit better than Adama Badji, founder of the Capoeira Association of the Gambia, when he marched up the hill to the peak of Gorée Island, a former European military fort called "the Castle," where cannon remain to this day. A motley crew of West African capoeiristas from the Gambia, Burkina Faso, the Democratic Republic of the Congo, Ivory Coast, Guinea-Conakry, Senegal, and elsewhere were waiting there to begin a workshop for Afreecapoeira's 2016 *encontro*. I started filming Adama on my iPhone and held down the repeated chorus with Cantador, a Gambian capoeirista who came up with a rhythm on the berimbau to hold a beat for Adama's riff on a Jamaican chanting style. Adama had me chant "Mbokk Capoeira" (Wolof for "Capoeira Family") or after each of his improvised lines. He sang:

Rastaman a tell dem!
Mr. President!
Mr. Vice President!
Donkey cries now! (*pointing to a donkey tied to a cart, causing me to burst into laughter*)
Martin Luther King!
Kunta Kinteh yo yo!
Inna Gorée Island!
Education Minister!
Defense Minister!
Foreign Minister!
Patrice Lumumba!
Afreecapoeira! (*sung when we reached the top of the hill and found a gathering of capoeiristas, all of us in our blue event shirts*)
Mama Africa! (*pointing to Senegalese women with puzzled expressions watching this strange mini-parade go by as they tried to sell us beaded jewelry*)
Likkle chil'ren! (*in his Jamaican patois-inspired phrasing*)
Yayah Jammeh!
Macky Sall!

Sharing capoeira was the rhetorical tool for social and political life, past and present, in West Africa and in the diaspora. The jewelry vendor began chatting with Adama when the song died down, and he deployed his few French words to share that he was Gambian and that "it's capoeira here," to which the woman replied, "You're from Gambia? Oh, OK. So it's capoeira here," confirming that a diverse capoeira gathering at the Castle was a normal part of daily life on Gorée Island.

This is the first book on capoeira's relatively recent emergence in African contexts. I am, therefore, also invested in expanding the conversation on the transnational dimensions of capoeira that works with the contemporary processes of globalization, consumerism, critical race studies, and embodiment (Aula 2017; de Campos Rosario et al. 2010; Delamont and Stephens 2010; Griffith 2016; Humphrey 2020; Robitaille 2007, 2014; Rosa 2015; Rosenthal 2009). While most scholars of capoeira have focused on the history of the practice in Brazil (Assunção 2005; Desch-Obi 2008; Lewis 1992;

Soares 2001; Talmon-Chvaicer 2008) and the networks extending from Brazilian capoeira structures into other countries (Delamont et al. 2017; Griffith 2016; Robitaille 2014; Taylor 2005; Varela 2017), only recently has any scholarly work been published on how the practice has circulated in Africa (see Wesolowski 2020). Centering my study on a youth organization, I also follow the body of scholarship that understands youth to be an imagined category of the postcolonial state (Diouf 1996; Ivaska 2011; O'Brien 1996).

The study of capoeira in West Africa is an inquiry about the ontology of Blackness in a postcolonial moment in process. Taylor's (2003, 15) formulation of performance is "as a theoretical term rather than as an object or a practice." Capoeira, therefore, is less the object of study than an angle from which to enter a historical process and a geographical palimpsest that is playing out partly in the concrete space of a Franco-Senegalese elementary school's yard (Smith 2016a). Capoeira also allows for exploration of the blurred line between Black performance and performativity because capoeira is always being staged, with or without a literal stage, both within capoeira and in literary, scholarly, and discursive constructions that have implications for how performance is always linked to racial formations (Acuña 2014; Höfling 2019; Rosa 2015).

Thinking Capoeira Transnationally

This project required a transnational approach to capture both the geographical range and imaginative reach of the people involved in these West African artistic networks. My strategy of multisite ethnography, conducted over twenty months between 2013 and 2022, was designed to chart a set of interactions and relationships in an inherently partial glimpse into how dominant narratives of diaspora, racial ideologies, and cultural resources circulate. Therefore, I followed this people-based network in a "mapping strategy" from one of its oldest and most stable nodes in Dakar to the larger nexus of capoeira communities in Abidjan, Ivory Coast; Cotonou, Benin; Banjul, the Gambia; and Lomé, Togo (Marcus 1995).

These cities are home to a network of practitioners connected by a goal to develop capoeira in their respective sites, as well as by a shared vision of one day creating a regional West African capoeira federation. By moving across these spaces, I established relationships with members of the network and their itinerant guests from around the world. I also tracked regional movement to follow the links of communities connected through their practice. While mobility was limited for many of these young men and women, others gained access to various forms of travel (pilgrimage, migration, adventure) (Clifford 1997). My interlocutors were primarily professionals and university students, mostly in their early twenties to mid-thirties from across West and Central Africa.

As an ethnographer and fellow capoeirista I have a responsibility not only to document what "is" but also to meet the imaginative reach of my interlocutors. I conducted in-depth interviews, recorded informal music sessions, and engaged in participant-observation of training sessions, local performances, and international events.[20] The pedagogical nature of the classes and gatherings revealed the group's ideologies in action while also illuminating key dimensions of contestation. By becoming an active member of this community and spending time with members in spaces of everyday life, I learned over time about their socialization techniques and requirements for inclusion, as well as the different barriers to and tools that expedite entrance. I spoke with members, founders, short-term participants, event guests, and other political figures and community members, asking questions about how they understood themselves, their political environment, their relationships, their interactions, their visions, and their practice.

My positionality as an Afro-Brazilian American who primarily identifies as a Black woman, and as the daughter of an Afro-Brazilian capoeira *mestre*, meant that I was considered by some to be an active member of their political and artistic projects before I was acknowledged as a researcher. The capoeiristas I worked with granted me two nicknames indicative of our relationship. One was "Google Translate" for my frequent role as translator among French, English, Portuguese, and, at times, Wolof; the second was "Espionne" (spy in French), signaling suspicion attached to my studying, observing, note taking, and recording, which seemed irrelevant to our shared goals as capoeiristas. At times, my semi-insider status meant taking for granted the ways that anthropological methods and categories have inherently colonial vestiges that demand active critical engagement at every step (Gordon 1997).

Chapter Overview

As the chapters that follow demonstrate, capoeira as an embodied performance shows how Africans were putting diasporic concepts to work long before—and, perhaps, more important, long after—diaspora itself "arrived." Each chapter probes how regionalism and migration within Africa affects the emergence of racialized concepts and the experiences of racialization in spaces such as Dakar.

Chapter 1 provides a history and overview of why capoeira in Senegal is significant for a theorization of diaspora without displacement. The chapter contextualizes and investigates the historical and contemporary social work that Senegal's first capoeira school does for the nation's position in the Black Atlantic and in the region. Furthermore, it lays out the transnational implications for how gendered performances through capoeira affect social implications differently in Brazil and in West Africa. Chapter 2 looks more specifically at the twentieth anniversary of Afreecapoeira to establish how celebrating the group's beginnings reveals tensions around ownership of the meanings generated in the racial murkiness of embodied performance. In the chapter, pro-Blackness through the celebration of Black performance has anti-African consequences, enacted by Africans and non-Africans alike. I develop the concept of diasporic chauvinism, an assertion of ownership and expertise that, ironically, excludes African participation in Black performance that has diverse and somewhat ambiguous African origins.

On the question of direct Lusophone links, chapter 3 explores the subset of capoeiristas in Dakar who were born and raised in Senegal but have heritage from Portuguese-speaking African countries such as Guinea-Bissau, Angola, and Cape Verde to provide one of the most direct examples of diaspora without displacement. It shows how they seek out capoeira as a form of diasporic performance and come to have more intimate knowledge of their own Lusophone African backgrounds as a result. In the chapter I also analyze the physical accessories essential to practicing capoeira as a way to think through the tangibility and intangibility of heritage.

Chapter 4 looks at the inverse process: how pro-Africanness and anti-Blackness coexist within a framework of modernity, masculinity, and Muslim respectability as they create friction with a call for Black liberation. I examine how Senegalese capoeiristas see the form as having both good and bad spiritual potential. Here we see diasporic tensions unfolding in the realm of spiritual concerns with capoeira in the Muslim and spirit-based landscape of Senegal, in which diasporic and local histories offer possibilities to elucidate each other. The chapter thus turns to the representations of diaspora that demonstrate racialized anxieties about the body as the site of the religious, the spiritual, and the liberatory. In chapter 5, I look at the phenomenon of capoeira pilgrimage trips to Africa, gatherings of capoeiristas from around the world who are guests or who organize summits in African cities. The chapter also explores how the regional ties ultimately reveal themselves to be the most solid group for preserving and maintaining the legacy of what West African capoeira schools created. The conclusion reflects on how the membership of Afreecapoeira is undergoing yet another unexpected shift, with implications for a new political moment in Senegal. The possibilities unfolding from the coloniality and promise of Black performance in Dakar continue to bear on West Africa as a space of both imaginatively embracing origins and refusing the burdens it produces.

CHAPTER ONE

WHOSE DIASPORA?
UNMAKING ORIGINS AND RENEWING REGIONALISM

One Saturday evening in 2016, as the sun slipped into the Atlantic Ocean on the Dakar horizon, Christopher (*apelido* Antilope) sent out a group text that read: "Hello capoeiristas, I hope you all are well. We will meet at Daniel Sorano at 9:40 p.m. to show the beauty of our art to the eyes of the world. Axé." The third annual La Nuit du Tatami (Night of the Mat), hosted by the National Association of Martial Arts of Senegal (L'anams), was dedicated to displaying almost every martial arts group in the country in front of a large live audience and an even larger one watching on television.[1] L'anams has hosted this event at the Daniel Sorano National Theater since its inception in 2014. In 2016, around 1 a.m., fifteen capoeiristas huddled offstage behind a set of curtains. They looked over in awe at the much larger group of kung fu practitioners presenting an elaborate spectacle. The performers crashed their heels through wooden boards. They formed a human tower, topping it with an apple before a woman in a stiff white uniform with her hair wrapped tightly in a black *fula* (headscarf) ran toward it, leaped into the, air and smashed the gleaming fruit into bits with a precise kick, her peers undisturbed below. Aziz, waiting in the wings with the other capoeiristas, picked up one of the pieces of fruit strewn across the stage, glibly saying: "See? I knew it. They cut it beforehand." Looking around at the hundreds of martial artists stretching and shouting battle cries backstage at the theater, I turned to Moctar Ndiaye, the founder of Senegal's first capoeira association, with a series of questions to calm my own nerves about the performance. When I asked whether any African martial arts were represented in the showcase that night, he responded, "Only capoeira."

Africa Capoeira–Ilha de Gorée (Afreecapoeira) performed toward the end of the La Nuit du Tatami event, at about 1:30 a.m., after half the audience had packed up and gone home. Following the kung fu group was tough. Their onstage smashing of boards and apples was accompanied by dramatic movie soundtrack–type music. For Afreecapoeira, the goal seemed twofold: to prove the utility of capoeira in a fight/self-defense situation and to teach the public to value the multifaceted beauty of *their own African art form* in the midst of flashy foreign styles. The group projected an African universalism in its consideration of itself as "the only Black martial art" onstage that night. Through the use of an Afro-Brazilian martial art, these practitioners sought to "return" Senegal to a Black past— to reify not an essentialized notion of Blackness but one that is multiple and contested. In addition, the group was primarily non-Senegalese; there was a wide representation of West and Central African, as well as Western (French and American), performers.

Although our group was relatively small, Moctar made sure that the female capoeiristas opened and closed the solo performances; at the end of our set, Bigue, a Senegalese dancer and musician, held a *queda de rins* pose, resting all of her weight on one elbow, with her legs solidly extended in a diagonal V-shape. The capoeira performance was the only one with musical accompaniment built into the practice, which many scholars and practitioners believe to be one of the key features that distinguishes capoeira as African-derived, as well as movements that were as much for the purposes of beauty and collaboration as they were for self-defense and aggression. Thus, the group evoked curiosity backstage before and after our performance. Some people mocked us for what they saw as dance trying to pass as a form of combat. However, there was also a certain respect for the unique aesthetic of our practice; the other senseis and masters came over to bow and pay their respects to Moctar. Dozens of students told us that they always wished they could learn capoeira, despite their limited knowledge of the form's context.

Afreecapoeira's project in presenting capoeira at La Nuit du Tatami was not a matter of slotting in a Brazilian martial art alongside Eastern martial arts to match popular global media representations disseminated since the 1970s (e.g., the many kung fu films and the capoeira-themed movie *Only the Strong*). In fact, while both practices are globalized products that have been imported to West Africa, capoeira resonates with its practitioners as having great historical significance and connection. Instead, the group aimed to use the Afro-Brazilian art form to center global Blackness in Senegalese martial arts culture in the face of an East Asian monopoly of that cultural market. James Clifford (1997, 9) has viewed diaspora as "potential subversions of nationality—ways of sustaining connections with more than one place while practicing non-absolutist forms of citizenship." The national and gender diversity of the group, in conjunction with its identity as the only "African" martial art at the event, speaks to its postcolonial commitment to a cultural Pan-Africanism in which an Afro-Brazilian object created out of African diversity in the Americas belongs not only to Senegal in defining its cultural nationalism but also to all African countries.

In the sections that follow, I give a brief history of local capoeira institutions to show the regional ties West African capoeira practice has produced. I highlight Senegal's community because of its significance in the history of capoeira and argue that capoeiristas based in Dakar are attempting to rectify their relatively marginal status, despite being the site of the first "African return" of an Afro-Brazilian art form. Then I turn to the broader concern about capoeira's geographic and racial origins to argue that the tropes of African cultural authorship and African origins both make for a framework of Black performance that ironically provides more space for non-Black participation than for contemporary African participation. Capoeira's ambiguous origin lends itself to discourses of ambiguous ownership and obscures the racialized gendered effects of its circulation. I end the chapter with a discussion of the kind of political work West African female capoeiristas do to both assert the role of Blackness in Senegal and wield the potential of Black performance to solve social ills.

West African Capoeira: New Regionalism Through Diaspora

Senegal is the site of global capoeira's forgotten origins. Capoeira is one of the iterations of Black performance that contributed to how Senegal was imagined, performed, and enacted as a sovereign Black nation-state, as well as a Pan-African "homeland" of the diaspora. In 1966, Leopold Sedar Senghor, Senegal's first president and one of the founders of the Négritude movement of the 1940s, held the First World Festival of Negro Arts (FESMAN) as an instantiation of his philosophy. The Daniel Sorano Theater was built, along with several other cultural institutions, to inaugurate a new era of civic arts. Performers hailed from all over the African continent, the Western hemisphere, and Europe, mostly members of national ballet companies (neotraditional dance troupes). The festival marked a new era of African independence and cultural nationalism after seventy years of colonial rule. Among the array of acts to celebrate global Black performance and inaugurate Senegal's sovereignty, a small troupe of Afro-Brazilians performed capoeira at FESMAN. It was the first showcase of what we know today as capoeira on the African continent. Mestre Pastinha, a prominent figure in capoeira lore for his efforts to "re-Africanize" capoeira in the 1940s, was invited by the FESMAN organizing committee, along with a Brazilian cultural delegation, to represent Brazil's African roots. As Joshua Rosenthal (2007, 262) has framed it, "Apart from its much-debated origin as a martial art and cultural form of the Black Atlantic, capoeira's contemporary globalization dates back to at least 1966 when the incomparable master of Capoeira Angola, Vicente Pastinha, took his students to the *First International Festival de Artes Negras* in Dakar, Senegal."

Matthias Assunção (2005, 162) also pinpoints Senegal as the starting point for capoeira's globalization:

> The *mestre*'s ultimate accomplishment was, without doubt, his trip to Africa. His group was part of the Brazilian delegation attending the First World Festival of Black Arts (Festival des Arts Nègres), in Dakar, Senegal, in April 1966. The delegation demonstrated capoeira, traditional *samba de roda, lundus,* and modern samba presented by well-known artists (Clementina de Jesus, Ataulfo Alves and Elizete Cardoso), and also included outstanding *candomblé* priests (Olga from Alaketo) and academics researching Afro-Bahian culture (W. Freitas, E. Carneiro). M. João Grande still remembers how much the *capoeiristas* were moved when they saw Africans near the hotel dancing to a *balafo* (a type of xylophone) and executing movements that resembled those of capoeira.

Despite this originary moment, no scholarship has investigated the social impact of capoeira in Senegal as a result of the festival or how West Africans have imbued capoeira with new, complex meanings. In fact, there was no documented evidence of capoeira's institutionalization in Senegal until a white French woman surfaced on Gorée Island in 1997 with her five-year-old adopted Senegalese son, carrying capoeira in his body. Moctar described his first encounter with Samba:

> I met a little boy on Gorée who just moved there with his parent. I helped him do his homework, and he always had his legs in the sky. I asked the

mom, and she said sometimes he does capoeira—she described it as an Afro-Brazilian martial art invented by slaves, and this description really interested me. How could something like that exist that was created by Africans and it's known in Paris, but we don't know it here? She showed me an artisanal book about the history of capoeira, written by a big master that talked about the philosophy and the history of it. [It was] Nestor Capoeira's book [1995]. When I read the first two or three pages, my life was transformed.

I met this kid and discovered this art that was also my own history—a history that is African, Senegalese, and [of] all of us here in Gorée; the strongest symbol of the tragedy of this Atlantic trade. Despite this strong symbol, before this little boy came we didn't have the chance to know about capoeira, and when it came, all this created something very strong in me. But I realized it wouldn't have been simple. It is an undertaking that wasn't very accepted here, never seen here.

The child's mother, Dominique, expressed dismay with what she described as Moctar's ignorance of capoeira. Twenty years after first meeting him, she repeated this perspective to me by saying, "Africans don't know their own history!" Needless to say, this comment was a succinct artifact of the Hegelian logic of African historical absence and ignorance. However, Dominique's view echoed the way that the coloniality of Black performance shapes West Africans' access to cultural resources of racial self-making—a process rooted in a framework of diaspora that is inadequate for capturing the dynamics of race.

Coloniality can take the form of a mandate that Africans constantly measure up to something outside of themselves, pursuing external standards, whether from the former colonial "father" of France, or the global economic and cultural force that is the US empire. Moctar comes from a generation in which artists who tried to live off performance were "the state's orphans" who had lost the once strong support of creatives by the Senghor leadership (Kringelbach 2014, 44). Some of the capoeira vanguards in West Africa resisted postcolonial respectability by creating an alternative path through the construction of an Afro-Brazilian universe at home. Moctar was hit with both the *année blanche* (blank year) in 1988 (an election year accompanied by student protests in which all students were made to repeat the school year) and the *année invalide* (invalid year) in 1994 (another election year in which the devaluation of the West African CFA franc caused course credits to be invalidated, again forcing students to repeat classes), spoiling his effort to graduate from college. He described himself as never having been one to have "an office job wearing a tie" (motioning a tightening grip on his neck whenever he mentioned the stuffy bourgeois). "Senegal does not support its own at all," he said. "Only elites and millionaire foreigners." Now, French cultural centers dictate artistic production in the absence of state investment (Kringelbach 2014).

While this story is unique to Senegal, many West African capoeiristas cite the American film *Only the Strong* (1993) as their first introduction to the art form. The film, shown widely on television around the world, likely circulated in the region due to the advent of satellite broadcasting in the 1990s, which dramatically increased TV ownership among the non-elite in sub-Saharan Africa (Akyeampong and Ambler 2002). The film's popularity spread among the "lost generation" of disenfranchised youth in West Africa, and in Senegal in particular, who came of age in the 1980s and 1990s (O'Brien 1996). Sports and martial arts play a central role in enacting national imaginaries, as well as in the construction of hegemonic and complexly situated neoliberal masculinities (Besnier and Brownell 2012). In Senegal, following youth riots that ravaged the country in 1988 and 1989, the state placed more emphasis on structural support for youth activities through Sports and Municipal Associations (O'Brien 1996). In Dakar, capoeira exists only as a youth association and therefore outside the realm of commercial sports, such as soccer, that have professional leagues and financial backing. Nonetheless, the scrappy capoeira association has repeatedly sought to register with the Ministry of Sports to receive formal state recognition and sponsorship.

All the while, these new Black imaginaries collide with the structures of class, citizenship, and racialized and ethnicized neocolonial categories of personhood. The FESMAN event was a particular moment in Senegalese history and in the broader anticolonial independence movements that celebrated a vision of global Pan-Africanism and Black modernity in the arts (Jaji 2014). The twenty-first century, in contrast, has been thus far characterized by disillusionment with the promises of political sovereignty of that earlier moment and riddled with economic precarity and mass migration brought on by neoliberal restructuring. These political processes engender what Deborah Thomas (2016, 13) identifies as "the simultaneous denigration of Blackness and its celebration in popular culture" (see also Smith 2016a) that we see occurring in conjunction with structural and spectacular violence in other African diasporic geographies. Yet in Senegal, we see the denigration of Blackness at the regional African level, while diasporic (read, foreign) Black cultural forms are drawn into the social environment to renegotiate the parameters of postcolonial belonging. Making definitive statements about the essential definitions of the terms *African* and *Black* is less generative than examining how they are deployed in certain contexts, with special attention paid to their shifting relationship to each other. These categories and their referents may not always be explicit. Andrew Apter's (2005) analysis of the second iteration of FESMAN, hosted by Nigeria in 1977, spells out the complexity of the debates among festival organizers and invited guests about who was considered "Black." The distinction between "Black" and "African" was taken for granted. It is precisely the irony of Afrophobia existing within an artistic world based on a Black imaginary that attunes us to the lived experiences of young people in urban West African.

Moctar's commitment to spreading capoeira in Senegal, and situating Senegal as central to the global capoeira world, is a way of "performing the nation diasporically" (Livermon 2020, 52). Today, Dakar is full of former capoeiristas who either trained with Moctar as children or joined Afreecapoeira as adults. For such a small-scale form in Senegal's expressive cultural landscape, Moctar's capoeira initiative has had a wide impact; the number of times one runs into former capoeiristas can come as a surprise. As a result of Moctar's lifelong dedication to spreading the gospel of capoeira in Senegal, there are few residents on Gorée Island who are not familiar with the art form. Although it is not based in Dakar, Gorée remains Afreecapoeira's symbolic home in remembrance of the atrocities of the slave trade and to recover the innovative forms of survival and community building created under its brutal conditions. Moctar is known for making endearing, if somewhat rambling, speeches, particularly at special events such as the graduation ceremony called the *batizado*.

Behind the Gorée Island fire station—in the center of a plastic tarp laid out after the members meticulously swept away any rubble from the cement floor—Moctar presented the new belts to his students. When Lamine's turn came, he walked to the center of the circle to a chorus of whoops and hollers, some urging him to perform a *salto* (backflip). Lamine's skill in doing backflips, especially on command before an eager audience, is an element of masculine virtuosity in capoeira for which both men and women strive. Lamine had earned the level of *gradé*, the only member that year to receive that belt, making him one of the highest-ranking active participants. Moctar welcomed him with a song he improvised in Portuguese that spoke of Senegal and the *batizado* event. Then he presented his belt with a speech:

> Lamine, it is hard to say, but I often regretted not having many Senegalese with me. And that gives me occasion to send out a call to all the young Goréeans that are here, who watch me with big eyes. For the many years that I have been in capoeira, I had the chance to be accompanied by a diversity of really good capoeira students. I only regret not having enough of a relationship with respect to young Goréeans. In any case, I am proud of Lamine, one of the rare Senegalese in the group.

The survival of Afreecapoeira is a serious concern not only for the active members working daily to keep the group alive but also for alumni who have moved away but remain invested in the group's future. The lack of Senegalese core members is puzzling for many—especially Moctar. For others, especially Senegalese capoeiristas who have felt marginalized in the group and those who have left the group, there is little mystery. They feel that, over the years, Afreecapoeira has favored African foreigners, making it no longer a viable creative space for local youth. Working-class Senegalese children and young adults often populate the surroundings of capoeira gatherings and even join in to sit in the *roda* from which they will almost inevitably be invited to learn a few moves on the spot. Lamine, however, is one of the few Senegalese nationals to advance in Afreecapoeira. His nationality and social status as a middle-class professional from Dakar, however, do not really align with Moctar's regretful reference to not having invested more in the most symbolic demographic: working-class residents of Gorée Island, where Moctar sees his work with capoeira as most historically significant.

As noted in the introduction, capoeira *rodas* are ephemeral and improvisational but also predictably structured. Capoeira temporality is both a performance of enslavement (carrying out movements that were originally criminalized for subversive Black embodiment and lyrically narrating scenes of enslavement in the present tense) and a metadiscursive performance that reflects on enslavement (the passionate involvement of free Afro-descendants and others in perpetuating capoeira's legacy). African capoeiristas pay homage to enslaved Africans who became Brazilians. As capoeiristas, they assume the position of the formerly enslaved, even as they are, by virtue of their continental Africanness, descendants of those who were never displaced. West African capoeiristas thus consciously play a dual role as origin bearers paying respect and diasporic subjects bend-

ing and singing through imagined enslavement. West Africans performing capoeira on Gorée Island thus also reenact the scenario of captivity
to bring about what they conceptualize as closure to the slave trade. As
"performances enter into a dialogue with a history of trauma without
themselves being traumatic," their practice simultaneously holds brutality
and levity (Taylor 2003, 210).

Lorelle Semley (2017) critically engages with an 1846 painting of
French Prince Joinville's send-off on his way to Brazil to marry Princess
Francisca. Semley discusses how the multilayered scene revolves around
a "dance indigène" that displays Gorée not only as a "Trans African City"
but also as a diverse locale in terms of race and free versus enslaved status. The painting tells a story of Black African and prominent mixed-race
women (*signares*) taking center stage in part through dance (Jones 2013).
In our contemporary moment, a man from Gorée and a cosmopolitan
group of West African martial artists helping to carry out his vision hold
capoeira trainings and ceremonies year after year at the same spot on the
island. Moctar has even performed on that site—without permission—for
Brazilian diplomats, including former president Luiz Inácio Lula da Silva,
former minister of culture Gilberto Gil, and former Senegalese president
Abdoulaye Wade. These performances aimed to bring attention to, and
honor the history of, the slave trade—how it links Senegal and Brazil and
Gorée Island's continued living legacy. Historians are increasingly debating racial categories and discourses with respect to the slave trade and the
formal colonial period in the region (Jones 2013; Ray 2015; Semley 2017).
Contemporary ethnography on the so-called postcolonial present is only
beginning to explore what I elsewhere have called *racial self-making* (de Sá
2023) and the *coloniality of Black performance* in Senegal.

While *diasporic capoeira* refers to capoeira schools around the world
that originated in Brazilian capoeira structures (Delamont and Stephens
2010; Griffith 2016; Robitaille 2014), *transnational capoeira* indicates
groups that developed without these direct links (Gibson 2014). I use the
term *global capoeira* to encompass both, referring to capoeira structures
outside the African continent. I also avoid the term *diasporic capoeira* to
reduce confusion about my use of the term *diaspora* in this book—that is,
I use *diaspora* to refer to the historical African diaspora rather than capoeira's diaspora. West Africa is one of the growing peripheral sites of global
capoeira. By distinguishing African capoeira from global capoeira, I do not
intend to further marginalize Africa, a framing that perpetuates coloniality. In fact, I aim to highlight Africa's complex role in the dissemination of

the practice. I set apart African capoeira (and particularly West African capoeira) to attend to the multiple, simultaneous burdens of origins, diaspora, and transnational relationships that adhere to African capoeiristas and their practices.

Furthermore, I posit that the term *African capoeira* is a critical geography that is not limited to the continent of Africa, even as I emphasize the particular experiences of Africans conceived of as "non-displaced." There is a growing literature that attends to the issues of non–African Black practitioners of global capoeira (discussed later in the chapter) and African capoeira is symbolically compelling for global capoeira, but West African capoeira associations themselves are still fairly new.

West Africans are committed to capoeira not just to access some kind of cosmopolitan worldliness. Rather, their view of capoeira as African and Brazilian, as belonging to them in the sense of a newly discovered heritage and as belonging to Brazil (related to Brazilian exceptionalism) shows how they hold multiple, and even at times conflicting, realities at once. They are drawn to what is cosmopolitan *because it is African*. Capoeira, for many West African capoeiristas, is the proof that what is African can also be modern and trendy and have mass global appeal, even if Brazilians are the ones getting the credit. That said, most new recruits are drawn to capoeira not because they hold aspirations for diasporic connections but, rather, because they are attracted to capoeira's pleasure, beauty, joy, family, and music. Through learning both the context of the practice and its social interactions, West African practitioners become attuned to the possibilities for racial self-making through a creative, embodied practice. *Ambiance* is the most common descriptor people use to describe what draws them to capoeira and what keeps them committed in the present and (they believe) the future. It is an atmosphere that is secularized but also offers a protective, creative, communal space for foreigners. People speak about the music transporting them to an imaginative space where they think about history or try on different identities: Capoeiristas have nicknames, personalities, and characteristics that are distinct from their identities out in the world (and sometimes this spills over). Rather than carrying the English connotation of a calm spa setting, *ambiance* in French implies an energetic mood; interestingly, it also has a particularly African bent. The eleventh edition of the Collins-Robert French Dictionary has three listings: *ambiance, ambiancer,* and *ambianceur*. While *ambiance* is generally defined as "atmosphere" or mood, *ambiancer* and *ambianceur* are designated as African regional variants, with *ambiancer* meaning to liven up (a party) and *ambianceur/euse* serving as its pronoun form (a reveler or partier).

Ambiance in Francophone West African capoeira spaces is not reducible to associations with leisure or consumption. *Ambiance* comes from the delight in a satisfying space of racial self-making and the discovery of pride in something that was uncovered as a hidden heritage (de Sá 2023). The ambiguity of the term—its history and different meanings—makes room for aspiration, for a Black inheritance being simultaneously discovered and expanded on. *Ambiance* is the energy generated from the interactions in the capoeira space, which are not frictionless but offer a space to do the ephemeral work particular to diaspora as a perpetual process. The art of capoeira lies not simply in beating one's opponent but also in collaborating in a "beautiful game." While the direct Wolof translation for the descriptor would be *rafet* (beautiful), the Senegalese capoeirista Bigue described what she values in a well-executed game as *set*, literally meaning clean, but also neat, as in properly, effectively, or even morally executed. *Set* became a rallying cry against corruption and a visual rewriting and repainting of history in the Set/Setal movement in Dakar in the late 1980s and early 1990s (Diouf 1996; Fredericks 2018). In capoeira, it becomes the achievement of a *jogo bonito* (a beautiful game, meaning one rich with interesting moments of interaction between both players), successfully demonstrating skill in the diasporic gift.

The farewell *roda* tradition also demonstrates how standard practices in global capoeira take on new regional meanings in West Africa. Capoeirista visitors from other West African countries are given a farewell *roda* after a visit to train with Afreecapoeira. The group leverages the ritual of the *roda* to mark the memory of the visit and to signal a connection for the next visit, building relationships and networks one *roda* at a time. Further, a visitor from the Gambia who might be new to capoeira receives the same treatment as a high-ranking capoeirista visiting from France. Once again, the "work" of West African capoeira is given equal value to the legitimacy of global capoeira, breaking down the ways that capoeira hierarchy can reproduce existing structures of power.

While the practice of a farewell or welcome *roda* is normal in capoeira, in this context it not only fosters stronger regional ties but does so in ways that go beyond the kind of "work" of solidarity that shared language or ethnicity are presumed to do. Take, for instance, a visit by a few Gambian capoeiristas to Dakar in which a young woman, Aissatou, was housed with Kadi, a longtime Afreecapoeira member, during her stay. The two women were not able to communicate in the house because Kadi, who was originally from Guinea-Conakry and living in Dakar, and Aissatou, from the Gambia, did not have a shared language. As capoeira peers, however, they got along well, spending days together without clear verbal communication until they discovered they were both of Pulaar ethnic heritage, a common group in the region, although they spoke distinct dialects. Kadi told the story, laughing at the fact that she and her now sister in capoeira went days before they realized that both spoke Hal-Pulaar. A diasporic practice reintroduced them to the intimacy of their ethnic heritage and language, which they rarely got the chance to speak while living in diverse urban environments where Hal-Pulaar was not the main language.

West African capoeiristas may dwell in the capoeira world's margins in some ways, but they are deeply attuned to what is going on in more mainstream capoeira nodes. Major capoeira schools founded in Brazil often become franchises that open branches around the world. West African capoeiristas are often connected to global capoeira through the channels of these foreign branches. Yet the regionalism diaspora inspires is manifested in the work of the founders West African capoeira schools. At an event that brought together capoeiristas from the region, I approached a man named Alpha when I saw him standing alone, clutching berimbaus. He was visiting Dakar for the first time from his capoeira school in Guinea-Conakry. After we greeted each other, he said he had felt lonely until he saw me wearing my capoeira uniform. Capoeira comforted him with the familiarity of kinship, easing the discomfort of the foreign atmosphere. He had learned about Moctar's reputation from Chapeu, his teacher in Guinea-Conakry. "Chapeu spoke so much about the great master of Senegal," he said. "Such an honor. When you come to Guinea, we'll welcome you with open arms." Although he did not hold the official title of *mestre* that is granted through the capoeira structures rooted in Brazil at the time, Moctar has long been a regional hero among the West African schools.

On Gorée Island, capoeiristas take advantage of existing historical structures to produce origin stories and reclaim spaces of historical violence. The Gambia provides another example of the construction of sites that not only meditate on the past but literally produce new regionalisms stemming from a desire for diasporic connection. In 2009, the Capoeira Association of the Gambia built a space for its daily training sessions that it named The Door of Return to create a site of welcome for exiled Africans.

This is the architecture of their diasporic imaginary. The concrete structure the association constructed is not only a response to the relics of slave forts on the Gambia's Kunta Kinteh Island (once called James Island and thus itself a historical object of reframing West Africa in diasporic terms), Ghana's Elmina Castle, and Senegal's Gorée Island. Nor is it only the Gambian association's manifestation of a site of diasporic origins and return, to welcome home descendants of the enslaved. The Door of Return is also a site for the mundane practice of origins as diasporic. Members train almost daily in the space, making it a central fixture in the routine of their everyday lives. West African capoeiristas make certain kinds of claims on space when they play capoeira in sites of the historical slave trade, but they also bring their boisterous practice to make claims on mundane spaces, such as outdoor markets, national monuments, upscale restaurants, rural village squares, and the dusty alleyways of crowded urban neighborhoods.

The work of upholding and disseminating this diasporic legacy, perhaps confusingly, also manifests as leisure activity. Scholarship on neoliberal Senegal has examined youth-led movements as acts of performing and reclaiming the practice of citizenship (Diouf 1996; Fredericks 2018). The Set/Setal movement in the late 1980s centered on a discourse of moral cleanliness and hard work, manifesting in its youth leaders' "clear[ing] out spaces of leisure such as soccer fields and playgrounds, buil[ding] monuments, and plant[ing] gardens. . . . For Set/Setal youth, the city became a do-it-yourself workplace" (Fredericks 2018, 68). Without diminishing the critical lens of political economy and youths' economic marginalization, being a young person in Dakar, a city that takes pride in its leisure activities, is exciting, even as young people are sometimes perceived, and chastised, for being overindulgent. Instead of theorizing what kind of youth politics West African capoeiristas produce in Dakar, capoeira reveals spaces of leisure, play, and even apolitical reprieve—in some cases, accomplished partly through a displaced politics centering on a past in a diasporic elsewhere. This practice of leisure—improperly using or disrupting space to create a spectacle of friendly sparring—is resistant in its "wastefulness." There is no end goal other than to be a capoeirista, a process that is both always incomplete yet already accomplished from the first days of training. To outsiders, and even loved ones, capoeira is the furthest thing from a productive use of time or of the gendered body. Men have a controlled space to perform hypermasculinity, but one that is more about building friendships with other men than competing. Women play with their own gender performance in the sense that they prove—most surprisingly, to themselves—that they are not as delicate as the discourse of their male peers would suggest.

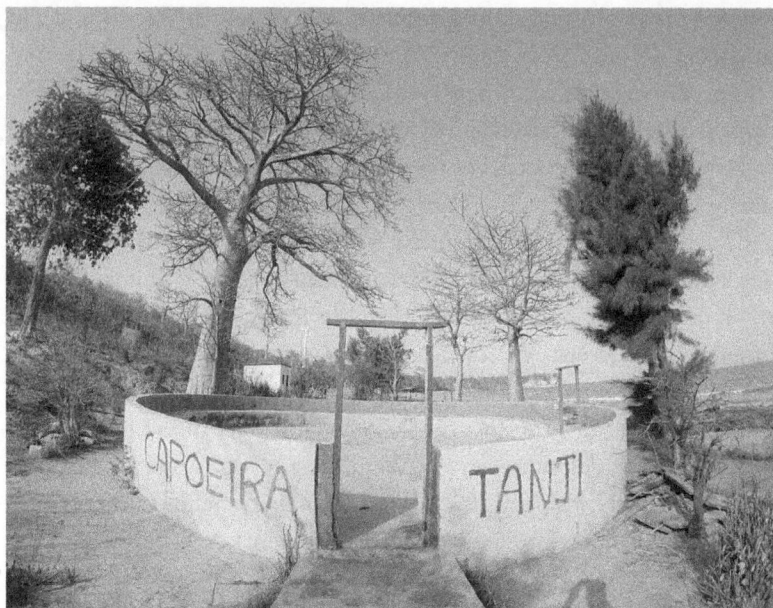

1.1 The Capoeira Association of the Gambia's structure for training in Tanji. Photograph from the Capoeira Association of the Gambia Facebook page.

In Senegal and the Gambia, we see the conscious practice of continuation, maintaining historical memory through performative acts. The circle of capoeira practice is created by moving bodies on cement, within brutal enclosures of slave forts, or in open spaces. Creative leaders such as Adama, the founder of the Gambian school, construct physical structures and carry out bodily choreographies to bring the techniques of resistance and survival necessary under enslavement in the Americas to contemporary life in West Africa (figure 1.1). These efforts are markers of the production of diasporic origins and the expression of a diasporic process of searching, longing, healing, and community building. Loïc, a Gabonese capoeirista who rose to high ranks in Afreecapoeira, characterized capoeira as evidence against African marginalization:

> Many express this, that capoeira is a triumphant story of the inherent value of African expressive culture finally being recognized. It turns the narrative of slavery on its head. We were not just enslaved; we also had agency. We were not just lacking, extracted from; we also created beauty, and even the conditions for our own liberation, out of nothing.

We should not just be relegated to the position of the tragic "Other" in history, but we are now applauded and desired around the world for something that came out of that same condition. *These are the reasons for which capoeira must remain "African" in the minds of certain capoeiristas, because it is ultimately proof of the value of the African will, not just a comment on the contribution of African heritage to what is ultimately a story of Brazilian national patrimony.* (Emphasis added)

Why might African practitioners feel particularly entitled to claim ownership of capoeira? Further, does the historical evidence of the enslaved Africans who created it bear any weight on the relationships between Brazilians and West Africans today, especially given that the capoeira network consists primarily of Francophone African countries, with little connection to the sites of capoeira's "origins" in Africa?

African continental regions have recently become stand-ins for capoeira's African origins and a destination for Brazilian capoeiristas and their vast network of students in the Global North. West Africa is fast becoming a privileged site for capoeira roots tours, as well as for Brazilian and European teachers' aspirations to develop branches of their own schools. West Africans themselves, particularly in Francophone contexts, have created their own, independent capoeira groups and associations. Some founders cite the mediatization of capoeira through the TV movie *Only the Strong*, while others recount brief encounters with Brazilian capoeiristas who were vacationing in the region. The regional project to grow capoeira over the past twenty-five years begs consideration of the central role of West Africa as a region and of Dakar, in particular, as a central site for thinking about Black expressive art forms created as a result of the transatlantic slave trade and, subsequently, how people mobilize in postcolonial Black spaces.

In a sense, the schools that make up the network of West African capoeiristas are all oriented toward Brazil, but each defines its unique relationship to Brazilian capoeira in different terms. Some have more direct links than others, highlighting the distinction between legitimacy from global capoeira and the "work" of West African capoeira. Mamadou Fassassi, who founded Ogun Eru, the first capoeira school in Benin, was also the first African to become a capoeira *mestre*. I approach the designation of "first" with attention to the fact that early capoeira in Brazil was disseminated by Africans who reached the level of venerated teachers but were not given the official designation *mestre*. Mestre Fassassi was baptized by Luiz Luiz Renato Vieira, a white Brazilian *mestre* and sociologist of capoeira; the

1.2 The front of Mestra Marcia Kablan's capoeira school and cultural center. Photograph by the author.

two were put in contact through the Brazilian Embassy in Benin. Fassassi's status as the first African *mestre* is somewhat contested, as he is younger than, and was preceded by, Moctar, who only recently received the title of *contra mestre* (the level just before *mestre*). It was granted to him by Mestra Marcia in Abidjan in 2022. While Fassassi's title speaks to his status in the global capoeira world, Moctar's longevity and initiatives, which were foundational to the regional network of capoeira schools, grant him the highest status in regard to the political "work" of West African capoeira.

The Ivorian school, Owlavé, was founded and run by a Brazilian *mestra* (female *mestre*) (figure 1.2). Other schools are connected more through historical symbolism or heritage, such as Nukunu in Togo and Ogun Eru in Benin, both operating in national contexts influenced by Afro-Brazilian returnees in the nineteenth century, and the Senegalese school that claims Gorée Island as a symbolic home of capoeira. Capoeira in contemporary West Africa reveals an ironic formulation in a global hierarchy that situates African institutions on the bottom even as they are valued for being linked to the art form's origins. This hierarchy is evident in how West African practitioners work their way out of the margins, and assert themselves as contemporary authors and legacy contributors. The African-founded groups and associations in West Africa exist both in somewhat marginal relation to, but also independent of, the global capoeira network centered in Brazil.

The capoeira groups in West Africa not only provide mobility by way of travel for those with limited travel opportunities. They also demonstrate how desires for mobility and travel exhibit a remapping of space and invent new ideas about what constitutes opportunities based on this newly imagined social sphere. For example, Ivory Coast and Senegal share a history of movement back and forth between the two countries. Whereas Senegalese migrated to the bustling metropolis of Abidjan after independence, the recent sequel to the Ivorian civil war reversed migration patterns, with Ivorians looking to settle in Senegal. In the West African capoeira world, Abidjan, as a result of the stability of Mestra Marcia's highly productive Brazilian cultural center, has become one of the main network nodes. Moctar had a lifelong dream to institutionalize capoeira in Senegal, but because that had not quite materialized and to assess the potential of developing branches of Afreecapoeira in satellite sites, he decided to check on the progress of his former capoeira students who had originated from other countries in West Africa (such as Gabon and Cameroon) and returned home after finishing schooling in Dakar. Moctar desired to reverse "normal" patterns of migration, an instantiation of how the capoeira community remaps West Africa, with entirely different "centers" and "peripheries" than might be assumed by outsiders.

The capoeira network acts as a support system for the creative development of young people devoted to learning this martial art and furthering the connectivity of like-minded creatives. Through pooling and distributing financial resources, these West African capoeiristas were granted opportunities to travel that they might not otherwise have had. Moctar, as an unemployed man in his twenties, for example, traveled to Brazil with a group of other low-income Senegalese for a month of cultural and historical apprenticeship with Brazilian capoeira *mestres*, sponsored by the Brazilian Embassy in Senegal. Roughly a decade later, Moctar made a similar pilgrimage to France with a group of his advanced students. Cheick, a capoeirista whose childhood in a low-income household in Guinea-Conakry provided few opportunities, has taken multiple trips to France and Spain and established an independent life in Dakar, thanks to his familial relationship with a French capoeirista who trained him from age fourteen.

Togolese capoeiristas who had never been to Dakar left their home city of Lomé for events in Senegal sponsored by Afreecapoeira. And with funding from a nongovernmental organization (NGO) that sponsors Africans traveling to other countries on the continent for cultural events, two Senegalese capoeiristas attended an event in Benin, developing relationships with a Brazilian *mestre* and his French students in the "home of Vodun" in Africa. Several young Ivorian capoeiristas took their first plane trip to neighboring Burkina Faso to connect with capoeiristas there. And dozens more have settled in Europe or the United States through learning, teaching, or developing close relationships with capoeiristas they met in West Africa. Whether these trips are to a neighboring country or across an ocean, they mark a growing circuit of movement and connectivity based on the shared desire for a new kind of cosmopolitan, Africa-based artistic community.

Mobility as a desire, as well as a physical displacement, marks a new moment in the postcolonial reimagining of place and migration, whereby African aspirations are reoriented from seeking opportunity in the United States and Europe to other countries of the Global South (Ferguson 2006; Piot 2010). This is a generation that does not hold naïve perceptions of economic success and personal fulfillment in the West, as were once propagated by modernization theory, in which Western countries were painted as models of security and progress. Because the traditional "American dream" no longer carries the appeal it once did, rapidly modernizing Brazil, assumed to be free of race hatred, is emerging as an alternative to the United States. The number of Senegalese migrants to Brazil has grown significantly in the past ten years (Ndiaye 2020). Not only are Brazilian flags printed on almost everything in West African capital cities (mugs in the supermarket, baseball caps, board shorts, soccer jerseys, etc.), but a surprising number of people refer to Brazil as their dream destination to live, work, and even die.

Brazil circulates as a symbol of aspirational desire in large part due to its cultural presence in the media, from the airing of Brazilian telenovelas and films to the popularity of Brazil's globally beloved soccer team (Majumdar 2002; Werner 2006). Some West Africans have even adapted their lives to be closer to Brazilianness, even if they may never set foot in the country, by taking Portuguese-language classes in the hope of moving there someday or by engaging in Brazilian expressive cultural forms. Shifting their migration desires from France and the United States to Brazil demonstrates how young urban West Africans' aspirations are not just based on a "rational" explanation of better economic opportunity.

Ambiancing in Dakar

Much of Afreecapoeira's membership while I was conducting research consisted of students at the first Francophone African university, the Université Cheikh Anta Diop (UCAD), which is also known for being a "highly politicized space and avant-garde in its fight for democratization" (Gellar 2005). Student protests at UCAD in the 1980s brought national attention in Senegal to the value of higher education and the lagging job market for graduates. In 2003, the university implemented a series of reforms that brought in new financial resources and programs, and between 1994 and 2000, students formed ethnic associations for the first time since UCAD was established in 1957. These associations were primarily based on ethnic and language groups within Senegal. In recent years, however, new cultural and national groups have formed, accommodating the influx of students from other African countries who have come to study at UCAD. While not formally registered with the university, Afreecapoeira has been a cultural home for UCAD students for many years, in part because it is not bound to an ethnic or even a national identity. Instead, it is seen as an international youth club.

Afreecapoeira is also a space for white capoeiristas seeking "African" credentials similar to those who have sought "apprenticeship pilgrimage" in Brazil (Griffith 2016). Primarily Europeans, these white capoeiristas train with the group to gain credibility in the capoeira world. Many seem to build what they see as a more unique relationship to Senegal outside of the (stereo)typical entryways, such as through the Peace Corps, NGOs, study abroad programs, or surfing workshops, even when these are the avenues by which they entered the country initially. Because the group is so diverse in terms of African transplants, locals from various social strata, and white visitors, Afreecapoeira for a wide range of young people is an easy place to find social interaction and friendship.

I approach the category of "Senegalese" not as a given but, rather, as a site of inquiry to think through the intersecting desires, networks, and relationships that young Dakarois experience and create. The university is an appropriate backdrop—a cosmopolitan space that attracts students from all over the African continent and from Europe.[2] Political actions such as strikes impact not only Senegalese nationals but also students from Ivory Coast, Gabon, Benin, and Burkina Faso. Outside the political realm, friendships and spaces of leisure and extracurricular activities are formed between Senegalese and non-Senegalese students. Some spaces are designed almost exclusively for a Wolof-speaking Senegalese audience to enjoy both indigenously produced genres such as *mbalax* (a highly popular dance and musical genre based in neotraditional percussion and singing and influenced by Afro-Latin music), as well as transnational genres such as hip hop and, in earlier generations, salsa (Appert 2018; Shain 2018). Other spaces of leisure are devoted to specific expatriate communities, such as independence parties at the Ivorian embassy and Gabonese gatherings at the public Centre Culturel Blaise Senghor. Nonetheless, many other cultural spaces, such as dance troupes and kizomba classes, draw a more mixed crowd.

Senegalese youth "using the idioms of their time [are] a force to be reckoned with" (Lambert 2002, 49), yet they have never been tied to a bounded notion of Senegalese culture. Just as salsa influenced the independence movement, *mbalax* fueled the desires of young Senegalese, and more recently hip hop has been leveraged by sociopolitical movements. In this vein, capoeira is yet another medium that is produced by young people in Dakar and circulated within the Black Atlantic, where practitioners navigate personal lives, political expression, and ideas of the past and the present.

West African capoeiristas commune regularly across the urban landscape of Dakar, at historically sacred sites such as the Maison des Esclaves (House of Slaves) and at a fork in the center of the busy "populous neighborhood" of Ouakam (figures 1.3–1.4). During one of his numerous trips to Gorée Island, one instructor—a Guinean capoeirista named Cheick—kneeled in a crouched position in front of an informational placard on the second floor of the House of Slaves. Two players preparing to engage in physical dialogue in the capoeira *roda* always begin in this position: facing each other on each side of the percussion orchestra, waiting to play once the opening song is complete.

So much transpires in this brief liminal space of the "opening" of the *roda*, as the sequence of the singular voice and singular berimbau gives way slowly to the rest of the orchestra and then the surge of singing voices of everyone present in the circle. The two players might also sing along, but in this period they are particularly alert and yet calm, humbling themselves before the instruments as a sign of respect for the event, while meditatively preparing their minds and bodies for whatever might soon transpire. Yolanda Covington-Ward (2015) has written about how "everyday cultural performance" contains banks of overlooked, and thus undertheorized, forms of colonial resistance sedimented in mundane bodily movements.

1.3 Capoeiristas participating in an *encontro* hosted by Afreecapoeira who are about to take a tour of Gorée Island's House of Slaves. Photograph by the author.

1.4 An Afreecapoeira street *roda* in the Ouakam neighborhood in Dakar. Photograph by the author.

Cheick has devoted his life to the creative practices enslaved people produced under extreme duress. I saw his invitation to perform this weighty capoeira gesture as a means of paying respect to the memory of the enslaved. By embodying that legacy, Cheick also positioned himself as interacting with and memorializing the history of the slave trade, not just as a Guinean man, but also as a postcolonial African capoeirista answering the call of a diasporic legacy.

In West African capoeira gatherings, Africans, both members and nonmembers, participate. Children in the surrounding public spaces move around freely throughout the gatherings rather than being used as symbolic props of "Africa," as they so often are by European and non-Black Brazilian visitors. In West African–run events, we find the extraordinary: a display of the being and doing of an unrecognized iteration of diaspora—unrecognized because it looks like a predetermined set of relationships based on regionalism when, in fact, the practice of capoeira is what has brought together different generations, nationalities, and genders to learn about themselves through a Black martial art.

Waisted Anxiety: The Gendered Stakes of Capoeira in Brazil and West Africa

A key irony is that while capoeira is often discussed as an embodiment of the trope of the eroticized hypermasculine African man, West African men who practice capoeira today are commonly read as effeminate or gay. Capoeira is difficult to categorize and is referred to alternatively as a sport, a form of combat, a martial art, a dance, and a game. At the core of this ambiguity is how capoeira is gendered and how it genders its practitioners. Gendered and racialized processes feed into capoeira's ambiguity as capoeira makes global moves, but they do not define how it is interpreted and taken up outside Brazil. Gender is also a limitation on how diaspora without displacement in Senegal unfolds, making its particular form of hypermasculinity and even sensuality a barrier to its proliferation in places such as Dakar. Performance spaces in Dakar allow for "ambiguous masculinities" where the choreographed and performing body oscillates between gender norms. The gendered dynamics of capoeira pose a significant challenge to the otherwise enthusiastic adoption of diasporic registers and affects toward the goal of racial self-making. Normative gender performativity confronts how capoeira performance genders and is gendered.

Women's participation is crucial to the effective operation of Afreeca-poeira. Its self-sufficiency depends on women's labor, both by capoeiristas and non-capoeiristas, such as Moctar's wife, who feeds the entire group when an event is held on Gorée Island. While many members help put on events, these gatherings would not happen without the gendered labor of a rotating group of West African women, both those hosting and those visiting for the event. They clean and prepare sleeping accommodations for all capoeirista event participants; they cook all meals for the guests; and they often have to miss the workshops during the events to attend to these tasks and ensure everything runs smoothly. Despite their key role, and their genuine passion for capoeira, some members of Afreecapoeira characterized women's participation as disingenuous and strategic, believing that Senegalese, African, and European women join capoeira to find a husband and then take him out of capoeira to start a family. In fact, men and women confessed at fairly equal rates to joining capoeira partly to find romantic partners, according to my fieldwork. The perception that women have ulterior motives (and men do not) speaks not only to the pressure on women to find husbands but also to how women are read as not having genuine appreciation for leisure activities, joy, and personal development.

Capoeiragem, as the practice of capoeira was referred to historically—grammatically structuring *capoeira* as a noun and a process—was one of the biggest threats to urban public order in Brazil's white settler colony in the late nineteenth century (Reis 1997; Soares 2001). The archives refer to practitioners during that era as *capoeiras* (rather than by the contemporary term, *capoeirista*). Capoeira was criminalized not just for being African/Black, but also for inciting colonial anxiety about Black masculine transgressive corporeality. According to Daniel Granada (2020, 11), "The strong repression culminated in the penalty of forced exile for capoeiristas who were arrested for the blatant crime of the practice of 'bodily agility' movements."

The Portuguese empire and, later, the Brazilian republic feared capoeira as an activity and way of being that endowed some enslaved men with mobility and a sense of honor in their communities. While capoeira involved violence at times in the nineteenth century, it was, more importantly, part of a criminalization of a much broader set of targets. The attack on and eventual prohibition of *capoeiragem* was an intentionally ambiguous way to criminalize not just the activity of capoeira but also ways to dress, move, and be. Capoeiras were identified by the state by the red and yellow scarves they sported, likely because these colors were central to Bantu cosmology.[3] In nineteenth-century Rio de Janeiro, capoeiras embodied a form of urban dandyism, despite the fact that the anxiety around capoei-ras' being an unwieldy force of Black masculine rebellion resulted in their recruitment to the Paraguayan War to contain and mobilize the threat (Rosa 2015; Talmon-Chvaicer 2008). As a space of Black social vibrancy, an act of alternative masculine self-determination, and, increasingly, an urban threat, capoeira required containment in the eyes of the Portuguese, with recruitment of its practitioners into military service being one effort to achieve that. In this way, capoeira was a space for a spectrum of Black men's embodiment that ultimately was threatening to the colonial state.

Today the concept of *Suigue* (swing) is core to understanding Brazilian forms such as samba and other musical genres, as well as soccer. *Suigue* is a quality of physical or sonic flow that is celebrated in theory but in practice is a racialized term connected to Black African masculinity. Capoeiras' sar-torial expression and bodily agility, rooted in the swaying *ginga* movement, marked them as urban dandies (Rosa 2012). More generally, "The term *ginga* gains wider currency as a distinct swing of the body instantiated from the hips, culturally tied to blackness, enslavement, and social degenera-tion. . . . Males who 'swayed' as they walked on the streets were collectively identified as indecent figures that disturbed civic order or (threatened to) harm others" (Rosa 2012, 149). Black performance is never distinct from Black performativity, ways of inhabiting the body, interacting with others, as Blackness has been theorized as in excess of humanity (Cox 2015; Sharpe 2016). The threat of Black men overdressing, over-moving, hypervisible, and over-interacting, the excess of their bodies and the meanings they make with their bodies, become a valued commodity of capoeira's Black masculine appeal in global capoeira today.

Capoeira's most important movement, the base step called *ginga* that keeps the player swinging from left to right in a smooth flow, is linked imag-inatively to the seventeenth-century Angolan Queen Nzinga (or Njinga). By European accounts of the time, Queen Nzinga was a symbol in the Por-tuguese imagination of evil, savagery, and lecherousness; she possessed a threatening sexuality and unyielding violence. She was also reviled for "sub-ordinating" her husband to the role of queen and elevating herself as the king (Heywood 2017; Rosa 2015). At the same time, her name is imagined to be connected to the foundational physicality and performance of Black masculine power in capoeira. Despite the lack of linguistic evidence that the capoeira term *ginga* and the name Nzinga are related, the symbolic sig-nificance of Queen Nzinga persists. Queen Nzinga was a legendary military leader in seventeenth-century northern Angola who resisted Portuguese slave raiding and early colonization, in large part due to the exceptional martial arts of her armies. Linda Heywood (2017, 256) writes about Queen Nzinga's contemporary legacy that is, in part, "captured in the terminology of the capoeira martial art, where the term njinga came to signify the stealthy movements reminiscent of the training that Njinga's soldiers received." The military legend is also immortalized in capoeira songs that sing her praise (despite her controversial memory for Angolans).

Without proof of the material correlation between Queen Nzinga and the *ginga* movement, the symbolic connection tells us something about the imaginaries that are meaningful today. Capoeira in Brazil rests on gender-queer and transgressive premises that are right on the surface but go deeply underexplored. The form's reputation for hypermasculinity and heteronormativity does not hold historical water. Newspapers from the nineteenth century show reports of women who assaulted their husbands using capoeira, with the husbands' names excluded to avoid publicly embarrassing them. Madame Satã (João Francisco dos Santos), a mid-twentieth-century queer Brazilian capoeirista, is venerated in folklore for his *maladragem*, a kind of toughness and cleverness one needs to navigate life in the streets, especially as a gay man and a cross-dressing performer facing off with police. While capoeira lore celebrates him, he is singled out as exceptional. However, trial records from Bahia in 1900 also tell of Black female capoeiras defending themselves via *gingado* (doing *ginga*) to avoid knife attacks (Pires 2017). Presumably, the women mentioned in early capoeira history were Black women, yet race rarely co-occurs as a framework of critical analysis alongside gender in Brazilian scholarship on capoeira.

The Brazilian nation-state is deeply shaped by gendered discourses that are entangled in class and racial structures, and the broad umbrella of sports and other embodied public performances shape how those discourses are part of a discourse about the nation. Capoeira becomes one of the few spaces in which Black masculinity is at least superficially valued in the disproportionally white public sphere of Brazil, yet tying it to a form of combat and the moving body on display reinforces a connection produced in the colonial era of Blackness to aggression, musicality, and lasciviousness. Similarly, ideal femininity is linked to whiteness, and whiteness is desirable. Ashley Humphrey writes about a women-only Facebook group that refers to "Capoeira girls," which Humphrey (2020, 105) defines as "women who are superficially engaged in capoeira while not showing their skills or faces but have the primary goal of sexualizing a women's body with capoeira as a backdrop." A quick Google search shows that, in the visual culture of Capoeira girls, the women are predominantly thin, fit, and white. The counterpart to "Capoeira girls"—what I simply call "Capoeira guys" (*Caras* in Portuguese or *Mecs* in French)—are the shirtless, hyper-muscular, and spectacularly acrobatic risk-takers prevalent in the visual culture of global capoeira.

Globalization has also recontextualized the racial connotations of performance located in the body. This phenomenon is echoed in Lena Sawyer's (2006) work on Gambian migrants in Sweden, many of whom were never dancers or dance instructors in Africa. Nonetheless, these men have capitalized on their perceived cultural knowledge to gain economic standing under neoliberal restructuring by catering to female Swedish clients seeking a kind of primordial return to earthly femininity. Similarly, Brazilian capoeira abroad are eroticized and racialized through tropes of the Black body as characteristically more fluid, while their white students are read, and read themselves, as more "rigid" or "hard-waisted" (Delamont and Stephens 2008; Robitaille 2014). According to Laurence Robitaille (2014, 231), "The capoeirista's body becomes a marketing device, both for the promotion of capoeira and for the promotion of Brazil as a nation-state." Brazilian capoeira teachers' bodies abroad become racialized as a commodified asset, framing white bodies as requiring remolding.[4]

These teachers use not only capoeira but also dance to teach British men, in particular, how to achieve the flexible waist required for the trickery and fluidity of capoeira. In West Africa, there are also no teachers trying to break down, rebuild, and retrain people's bodies in the Brazilian fashion. Instead, white European men and women—those whose "hard waists" are being discursively and physically reeducated by Brazilians—become the most common teachers of capoeira in West Africa and, as a result, pass on those gendered messages. In addition, West Africans learn from what they see on the internet, where capoeira's gender normativity is most visible. Yet West African capoeiristas can perform "Capoeira guy-ness" only to a limited extent.

Dangay Fecc: Misperceived Masculinity and Dangerous Frivolities in Senegal

Black diasporic performance in Senegal is often defined by its performers in relation to what it is not—or, more precisely, how it is misperceived. While male hip hop artists often maintain that hip hop comes from a mythologized griot origin, rather than a specific neotraditional Wolof oral rhyming and improvising form called *taasu*, which is notably performed by women (Appert 2018), male capoeiristas in Senegal similarly distance themselves from the charge that they are "dancing" (*fecc*). In West Africa, male and female capoeiristas are open to ridicule in overtly gendered terms. Still, engaging in capoeira allows men and women to eschew some of these weighty gendered social norms and provides a framework for organizing life in non-normative ways. But it can also reinforce anxiety about gender or, as Ayo Coly (2019) has argued, about postcolonial distance from colonial logics that leverage gendered tropes. Dakar is not purely conservative, yet Islamic values of modesty influence public comportment. Tropes of African aggressiveness and hypervirility are flipped on their heads in capoeira spaces in Dakar. The Senegalese value of modesty sits in opposition to the perception that *tubaabs* (white people) are more open to vulgar jokes, discussing sex, and displaying sensuality.

In terms of eroticized bodies, capoeira holds different stakes in the Senegalese context from those in Brazil. There, men sometimes take their shirts off when a capoeira *roda* grows intense and pose sweaty and shirtless for photo shoots on the beach. The Senegalese context is not as conducive to exposing one's body, even for young men. Tshikala Biaya (Biaya and Rendall 2000) argues that in Senegal, eroticism is found in the adorned body and sensual contexts (food, scents, visuals, etc.) rather than in the nude or bare body. A shirtless man is not eroticized in the same way in Senegal as in Brazil: In the former, it is read as indecent. Irene Peano (2007) similarly argues that wrestling in Senegal reveals an erotic based on a male body that is adorned and put to work on display in an arena of national representational spectacle. Wrestling is a symbol for masculine traits of courage, but it also stands in for precolonial Wolof empires, when wrestlers were crucial for royal activities; nonetheless, the bureaucratic elite find wrestling inferior and uncivilized (Peano 2007). Wrestling in Senegal thus exemplifies the fine line that masculine bodily spectacle walks between honor and vulgarity in a predominantly Muslim country that is also navigating precolonial symbolism and modern notions of respectability derived from both Western and Islamic ideals.

To outsiders and loved ones of West African capoeiristas, however, there is a fear of idle or excess movement as an unconventional expression of masculinity. To waste time on unproductive pursuits, particularly those that are viewed as not economically viable—that, for example, would have men spinning and kicking on a beach in the middle of the day—is also a critique that relates to a man's role in his family, his relationship to public space, and how he is expected to embody Senegalese values. It is precisely this disruption of gender norms that provides capoeira practitioners with a sense of freedom. It is not a radical rethinking of masculinity, but it is perhaps a radical way of approaching the same normative goal. While it may be more possible for a Senegalese man in Dakar to aspire to the status of Capoeira guy, women in West Africa cannot as easily enact the role of Capoeira girl the way women do in the Global North. This was especially true during my research in Senegal, a moment that was marked by paranoia and disciplining around gender norms. Non-normative masculinity, women's bodies, and women's sexuality were nearly daily concerns for the media, particularly surrounding women in sex scandals but also in performance spaces, demonstrating the limits of performance in expanding gender expression.

Capoeira is sometimes jarringly and illegibly intimate for West African audiences. After leading a training session, Sylvèr, a Congolese native, opened up about a grievance that had burdened him for years: that people in Dakar regularly read him as effeminate for doing capoeira. "I've even been called a *pédé* [a slur for gay men]!" he said. "If only he [the person who used the slur] really knew what we could do, he would bite his tongue." Two years after this incident, I attended the thesis defense of a fellow capoeirista, Elena, who had officially become a physician specializing in dermatology and invited her capoeirista peers to give a short demonstration at the celebration dinner. She kicked off her heels and played a controlled and graceful few games, careful to limit her movements to mind her dress. After the party, she was deflated when she learned that several of her uncles were upset by the display. "A lady like you shouldn't do stuff like that," they said, "especially not in a dress." And when I played capoeira in public, I sometimes heard men passing by reprimand me in Wolof by saying, "Bul ko def Sokhna si" (Don't do that, miss).

Senegalese familiar with capoeira call it *Paranauê* (a reference to "*Paranauê*," the most popular capoeira refrain in the world) or *kapuera* (the Wolofization of capoeira), which recognizes the art form as something done in Senegal. Those who are unfamiliar with the practice often mock it by saying, "Dangay fecc" (You're dancing), which implies that capoeira is not a form of combat. Practitioners are often frustrated about the presumption that their martial art, which involves combat with an opponent (however playful at times), is a dance. West African male capoeiristas shared that Senegalese audiences unfamiliar with the form perceive their practice to be *feccu jigéén* (Wolof for "a woman's dance"). These types of comments are meant as gendered slights. In Togo, Ivory Coast, Benin, the Gambia, and Senegal, male capoeiristas have heard that their life's passion is "nothing more than a dance," effeminate and trivial. Yet female capoeiristas also experience gendered perceptions as too masculine, as embracing a dangerous "warrior spirit" that is unsuitable for a good Christian or Muslim woman. Embedded in these attempts to enforce gender respectability on the behavior and the bodily practices of West African capoeiristas is a social policing that is often at odds with what practitioners believe to be their cultural heritage and duty to carry on a legacy of Black expressive forms that were used to maintain dignity and social power under enslavement in colonial Brazil. The practice of capoeira in West Africa therefore is not only about martial arts training, or even the lived memory of history. Sometimes it becomes a construction of anxiety around Black Atlantic forms of masculinity and femininity that are taken on, resignified, and put to use by West Africans practitioners.

Senegal sits at the intersection of two discourses—Islamophobia and overdetermined tropes of African patriarchy—both of which assume that the country holds "backward" ideas about gender (Coly 2019). Gender, therefore, is not only inextricable from these charged discourses; it also becomes an overdetermined realm in public debate—either as a defense of Senegalese society from outside opinions that do not understand the more complex reality or in ways that reproduce and reinforce those damaging tropes. In other words, as Coly offers, gender becomes a key tool for the postcolonial state to distinguish itself from (even as it remains in dialogue with) the colonial. As a result, women's bodies—especially those that are in expressive motion—are hypervisible. The tension between *coosaan* (a Senegalese custom that is perceived as modesty) and *dund tubaab* (white/ Western lifestyles that are perceived as too sexual) plays out in discourses about bodily practices (Falcão 2014). This is evident in the debates around women dancing *sabar*, one of the most popular neotraditional dances and music forms indigenous to Senegal, at public events such as weddings, or the feminized space of neighborhood gatherings in which the sensual *lëmbël* dance is performed (Coly 2019; Kringelbach 2013). Here I emphasize the expressive and performative element because of how feminine spaces, particularly dance spaces, are often targeted for moralizing about the national reputation (Kringelbach 2013). What Coly (2019, 4) calls "a postcolonial African hauntology around the female body" is by extension also a preoccupation with the inappropriately feminine male body. She "identifies the African female body as an archive for the study of colonial and postcolonial discourses" (Coly 2019, 11). These are hauntologies, she notes, in which the postcolonial context is always in dialogue with the Western colonial standard and therefore is never speaking for itself or transcending the latter.

Performance communities in dialogue with global Black politics are also never free from colonial interlocutors. Capoeira is not as recognizable in terms of its gender norms as a practice such as hip hop, which is often perceived in Senegal as a foreign influence that oversexualizes young people but in ways that do not challenge gender norms. Xavier Livermon (2020) argues that the nature of diasporic (mis)recognition is gendered and sexual, particularly when artistic performances and performativities offend social mores. In fact, as he shows, transgressions of gender and sexuality are resolved by framing transgressive performers as foreign (or, in his study, as "less South African"). Similarly, Bimbola Akinbola's concept of "disbelonging" asks what women and queer subjects are asked to sacrifice to find postcolonial belonging in African spaces and how performance can be a productive site of intentionally not belonging (2020, 159). However, the queer possibilities of diaspora are foreclosed in capoeira in Senegal, just as they are in Brazil. The process of becoming a capoeirista is sometimes bound up with anxiety about non-normative masculine others. One member once refused my invitation of a *chamada* (when one player pauses with their arms spread to "call" their opponent toward them to touch hands or shoulders and pace back and forth in unison either for a rest, to reset the game, or as a trap). "No," he responded when I spread my arms. "I don't like *chamadas*. This whole thing [shimmying his shoulders] makes me think of homosexuals." "And you don't like homosexuals?" I asked. "No it's not that," he said before we were interrupted. After all, "being labeled *goor-jigeen* [homosexual; lit. "man-woman" in Wolof] is likely to result in social death" (Swanson 2019, 50). Capoeira produces fears for West African spectators of men being overly feminized and somehow also of women being overly masculinized. The ambiguity of the form makes it an illegible and strange diasporic target. Amy Swanson's work on modern dance in Senegal offers a way to think about how "artists creatively negotiate oftentimes contradictory sets of expectations at the interstices of the local and the global" with respect to gendered performativity in Dakar dance worlds (2019, 48).

If the West, embodied by visiting white European capoeiristas, provides a foil for what masculinity should *not* be in Senegal, then the capoeira body becomes an affirmative aspiration for those familiar with it who choose to train capoeira. When the *roda* picks up speed, many women feel that their male peers become less articulate and carelessly "throw their bodies around," as one Senegalese capoeirista, Oulimata, phrased it. They forget about their physical interlocutors and start to monologue. Susan Manning writes about masculinism, or "casting male performers as representatives of all humanity," while Amy Swanson extends this definition as "the production of an aesthetic that demands extremely high levels of physical strength more accessible to male bodies" (Manning 2004, 70; Swanson 2019, 158). Swanson argues that in early contemporary dance in Senegal, "[male performers'] physical aptitude shaped movement vocabularies and contributed to a standard more difficult—both socially and physically—for women to achieve" (2019, 158). More than what is available to male bodies, Oulimata's comment touches on the moral imperative for men to use their strength responsibly. From this perspective, the taken-for-granted value of masculine virtuosity is upended by considering its effect on peers in the space and its potentially negative consequences to sociality.

The possibility of acquiring hypermasculine and heteropatriarchal traits that draws some men, in part, to capoeira is situated in a context of postcolonial hauntologies about masculinity, sovereignty, and morality. Muslim Africa, and African masculinities more broadly, are tethered not only to a colonial interlocutor but also to one of ensuing coloniality that subordinates already marginalized, racialized subjects in Europe. In postcolonial African contexts, the state crackdown on non-normative sexual and gendered expression (perceived or otherwise) enacts a coloniality of narrowly defined modern subjects. In the wake of the 2015 mass shooting in reaction to the French satirical magazine *Charlie Hebdo*'s publishing cartoons of the Muslim Prophet that included sexual references, the magazine *Jeune Afrique* featured a cartoon of the Senegalese Saint Seriñ Tubaa with a punchline that had his tunic being misread as a dress. On the ground in Dakar, a group of young Senegalese women were arrested and accused of kissing at a restaurant, and the Senegalese pop star Waly Seck's face was plastered all over the headlines for months because he carried a fashionable unisex bag that was perceived as a woman's purse (Swanson 2019). The Waly Seck incident sparked debates about permissible gender expressions, reinforced ideas of impermissible homosexuality "in Africa," and led to a proliferation of jokes during training in the group Afreecapoeira. In an article on transgender and other queer folks in colonial Senegal, Babacar M'baye (2019, 166) argues for a recognition of the cosmopolitanism of non-gender-normative communities, "despite the racism and conde-scension that European expatriates exerted on them," as well as "the power of Afropolitanism as a means for overcoming the marginality that people with alternative sexual and gender identities faced in colonial Senegal." In addition to French colonial powers, he argues, the postcolonial Senegalese state (including its inherently Islamic institutions) and the citizenry "con-tinue to sanction both homophobia and transphobia" (M'Baye 2019, 166). In the capoeira space, we see an Afropolitanism at work that does not lean into queerness but, rather, braces itself against it in response to the percep-tion of the practice in West Africa as "dancing" and "womanlike."

Some male capoeiristas see capoeira as a kind of training in heroism, a simulation that will allow them to face threats in the "real world." Christo-pher, a member of Afreecapoeira from the Central African Republic, found himself trapped at home with his family in Bangui when imminent elections led to violent clashes. "When the airport opened up again and I was able to return to Dakar to continue the [university] school year, I started thinking very seriously about my [capoeira] training," he said. "What if the rebels had reached my family home? Would I have been able to protect them? I want to train more seriously now to make sure I can defend my family in situations like that."[5] Another Africa Capoeira member, Gery, a former in-structor from the Democratic Republic of Congo, described his motives as training for life: "We share, we exchange. And in exchange and sharing, you need aggression like I said to push and evolve. . . . Look, we simulate a real situation, if I don't put aggression in it, you will be soft and you will think that everything will happen like that, so outside it will happen like that and the guy who will attack you, he will not have pity, you see." Thus, some men in Dakar train capoeira for the express purpose of preparing for real situ-ations. This also may be viewed as a rationalization of their passion: They construct it as "productive" so it is not seen as simply a youthful pastime that takes them away from starting families or their careers.

Allez les Amazones! The Body and Community Work of West African Female Capoeiristas

Years after several of the most talented men in Africa Capoeira formed an acrobatics training group on the beach called Les Spartiates (the Spartans), equipped with T-shirts and all, I joked about creating a counter-group called Les Amazones for women to teach one another these challenging skills.[6] In fact, women were welcome to join the Spartans, and anyone who had the time and will to show up for an extra training session on the beach on Saturdays to work on achieving a backflip could participate. The call for Les Amazones (which after Bigue's playful Wolofization of the French phrasing morphed into "Zamazones") became a rallying cry for women to encourage one another in training and at *rodas*. A woman facing off with a man in the *roda* would be boosted with shouts of "Zamazones! Allez!" from her capoeira sisters on the sidelines. Gendered approaches to teaching capoeira were unremarkable in Afreecapoeira. In many capoeira schools around the world, you can find the same kind of passive sexism: men "going easier" on women in the *roda* while encouraging them out loud; men choosing to play with one another in the *roda* and leaving the women to play with one another; sexist jokes during training; and women choosing to stop playing while men pushed past one another to show off spectacular acrobatics and fearless aggressiveness when the *roda* picked up speed. What was remarkable in Dakar was how women put capoeira history and symbolism to work outside official training grounds, a rare but growing trend for Black women in capoeira elsewhere (Humphrey 2020). Turning to the projects of two female capoeiristas, and the heroic figures who inspire them, we can examine the diasporic and African sources of political visions for women in Dakar and their radical potential.

Senegalese women, I was told by active members, used to make up a major portion of the group when it consisted mostly of Senegalese members. Some women were discussed as almost mythical within Africa Capoeira's history. Coumba, for instance, was famed as the one woman who, years ago, could compete at the same level as the best male players. Members glorified her as a force to be reckoned with, lamenting the dwindling numbers of committed African women in the group at the time. With the rupture of Senegalese participation from which capoeira has yet to recover, dreams of powerful local women rising through the capoeira ranks again have not been realized. Despite the dynamics in the capoeira group, female-led artistic spaces in Dakar are becoming key sites in the construction of class, national, gender, and racial politics. Diverse approaches to Black cultural production by Senegalese and other African capoeiristas show how race, gender, diaspora, and regionalism shape who is imagined to be the community in need of improvement.

Elena, discussed earlier in the chapter, moved from Burkina Faso to Dakar to attend medical school, where her passion for capoeira began. She advanced to become the top-ranking woman in Afreecapoeira—the only

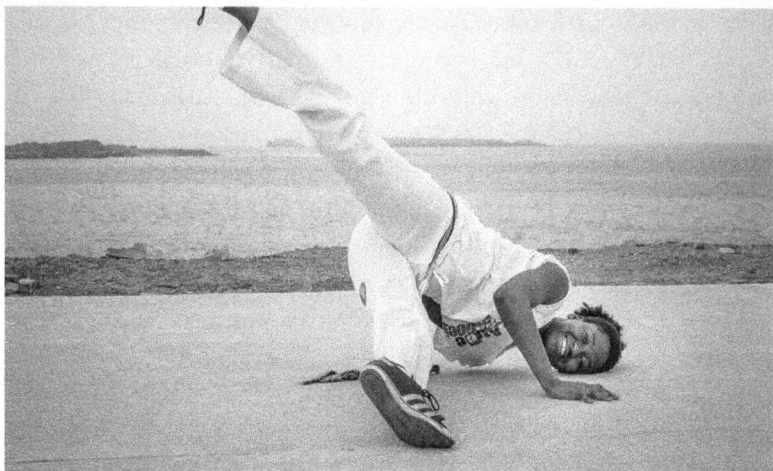

1.5 Elena holding a *queda de rins* capoeira pose on the coast in Dakar. Photograph by Ibrahim Photography.

woman to reach the advanced level of *gradé* and one of the few to master certain challenging acrobatic moves (figure 1.5). She was also one of the few women to advance her skills in playing berimbau, which offered her a leadership role in directing *rodas*. As a dermatology specialist, she became interested in skin through her curiosity about hair health. Her mother had straightened her hair when she was in high school, although she was a tomboy (*garçon manqué*) and never wore makeup or dressed in a feminine manner. Three years later, she decided to follow the "nappy" movement and wear her hair naturally. Her celebration in 2015 after completing her medical training was the culmination of her three passions: capoeira, medicine, and intersectional Black feminist politics. Elena had been promoting issues such as zero waste, supporting Black female entrepreneurs, and veganism through Kimpa Vita, an organization she created with a friend and business partner in 2021 (figure 1.6). Kimpa Vita organizes events, each associated with a different country in the Black diaspora and kicking off with Brazil as the theme for the inaugural event. The parties feature booths run by female business owners to support them through exposure and sales.

In 2024, Elena was invited to the UN Summit in New York City to speak on a transnational feminist panel to speak about Kimpa Vita's work to protect abortion and other reproductive rights in Senegal. At the UN, she had a tremendously rare and high-status platform, a position she was

KIMPAVITA

PROGRAMME

16h
Ouverture des portes

16h–18h
Exposition photos, stand de photos à l'ancienne, vinyles,
littérature, friperie en plein air, ventes d'illustrations,
boutique Zéro Déchet, food corner, menu et boissons
spéciales Brésil

18h–19h30
Projection de films

19h30–20h
Spectacle de capoeira et de maculélé

20h–00h
DJ Set [Djaymel // Mamie // YEAHMAN]
Stand de body painting

Entrée 3000 fcfa
Gratuit pour les enfants de 0 à 12 ans

Événement labellisé Zéro Déchet

1.6 A flyer for one of Kimpa Vita's events that features a capoeira show, a Zero Waste shop, and Brazilian specialties for food and drinks.

even surprised to find herself in. Yet the more mundane work of reaching locals through the organization back in Dakar proved challenging. Elena lamented how hard it is to organize events like this. "You would never imagine that there would be no Black men, and 50 percent white people for an event in Africa," she said. "It's hard. It's hard." As a middle-class expatriate from Burkina Faso, she sought to connect with an imagined community of locals in Dakar, where she has lived for much of her adult life. She shared vulnerably that if she were back home in Burkina Faso, she would not have had the courage to do the kind of female empowerment work she was doing in Dakar. Feminist politics, therefore, are always contextual. Brazil and its accompanying Black cultural forms such as capoeira are racialized, a pro-Black symbol for Elena, along with the Kingdom of Kongo female spiritual warrior Kimpa Vita, for whom she named her company. But the puzzle of "Why no Africans at my event?"—an event that is prohibitively expensive for most Senegalese and centers environmental issues in logics and frameworks in line with NGOs that place the blame on poor African women—remained a mystery to her. Just as an outsider perspective facilitated Elena's feminist projects in Senegal rather than back home in Burkina Faso, her position made it easier to wield and defend Blackness against white oppressive forces. However, the racialized, classed, and gendered dynamics intersecting in her own residential context of Dakar was harder to see—or, perhaps, to face.

Promoting aesthetics of Black African womanhood—let alone entrepreneurialism—is no easy feat in a global context of aspirations to whiteness that are sold through the beauty industries (Faria and Fluri 2022; Ochoa 2014). The harm of white supremacy even shows up in the relationship between Africans and diasporic Black people, demonstrating "the commonsense ideas about the *transnational* significance of race" (Pierre 2008). Symbols such as Kimpa Vita reroute the "spatialities of beauty" to center African female historical figures (Faria and Fluri 2022), disrupting the global beauty industry that targets African consumers to profit from beauty standards of whiteness and lightness (Pierre 2012). Furthermore, the African diasporic modality of queendom can be an empowering and subversive performance of feminine social power (Akinbola 2020; Ayobade 2019). Divine feminine tropes animate capoeira history and symbolism, as well. At the same time, the mundane practice of capoeira training relies on discursively masculine qualities that become the currency (and the entry point) for women's participation. Showing one's toughness, one's ability to be harmed and inflict harm for the sake of competition, and the emphasis on acrobatic and combative movements over aesthetics often misread as "dance" are just some examples of the masculine mandate in capoeira. Humphrey locates the masculine trajectory and subsequent marginalization of Black women once celebrated in capoeira to the recruitment of capoeiristas to fight for Brazil in the Paraguayan War. She writes, "Capoeira as a warfare tactic is also in my assessment why the narrative of capoeira continues to omit the Black women. . . . War, masculinity, and Statehood began to erase the contributions of Black women and turn the game into a competition and battle for livelihood and power" (Humphrey 2020, 38). Hypermasculinity, therefore, not only permeates the visual life of capoeira. It contributes to the erasure of Black women's role in the historical development of the form itself.

I want to think through Elena's preoccupations alongside those of her peer in Africa Capoeira, Bigue, a Senegalese woman who is both stunningly adept at contemporary dance and an eclectic musician. Bigue used her training to start her own acrobatics-focused capoeira-based group with Senegalese children and youth. At the time of my research, she was beginning to realize her long-standing dream of building a capoeira and dance institution in her grandmother's village of Palmarin. She began holding events at no charge to Senegalese locals, where children who attended went

1.7 Bigue (*right*) performing in her festival in Palmarin, aimed at educating the public about climate change. A capoeirista trails behind holding berimbaus in the background. Photograph by Claude Senghor.

home with a free packet of school supplies. By 2023, her event had become an annual festival in Palmarin that educates the public about environmental issues through processions and performances of modern dance and capoeira (figure 1.7). What she did keep from Africa Capoeira is her *apelido*, Iemanja. Known as Yemoja in a Yoruban context, Iemanja is the Brazilian iteration of the Black Atlantic goddess associated with the ocean or other bodies of water. Bigue carries herself with regal poise, which is likely why she acquired this nickname: It is a nod to the divine female power that her uncommon independence suggests. Bigue, the Iemanja of Senegal with the goddess's characteristic grace, challenges the contested but ubiquitous depictions of the Iemanja in Brazil, who is sometimes depicted as Black but also often as a white exemplar of beauty and femininity. The challenge sits in the space of diaspora without displacement, drawing on and resignifying the Brazilian figure rather than the West African iteration. Her embodiment of the goddess's associations with nurturing, motherhood, and family life reveal a tension of Bigue's artistic devotion as a working-class woman in Dakar. While deeply connected to her own family, Bigue lives an exceptionally independent, self-reliant life and has chosen to remain unmarried for much of her adult life. She is a creative, living partly from her artistry as a single Senegalese woman while also trying to inspire other Senegalese and bring resources to support them.

In her early experience with capoeira, her constant rehearsals provoked animosity from her father, who thought she was wasting her time and that women should not be "out in the street at night." At the time, Bigue was one of the few working-class Senegalese Muslim women in the group. Part of what allowed her to engage with this space was that she had already flouted many social expectations: She was single; she worked as a household chef and professional artist; she danced in multiple troupes; she played in the Dakar-based Brazilian *bateria* (parade percussion group) Sambaobab; she worked on Youssou N'Dour's music video; and she put on her own events. In thirteen years, I never encountered another working-class Senegalese woman who regularly trained with Africa Capoeira. While there is a larger issue of there being few steady Senegalese capoeiristas in the group in general, Senegalese women face the stigma of capoeira being deemed inappropriate movement for them—they are bodies out of place—as well as the pressures of domestic life. Several other women mentioned arguing with fathers who felt their capoeira activities were a waste of time. *Repetition* in French—rehearsal or training in English—speaks to the external perception of capoeira as dangerously tedious for young women. Bigue said, "My father would say, 'You do *repetition, repetition*, but what is all of it for?' But I still do it." She said she dreamed of becoming "a great/significant capoeirista."

Despite her big dreams, Bigue also understood the challenges in approaching social justice through performance. She was recruited in 2022 by the International Organization for Migration (IOM) to put on theatrical shows in the *regions* (the interior countryside of Senegal) to raise awareness about the danger of clandestine migration to Europe. She recounted that the troupe put on intricate and poignant dramas that resonated for many people. Mothers who had lost sons would thank her with tears in their eyes. Nonetheless, on occasion she would be confronted by young men, angry at the moralizing intent of the plays. *What choice do we have as men? How can you try to dissuade us? Who are you to tell us this message?* Coloniality does not operate along traditional boundaries of former colony/ colonial subject and former metropole/colonizer. Rather, it is reproduced intra-diasporically, regionally, and within even the national boundaries that separate Senegal's urban working class from its rural working poor. This phenomenon is also gendered, sometimes in unexpected ways: Young men are pressured to leave, but Senegalese women's professional opportunities in the "care" and humanitarian sector sometimes disrupt men's presumed duty to be breadwinners through transnational migration (Andersson 2014; Hannaford 2017; Ticktin 2011). The relationship of global Black politics, gendered configurations, and social change is rooted in artistic expression.

Juxtaposing Bigue's and Elena's projects is productive for understanding the dynamics at play. Both Elena and Bigue have confronted the space between their intentions and the limitations they face in materializing them. Elena expressed being plagued by the gap between her imagined and real audience for Kimpa Vita events, longing for the materialization of what her politics aimed for. They both struggle against colonial and postcolonial ideas about West African women to become outspoken and independent and pursue professional and artistic endeavors. Elena's project demonstrates the cachet of pro-Black discourse, while Bigue's illustrates the subtler way that racial empowerment emerges in and through Senegalese contexts, rooted in forms of Black power but not always explicitly stated as such. Bigue has struggled just as Elena has, but in different ways; while her projects are also anticolonial and racially grounded in form, they are not articulated as such in the same way. Bigue had to confront the reality of what she portrayed artistically: young men who have migrated, or planned to migrate, and found the gap between what was "right" with the tough choices many young men have to face. Rather than framing this as a failure, I see Bigue's experience as setting out to teach and instead being taught to listen as a political feminist act. She did not necessarily agree with the perspectives of these young men, but she adapted to the realities of a complex social issue unfolding in real time before her.

Conclusion: The Fear of Being Swallowed, and Protecting the Work

West African capoeiristas are carrying out a substantive project that seems to exist independently of more official forms of networking on a global or regional scale. Many have respect and admiration for the efforts of Brazilians to institutionalize their art form around the world. As West Africans who are new to this system, they often do not have access to resources or platforms and at times feel actively excluded. However, they have created their own value systems to chart their students' progress. In any case, we should question why they require outside approval. Yet beyond the self-sufficiency of these schools is "work," the idea that African capoeiristas are charged—or, perhaps, charge themselves—with a special set of tasks to cultivate a social network and education around capoeira in West Africa. This task answers the call that African groups deserve respect and recognition, despite their lack of global legitimacy, and is fueled by unannounced visits to one another's schools and pedagogical interactions that privilege affective rather than material concerns. While the aspirations to create an African federation, or to have their schools be legitimated by the Brazilian system, could undergird their work, this alternative type of work is more nuanced, characterized by its lack of a clear end goal other than perpetuating the work itself. It is a project that does not require outside authentication. Despite the subtlety of these seemingly unspectacular trips, events, or friendships, these networkers find their work to have global implications of historical proportions. In this case, connectivity to a global sphere starts by building community with neighbors, using a diasporic cultural tool of liberation created by enslaved Afro-Brazilians more than two hundred years ago. It continues to liberate West Africans from entrenched tropes that they are frozen historical subjects.

From time to time, the global capoeira world stops in to pay a visit, but few from that world have invested in building a partnership with the West African schools. Their continued survival and hopes of being institutionalized seem to depend on that legitimacy, a direct link to the Brazilian schools, since their own countries do not seem interested in funding this cultural project. Yet many West Africans have refused foreign partnership. Their goal is freedom, something they believe to be a central principle of capoeira itself—and history backs them up. While performing capoeira, Africans enslaved in Brazil were chained by their hands (or so the pervasive myth goes), and they had the will and ingenuity to use only their legs as a mode of defense, eventually crafting a martial art disguised as a dance. Chained men thus once transformed their bodies into weapons and used them against their oppressors as a means of obtaining freedom.

The vanguards who created their own capoeira groups in West Africa did so practically on their own. In the Gambia, Senegal, Togo, and Benin, the story is almost identical: A young man started training a few moves on the beach that he had learned from a foreign visitor or a popular film and slowly recruited others until a group was formed. Ten, fifteen, or twenty years later you have the African capoeira groups you see today, which have developed generations of capoeiristas with only infrequent visitors from the global capoeira world to guide them. While some of these African founders have actively sought out Brazilian *mestres* to baptize them into the formal Brazilian system, others have resisted offers from prominent international schools in the name of "freedom." They want to route themselves into the global network but without giving up their unique identity and control of their autonomous creation. In making these demands, they are risking the survival of the group. Without stable practice locations or funding to host and attend events, the number of these schools is dwindling. Some fear that many of the people who show up now are more interested in meeting romantic partners or getting in a fun workout than in advancing in the capoeira world.

Not all West African capoeira leaders are interested in working toward Brazilian-granted legitimacy. Nor do they particularly aim for any kind of state-based recognition as professionals, even in their own countries. What these folks have put into practice is a concept of work that exists independently from professionalization. Outside groups come and go, and, as Gery suggested, his group uses this fluidity of visitors to maintain their own, unique style in the spirit of communication and freedom from the constraints of fixed, external standards:

> I learned capoeira here in Senegal, and it's a context that is a little particular. My teacher learned with a master from Senzala. After that, [the master] left, *and he stayed to do a certain work.* My teacher always taught us to not limit ourselves to one single group or one single style. He wanted us to be able to communicate with everyone. And I believe that it's that spirit that we are trying to stick with today.

Sylvèr, a former Afreecapoeira instructor who now lives in Ivory Coast, held a similar view of the spirit of the group: "Like, for example, for us at Afreecapoeira, not everyone plays the same way. You know, if you take Abadá—at Abadá, they are all . . . the same. Afreecapoeira, everyone has their own style. Those who give class, each one has their touch. Each one develops their own style in the group. I find that it makes us richer." It is no accident that Sylvèr chose Abadá as his counterexample. The group is one of the best-known Brazilian schools, with a reputation for rigid standards and a business model that replicates the same style in all of its players in more than one hundred branches around the world. In a way, Abadá is a symbol of the rigidity of Brazilian capoeira, which Sylvèr strategically juxtaposes with his own Senegalese school that he positions as more diverse, organic, and free.

The reality is that the West African network is not entirely self-sufficient. The folks who "pass through" are a substantive part of its program; sometimes outsiders stick around long enough to seize control of groups. The Capoeira Association of the Gambia, for instance, was created by the Gambian Adama Badji in 2006, but ten years later, in 2016, the group's main teaching and administrative responsibilities seemed to have been taken over by Josselin, a white French financial consultant. Through his connections, Josselin set the group up with a regular sponsor, a company that produces the energy drink XXL, which pays the association to host a public *roda* once a month wearing XXL gear to promote its product. Outside the Gambia, the perception is that Josselin runs the association, and he is often the group's main contact. Josselin and his wife, Sandra, often travel in the region in their four-by-four, and Josselin leads trainings when he stops by Afreecapoeira, often announcing upcoming events in the Gambia for which he has found funding. I made the mistake of asking Adama how Josselin came to be the leader of the Capoeira Association of the Gambia, especially as a French foreigner and temporary resident of the country. He corrected me, saying: "We want to have some knowledge. So that's why we give him the chance, for him to lead us to train. . . . But not that he is our leader. I am the leader. And my assistant is Jungle. Josselin is trying to help us to *stand like any other capoeira groups in the world*, and support us. When he leave[s] tomorrow, we can sustain ourselves." Adama's association currently receives major structural support from Josselin's presence due to his connections and his status as a relatively well-off white European diplomat. Despite this, Adama made it clear that the aim of his group is self-sufficiency, being recognized as on par with global capoeira and maintaining Gambian ownership over the group's work.

Despite the pride they demonstrated in having connections to Brazil-based capoeira institutions, people I spoke with regularly said they "don't want to be swallowed" by them. Many of the capoeiristas, particularly in Afreecapoeira, feared that agreeing to a partnership with a Brazilian school meant they would lose creative control. Instead of networking, a partnership, they felt, was in reality a "swallowing" in which a foreign school would take over what they had built locally. This takeover was often expressed as a form of neocolonialism. Since the turn of the millennium, Africa has been painted as a new economic frontier with untapped market potential, even while political conflict and economic instability on the ground has left some people nostalgic for the colonial period (Bissell 2005). The discourse around the relative benefits or drawbacks of neocolonialism is a lens through which West Africans make sense of their relationships with foreigners on every scale.

French and other European teachers in West Africa are "authorized" by their training with Brazilians, as capoeira is highly developed and institutionalized in Europe by Brazilian immigrants. However, most of the capoeiristas I spoke to seemed surprisingly uninterested in and, most important, unthreatened by Europeans. The frequent repetition of the phrase "We do not want to be swallowed" occurred *solely in reference to the possibility of being taken over by a major Brazilian school.* White European capoeiristas often stepped easily into leadership roles in Afreecapoeira, with increasing managerial control over the direction of the association in recent years. It is interesting that the neocolonial gloss of these fears of being consumed by outside forces was ironically applied to Brazilians, their counterparts in the Global South and diasporic brethren at the center of this Pan-African pursuit, and not necessarily to the French capoeiristas who came to teach or run the African associations. For many of the leaders in this regional network of schools, the final dream prioritized the continent: to establish the first African capoeira federation. The idea of federating came from the example of many Brazilian capoeira schools that have done this in recent decades. There is even a World Capoeira Federation, an international non-profit organization that holds yearly competitions in Azerbaijan and whose mission is to convince the International Olympic Committee to recognize and include capoeira in the games. However, African capoeiristas find themselves feeling trapped between being marginalized for their innovations in Brazilian capoeira and mimicking or swallowing the Brazilian styles whole, which then erases their seemingly privileged position as Africans in the narrative of an Afro-Brazilian art form that "returned home."

Still, Moctar, Souvenir, and others imagined Dakar as the ideal base of a theoretical African federation, and Moctar has made efforts to realize this dream. In recent years, he has gathered several regional leaders, who held a meeting to discuss the possibility of federating, which speaks to the seriousness with respect to this pursuit. Furthermore, the meetings themselves were historic. They marked the beginning of a regional partnership among a diverse group of West Africans who otherwise might have had nothing to do with one another. The leaders of these groups have devoted their lives to the development of capoeira in their corner of the world. Despite the lack of recognition, resources, and other financial support—and perhaps most significant, despite their repeated marginalization by outsiders who control the "real" capoeira world—they have persisted since 2018 in working toward the creation of African schools and an African capoeira federation. They do so because they believe the presence of capoeira in West Africa to be a historic phenomenon, and they recognize the precious legacy that they essentially came to on their own.

The fear of being swallowed activates a larger discourse of African marginality and alterity in the global world order, although Black performance networks linked to the diaspora are an unlikely source of these fears. In the next chapter, I disentangle the affective politics surrounding the sense of ownership and authorship, mentorship and menteeship felt by capoeiristas during a key moment in the commemoration of Afreecapoeira. At various scales—Brazilians and Europeans swallowing what is West African, as well as West Africans swallowing what is Senegalese—this event highlighted the intersecting politics of diaspora and regionalism that animate performance communities.

CHAPTER TWO

WHITENESS, BLACKNESS, AND BUSHNESS

THE COLONIALITY OF BLACK PERFORMANCE IN DAKAR

Njaajaan Njaay existait. . . .
[Étymologiquement] Le Sénégal n'a jamais existé.
C'est une fabrication absolument *tubaab*.
—BIRAGO DIOP (quoted in *Birago Diop, Conteur*, dir. Paulin
Soumanou Vieyra, 1981)

In 2018, a group of martial artists traveled from France and across West Africa to participate in a weeklong series of workshops and presentations commemorating the twentieth anniversary of the founding of Afreecapoeira Senegal's first homegrown school dedicated to Afro-Brazilian martial arts. That week in July, the congregation of Brazilian, French, Senegalese, and other francophone West African capoeiristas held a performance at the Place de l'Obélisque in Dakar, a show that was broadcast by the Radiodiffusion Télévision Sénégalaise (RTS) during a World Cup screening event. As the performers caught their breath once the cameras left, a man stormed past in a fit of anger, shouting in Wolof. Dieudonné, a capoeirista from Dakar, translated his words for the mixed crowd of West

Africans: "[The man] just said, 'You don't have the right! Stop this monkey thing!'"

In a brutal irony, the comment echoed remarks in 1826 by Jean Dard—French colonial West Africa's first instructor—describing Europeans' general sentiment toward the Wolof language: "We have gone so far as to say that negros in general only speak a kind of chuckle without rules, without principles; a jargon almost similar to that of the orangutan" (quoted in Calvet 2010). The monkey analogy also resembled the description of James Wetherell (1860, 119–20), an Englishman visiting colonial Bahia who wrote a subsection in his travel journey "The Fighting of the Blacks": "They throw their legs about like monkeys during their quarrels. It is a ludicrous sight." The historian Matthias Röhrig Assunção (2005, 101) analyzed a section of this quote, noting that it reflected both Wetherell's Eurocentric assumptions, but "could nevertheless also express some degree of objectivity, since the imitation of animals' moves is a recurrent theme among capoeira practitioners." Wetherell, however, would not likely have taken emic perspectives into account. The Black cultural activist and iconic Afro-Brazilian capoeira leader Mestre Moraes addressed this type of cultural explanation in a TEDx talk on the practice of giving capoeira students *apelidos* (nicknames).[1] Moraes highlighted how many common *apelidos* are racist yet become normalized under the guise of "tradition" in tandem with the metanarrative that capoeira is free of prejudice. Mestre Moraes reminded his audience that the Catholic Church and the slave trade used the weapon of renaming enslaved Africans as a form of control. He described *apelidos* as originally a practice of countering oppression by tracing nicknames in capoeira to a broader African practice of honoring a child with a name that links them to their ancestors. However, the capoeira world has shifted to a tradition of giving names to students, and Black children in particular, that equate them with animals, disabilities, or inanimate objects. He offers examples of how *mestres* wield their authority to perpetuate harm through donning students with nicknames such as vulture, rat, frog, monkey, and chimney. I have also encountered shadow and even slave as common *apelidos* in capoeira.

During the performance of capoeira that ensued, the RTS news crew asked Mestre Boa Vida to play a musical solo, likely to showcase an "authentic" performance by the special Brazilian guest. Another Brazilian guest, Mestre Juruna, an Afro-Brazilian man trained in *capoeira regional*, stood quietly to the side while Boa Vida struck up the berimbau for the crowd at the Obelisque and for the countless TV viewers. Instead of engaging in what is almost always a collective activity, Boa Vida was isolated for a solo performance, singing and playing a slow *ladainha*. After a few minutes, a Senegalese man standing in the crowd burst into Islamic prayer song, complete with cascading melodies and vocal prowess. The two began trading off verses, alternately singing sorrowful themes about slavery in Brazilian Portuguese and worship music for the Murid saint Cheikh Amadou Bamba. Rather than becoming angry, as the first man did, this enraptured spectator took a different approach, weaving elements of Islam into an unrecognizable activity, rendering it legible to a Muslim Senegalese audience, and saturating it with religiosity.

The coloniality of Black performance is premised on the reality that Black corporeality is inescapable from racial tropes. The creativity of Black bodily performance is inextricably colored by racial tropes by both Black and non-Black spectators. The anger of the first Senegalese man at the illegibility of the gathering he witnessed may have stemmed from specific conventions of respectability, such as an Islamic framework for indecent displays of the body in public, the nature of gendered interactions, or the use of secular music in a predominantly Muslim context. Getting to the bottom of racially encoded criticism does not rely on an analysis of whether or not Islam is at the heart of the matter—neither is it necessary to prove race is the preeminent or sole marker of social difference in Senegal. Instead, I explore how the perception of an unrecognizable moving body as inappropriate is a form of hauntology—a rhetorical device that targets these bodies in a postcolonial discourse haunted by "lingering colonial interlocutors" (Coly 2019, 5). The racialized grammar (Ochonu 2019) of the man's outburst drew on well-established racialized tropes (the inappropriate use of the body being deemed "monkey-like"). References to animals read as subhuman behavior should be contextualized within the broader framework of what is common sense in postcolonial West Africa: comparisons to "nature" or to rurality ("bushness") are inextricably linked to the racialization of enslaved and colonized subjects (Faye and Thioub 2003; Mbembe 2001; Pierre 2020; Quijano 2007). The comment demonstrates how racialized discourse is readily available as a tool of social differentiation, and more specifically as a condemnation of bodies out of line.

The passerby's affective response and word choice trigger a set of questions about the possibility of white supremacy operating in Senegal, even without direct white actors. White supremacy rests on the surface of the everyday in urban West Africa. It lives in linguistic ideologies, the circulation of common phrases, and the categorization of bodily movement.

Coloniality is a framework to capture the enduring logics of the colonial encounter that survive the ostensibly liberatory events of independence or abolition (Mignolo 2012; Ndlovu-Gatsheni 2013; Quijano 2007; Wynter 2003). If we take seriously that coloniality is a mechanism for white supremacy to remain normative and germane, even in contexts without a significant presence of white people, then we see this discourse playing out in the most pronounced way concerning ideas about and uses of the body. The realm of performance calls attention to the body as an important site for the production of social categories. However, the performing body's materiality can be deceiving in its reification of "culture," "tradition," or nationalism, all concepts that traffic in racialism even without doing so explicitly. Black performing arts create spaces that center racial discourse, the body, and historical narratives that often result in a dangerously over-simplified public spectacle, erasing contemporary racial dynamics and minimizing the politics of cultural authorship. What I offer as *the coloniality of Black performance* reveals an iteration of white supremacy in postcolonial African sites that thrives in a context in which beliefs about Black or African inferiority are revealed within multiracial artistic spaces designed to celebrate Black cultural production. The coloniality of Black performance is the Trojan Horse effect of the infiltration of white authority through Black cultural expertise. Black performance is a practice in utopia, a choreography in process of a more liberated future (Cox 2015). Its utopic quality is a seductive force that attracts non-Black fascination and even dedication, and can even be used as a way to cleanse white guilt, perhaps even in sincerity, for historical wrongs (Jackson 2005). In short, the coloniality of Black performance highlights the exercise of devotion to Black performance arts with little to no acknowledgement of present racial exploitation.

A few performers from the group expressed only mild annoyance at the monkey comment, seeing it as another instance of critique from someone who "doesn't understand" their practice. In Dakar, racial discourse is not linked to structural dehumanization and its accompanying precarity of the bodily integrity of its targets, as is the case in white settler colonies such as the United States (Sharpe 2016; Ticktin 2011). What is specific to the dynamics of white supremacy here, and between differently positioned Black Africans, is the fact that racialized grammars are so deeply embedded in everyday ways of thinking, perceiving, and interacting that they are often ignored (Ochonu 2019; Pierre 2012). The fact that the capoeiristas reacted with mild irritation to being told they were behaving like monkeys is not proof of the incident's insignificance. Rather, it demonstrates the degree of normalcy and common acceptance of racialized insults as they circulate in everyday interactions.

The relationship between globally legible racial schemas and regionally specific discourses of difference in African contexts is increasingly under investigation (see, e.g., Lecocq 2005). Still, the debate has created a clear divide between those who find race to be relevant only to diasporic, but not continental, contexts—and by extension those who see the origins of racial ideologies in Africa as predating Euro-African contact—and those working to demonstrate the interconnectivity of race as a global phenomenon that impacts *all* African postcolonial societies. Coloniality in the form of the continued privileging of whiteness and the structuring of postcolonial societies into racial hierarchies is inextricably linked to schemas of social difference often framed as ethnicity, class, or caste (often perceived to be outside of or prior to European ideas of race). Autochthonous schemas of difference, such as the enduring attachment to ethnicity, and race as a phenomenon rooted exclusively in the diaspora, co-occur in sites such as Dakar, seemingly side by side and as two separate, unrelated phenomena. Yet their inextricable relationship becomes evident in the coloniality of Black performance.

Race is a fundamental technology of colonial and postcolonial statecraft in Africa, or what Jemima Pierre (2012) has called *racecraft*.[2] Ghana is a cosmopolitan site built on political and cultural ideologies such as Pan-Africanism that are inextricably linked to transnational capitalist development aspirations. Senegal is similarly global, yet is also a construct of Islamic statecraft, the administrative headquarters for all of French West Africa, and therefore subject to the legacy of direct *assimilation* efforts of the French civilizing mission (Conklin 1997; Diouf and O'Brien 2002). Therefore, processes of racialization are entangled with religiopolitical structures and Wolof cultural hegemony that often eclipses ethnic diversity in Senegal (McLaughlin 1995; Villalón 1995). I build on Pierre's argument that diaspora can sometimes act as an obstructive force that decenters postcolonial African racial realities. There are therefore two entry points from which to examine coloniality. One is the racialized grammar and categorization normalized in Senegalese society, and the second is the presence of foreign guests that are not spotlighted in discussions of whiteness because they are not directly tied to colonial rule.

The second iteration of the term's use stems from a critique of capoeira's inclusivity ethos that breaks down most starkly when global capoeira encounters African capoeira contexts. More broadly, the coloniality of Black performance is not simply the zealous consumption of Black performance. It is not even white people's participation in Black forms. It is also their embodiment as bearers of diaspora, and by extension, the performance of Blackness itself. White participation has always been at the roots of diasporic return in Senegal. Mestre Pastinha's presentation of capoeira during the World Festival of Negro Arts in Dakar in 1966—marking the first time it was played in Africa—included an interracial troupe of his students (figures 2.1–2.2).[3]

Capoeira has attracted white practitioners since at least the late nineteenth century, so by 1966 it would not have been uncommon to have a mixed group of students. The representation of capoeira's return to Africa, however, marks another layer in the larger debates among organizers and spectators that relates to what Andrew Apter (2005, 2016) calls Black cultural citizenship and the contested definitions of Blackness and Africanness at the historical event. Rather than argue for an essentialism that limits Black performance only to Black subjects, I want to draw attention to the unforeseen consequences not only of white participation but also of white expertise and diasporic embodiment in Black performance that this moment suggests. Not only has white leadership become normal in African-founded Afro-Brazilian capoeira associations in the twenty-first century, but the historical precedent for it is never openly discussed.[4]

Brazil has strong cultural purchase around the world, while the racial implications of its cultural exports are often radically and intentionally ambiguous. White subjects who are experts in Black cultural forms, such as the French, Brazilian, and American capoeira *mestres* who regularly visit West Africa, have been active consumers of Black cultural production for decades. Their expertise positions them as embodiments of "Black culture" for West African practitioners who are somewhat marginalized from global capoeira networks. As a result, whiteness in the postcolonial social landscape becomes flattened and depoliticized, especially in and through the realm of popular cultural production that centers racially obscured influences from sites such as Latin America. Beyond formal political systems and state-sponsored cultural events, grassroots, transnational artistic networks show how race is desired, rejected, and invisibilized in everyday life in urban West Africa through discourse and the affective experiences attached to performing bodies. I argue that race is often perceived as something external to West Africa, which obscures the problematic ways Black performance is perceived, embodied, and has the potential to revive colonial logics.

2.1 Mestre Pastinha's capoeira troupe arriving in Dakar in 1966.

2.2 Mestre Pastinha's capoeira troupe performing at FESMAN at the Daniel Sorano Theater in Dakar in 1966.

Casting Sinhazinha: Regionalizing Race

Afro-diasporic spaces on the continent, as Xavier Livermon (2020) has called them, can also result in the misrecognition of postcolonial Africans' own racialization. At a rehearsal for an upcoming show, Afreecapoeira rehearsed a dramatization of the capoeira song "Sinhazinha," which tells the story of a white slave master's daughter (Sinhazinha) who falls in love with a Black man her father owns, named Benedito.[5] When discussing roles, Yaya, an Ivorian law student, joked that Christopher (*apelido* Antilope), a master's student from the Central African Republic, should play Benedito. He commented, "He has the profile of a slave, look at him!," eliciting chuckles from the others. No one stepped up to play the slave owner/father, so the role remained unfilled in that moment. While many Africanists have argued for the centrality of domestic slavery (or "African slavery") as enduring in postcolonial sociality, all references to slavery in the Dakar-based capoeira school referenced the slave trade to the Americas.

When it came time to decide on Sinhazinha, the women unanimously decided on me. I noticed that Marianne, a reserved Senegalese capoeirista, had been more motivated in practice lately. I wanted to encourage her confidence, so I recommended she fill the role instead. Marianne responded by shielding her torso with crossed arms, saying, "It's better if you do it." This show required basic capoeira and dance moves that all the women present were more than capable of performing. As a light-skinned Black Brazilian American, and a confident capoeirista (even if my skills had not caught up with my confidence), I was often *expected* to have valuable contributions for creative projects, and *entrusted* with important positions. My proximity to whiteness—even stemming from diasporic Blacks—elicited "difference and deference" from West African interlocutors (Pierre 2012). In part, my proximity to capoeira as the daughter of an Afro-Brazilian master made me a logical choice for a creative adviser. Yet by 2018 I had forged friendships with the other members for nearly a decade, and they knew my capoeira skills and Portuguese proficiency to be far below what might have been expected. As a Western "guest," I should likely not have had so much influence in performances and administrative decision-making within this twenty-year-old West African cultural institution.

My racial identification in Senegal shifted depending on context. At times my status as a mixed-race, middle-class Black woman from the United States branded me as a *tubaab* (white person/Westerner).[6] At other times—most especially due to my Brazilian background and my experience as a capoeirista—I was seen as a diasporic Black and therefore racial kin. However, my proximity to whiteness relative to the African woman rendered me—by the normative schema of white supremacy—more central than I deserved to be. Later on, Aziz, a Burkinabe doctoral student in physics, mentioned Marianne as someone with the poise to play Sinhazinha. Aziz perceived her as being suitable for the role of the slave master's daughter, the object of desire and symbol of femininity and unattainability for an enslaved Black man. And yet, as a collective, we allowed for the foreign anthropologist to take the role.

Defining race exclusively through the vector of "slavery" in an imagined Brazilian past misses the ways that the creative process necessarily draws on local ideologies about how to think, talk, joke about, and embody race. Context shapes the way race is discussed, or hidden from plain view. What other logics would come into play in the absence of a Black Westerner? Would the national differences that were central to rifts in Afreecapoeira's past determine who could embody which racialized character in the dramatization? What does it mean that Christopher, who was from the Central African Republic and had notably lighter skin than Yaya, was humorously read as possessing "the profile of a slave?" African regionalism becomes the basis for a racialized grammar amongst West Africans in Dakar.

Here, capoeira is a Black safe space and creative outlet for those playfully and politically minded about their pursuit of Black identification. The joking part of play reveals the process of making the diasporic imaginary and Black elsewhere come alive and make sense in terms of the social categories at stake in Dakar. The framework of plantation hauntologies has gained traction for analyzing what Christina Sharpe (2016) theorizes as the "wake" of slavery in the Americas. Black performance in Dakar is often a conscious practice of learning about and creatively building from plantation hauntologies in the Americas, while the continuation of colonial hauntologies of race in African contexts operate largely invisibly in creative and mundane interactions (Coly 2019). The wake of the racial specter in the Americas is more visible than that of African histories themselves. Louisa Lombard (2016, 1) describes the reputation of the Central African Republic (CAR) in the colonial era in the following way: "CAR was known as the Cinderella of the French empire (big game hunters loved its vast spaces home to few people, but lots of other animals), or, less charitably, as the 'trash can' (of little strategic or economic importance, it was the dumping ground for colonial training school graduates with the lowest grades). Either way, it was a backwater." Dakar, on the contrary, where both Yaya and Christopher migrated to for higher education, symbolized "colonial solidarity," a beacon of the civilizational mission for France's imperial territories in the eyes of its colonial administrators (Delavignette 1950, 15). On a group trip to a capoeira event in the Gambia, Christopher and another capoeirista from the Central African Republic were held up at the border, and told despite being university students in Senegal for many years that the recent political conflict in the Central African Republic made them potentially dangerous. They were forced to sleep in the street until the issue was resolved in the morning, while Souvenir, a fellow Afreecapoeira member, spent the night with them in a show of capoeira community solidarity.

In order to produce an artistic representation of interracial love on an imagined plantation in Brazil, the capoeiristas must negotiate the available racial and gendered resources. The discursive and embodied resources are legible as gendered givens (the "girls" will play Sinhazinha) but also gendered intersections. As the Afro-Brazilian-American woman embodying a Brazilian-enough expertise and capoeira skill, I made sense as the choice to play the white plantation owner's daughter, and more importantly, the love interest, who is a symbol of ideal femininity and desirability. Christopher's Central African Republic nationality is not mired in a New World positionality of Black Otherness, but is positioned as Other in the colonial hierarchy of West Africa, in which Ivory Coast and Senegal are model mimesis (former) colonies, and the Central African Republic is not. Poking fun at Christopher as the best option among them to be the enslaved Benedito speaks to the racialized status of ñak, a derogatory Wolof term for non-Senegalese Africans. While not Senegalese and not a Wolof speaker, Yaya's status as an Ivorian, hailing from what was known as the "Paris of West Africa," depends on positioning himself as not a ñak, a slight his own sister (Ferelaha, also a capoeirista) has experienced.

Ambiguous Anniversary: Competing Claims of Racial and Creative Authority

The twentieth anniversary event produced performative acts that revealed the high stakes of Black cultural events in West Africa, even beyond the state-sponsored global spectacles (Apter 2005). Each day involved capoeira movement and music workshops, but also speeches from the visitors and the key hosts. One day after a morning workshop on the Castel on Gorée Island, the round of speeches ensued, set off by Boa Vida (figure 2.3).

2.3 Mestre Paulo Boa Vida giving a workshop at the top of Gorée Island for the twentieth-anniversary event. Photograph by Ibrahim Photography.

Mestre Boa Vida was the first capoeira expert to teach Moctar over a two-week workshop in the mid-1990s that led to Moctar founding Afreecapoeira (originally called Les Messagers du Vent). Their relationship ended when, as Moctar tells it, he refused to adhere to the strict requirement that he only practice the *capoeira angola* genre that Boa Vida practiced. Diaspora without displacement rests on proliferating ironies. A white Brazilian *mestre* refused to work any further with the first known Senegalese capoeiristas in history because they did not wish to be limited to the genre considered to be the "re-Africanization" of capoeira. Mestre Pastinha, the genre's creator, named it "Angola" after capoeira's foundations. Founder of the *capoeira angola* genre, he first brought it to Africa, performing it not in Angola, but in Senegal.

Boa Vida, now back in Senegal, spoke of a "rupture" that we must acknowledge happens often in capoeira circles, referring to his break with Moctar twenty years earlier. He reiterated his position that the African members were free to do what they wanted, and if they wanted to do more *capoeira angola* there was a lot to "correct." He expressed that he was willing to make those corrections, and if not, that they could still maintain a friendship. When he first came to Senegal, he had himself just transitioned from fifteen years of *capoeira regional*, the genre often opposed to *capoeira angola,* with the famous Senzala group. "I never gave a single belt to Afreecapoeira or anyone," he said. At that point, Samba, the Senegalese capoeirista who had been adopted by a French mother as a child and had introduced capoeira to Moctar, raised his hand timidly to say Boa Vida did in fact give him a belt a long time ago. Mestre Juruna took a humble approach, stating that as an Afro-Brazilian, he had wanted to come to Africa all his life, so he had come here to discover it. He emphasized that he came to give, but also to receive. His position as a capoeira expert (*mestre*) and a diasporic returnee were not used to assert what I call *diasporic chauvinism* (elaborated on in chapter 5), but rather to establish mutual cultural exchange.

After a few more speeches, Souleymane (known by his *apelido* Apollo) took the floor. A key figure in the history of Africa Capoeira, and one of Moctar's most advanced Senegalese capoeira students, he spoke intentionally in Wolof, and Gabrielle stepped in to translate. Boa Vida then told me to translate what she said in English, perhaps for the sake of the Gambians present. During Apollo's remarks, Boa Vida interrupted to ask him to speak French instead, and Apollo responded that he would, but only once he had finished with the full Wolof version. Apollo shared that he was African above all else. He spoke about conflicts he had with Africa Capoeira in the past, how he rejected his "family" and how they rejected him, but that capoeira was already a part of him. He recounted that his parents never paid for him to immigrate to France, that it was due to capoeira that he was able to travel around the continent and build a life in France.

Here, diaspora without displacement is a performance of inherent African worthiness. Apollo spoke into legitimacy the idea that West Africans are rightful heirs of capoeira rather than subordinated apprentices waiting two decades for instruction and guidance. What was at stake was not contained within the structure of capoeira hierarchy, as Apollo signaled. He brought to the fore the context of the event itself, as well as its historical and racial implications. Intervening in this "international" event centered in Dakar, and Gorée Island specifically, with a discourse in Wolof demonstrated an act of decolonization to the new face of coloniality (figure 2.4).

At one of the shows commemorating Afreecapoeira's twentieth anniversary, Paulo Boa Vida, the Brazilian *mestre*, led the presentation but RTS television crews interviewed three Senegalese capoeiristas so they could describe the martial art to viewers. In the capoeira *rodas* that ended up broadcast on national TV, African women capoeiristas—who had participated throughout the week's classes and workshops—joined in only briefly. In contrast, two French women capoeira players jumped freely in

2.4 Moctar and Elena playing in a *roda* led by Brazilian and Senegalese guests (who live in France) at the Place de L'Europe on Gorée Island, where the Brazilian flag was raised for the event. Photograph by Ibrahim Photography.

and out of the *roda* multiple times. In the final cut of the aired segment, RTS repeated a reel of the French women, spliced with scenes of three interviews, two of which were with Senegalese participants based in France who spoke with metropolitan French accents. Both white subjects and the Senegalese media effectively centered whiteness in the footage editing, shaping the way the collective of West African capoeiristas presented their cultural work to the broader public. Discussing the footage with a group of Africa Capoeira members while we messed around with the instruments during a lull in the day's activities, Gabrielle, a longtime member of Africa Capoeira, discussed why she thought Lamine was chosen for the interview: "They wanted a real Senegalese face." We all chuckled, and Lamine pushed back, "Does that even exist?" Everyone else chimed in that true Senegalese are tall, thin, and dark. Gabrielle stated that she was none of these, reminding us about the struggles she voices regularly of being of Cape Verdean descent, born in Senegal, and a second- or third-language Wolof speaker. Her nationality is consistently questioned, neither Senegalese enough nor Cape Verdean enough, she said. The RTS representation of capoeira—focused on the "true" Senegalese, the Brazilian *mestres*, and white French women—revealed the layered forms of racial coloniality that Black performance brings to the surface.

The scales of exclusion collapsed when the cameras shut off. Mestre Juruna struck up the berimbau in a fast-paced rhythm signaling *capoeira regional*, the genre that is often perceived as more exciting to watch because of the standing acrobatics, rapid-fire kicks, and dramatic takedowns that resemble East Asian martial arts. Suddenly, all the West African women capoeiristas that only clapped their hands to support others playing when the cameras were rolling sprinted to the orchestra to have a go in the *roda*. More representatives from the visiting West African schools outside of Senegal jumped in to play too, especially those who were at different skill levels. This inclusive off-screen *roda* was vibrant with participation, and it was not for lack of skill or confidence that they did not appear earlier. One Gambian woman, Aissatou, faced off with Gabrielle, showing off moves she had learned since the last collaboration between the Gambian and Senegalese schools. Another Gambian young woman, Seynabou, jumped in to play. Her kicks were much higher and more stable than the last time I saw her. Watching her, I realized this was my first time seeing her play in a *roda* during the weeklong event that had begun days ago. She faced off with a man much bigger than her, and yet she remained direct in her attacks. After backing him into a corner, she even called for a *volta do mundo*, a kind of reset in capoeira sometimes used to gloat and signal to the audience that you could do worse to your opponent, but have decided to be merciful.

Boa Vida opened most of the events that week with a speech to set the tone. He claimed he "planted the seed" that became the group that exists today. Boa Vida had not been back to Senegal in the twenty years since his initial visit that helped spark Moctar's group, citing a disagreement with Moctar over the artistic direction of the brand-new Senegalese capoeira school. Ousmane, a Senegalese participant at the event, commented in frustration, "The seed metaphor is a bad one. Did he water the seed? Check on it? No. He just planted it and then came to harvest." Those enacting diasporic chauvinism must lay claim to diaspora, which requires an orientation to an African origin. Later in the speech, Boa Vida stated that he "too was a child of Gorée Island," drawing on a Brazilian myth of racial harmony in which all Brazilians can lay claim to Indigenous, European, and African heritage. The capoeira world in these moments of "return" epitomize how Black performance has been divorced from Black cultural authority.

Boa Vida had recourse to a Brazilian racial ideology of creolization, in which all who possess Brazilian nationality are understood to carry the blend of Indigenous, European, and African heritage—a discourse that obscures the country's deeply racist structures. Writing about white Portuguese practitioners of Afro-Brazilian Candomblé, Roberto Strongman (2019, 222) theorizes how "participation in Candomblé might serve as an expiation of colonial guilt for the Portuguese participants and explain the dearth of Brazilian migrants—who might be more interested in acquiring respectability through assimilation—in Portugal." Black performance trajectories reveal a postcolonial phase of reabsorption by colonial logics and by those positioned to embody its legacy. Black performance is an avenue through which non-Black and specifically white subjects from the heart of Empire transform themselves, their bodies, voices, and even identifications, through the open door of artistic expression to resolve collective white guilt of their position as a former internal or external colonizer. Their intentions are to rectify harms of the past, and yet the cannibalism, and often self-centering, of white performers and practitioners engenders new harms as these forms grow, circulate, and change.

Just hours before the pinnacle event, the *batizado* (baptism) ceremony to graduate each student to the next level as capoeiristas, Boa Vida banned the belts at the center of the event. This was, as he framed it, to push the group to accept *capoeira angola*, the genre of capoeira he ascribes to that does not use a belt system. I heard about the ban in the women's sleeping quarters where the diverse group of about ten West African young people, many of whom did not know each other and did not have a shared language, had organized teams to clean the mats, the floor, and the bathrooms. As they were joking about how the men were likely not even attempting to clean their own quarters, Elena came to break the news that the ceremony would be deprived of the belt ritual. Some folks grew sad and quiet, others angry, and dissemination of this information provoked animated discussions. No one confronted Boa Vida about the decision, and only a few chose to wear their belts in protest.

In an act revealing the irony at the heart of the coloniality of Black performance, Boa Vida revoked the core objects that materialized the creative work of Africa Capoeira in the name of imposing a version of capoeira widely considered to be its most "African" iteration (Höfling 2019). Africa Capoeira has struggled for twenty years to institutionalize their association and have yet to own their own training grounds or establish cultural centers. In light of this, symbolic objects such as belts and ceremonies such as the *batizado* take on a deeper significance and function as evidence of their consistent efforts over the years. Boa Vida's restriction was deeply unsettling for both experienced members of the West African school, who took great pride in the belts they earned, and for the newest recruits who worked all year to earn them. The ceremony proceeded without belts. I spoke about Boa Vida's decision to Lamine, who provided an analysis minimizing his role in their everyday affairs outside of these symbolic, infrequent events. He described the hierarchy: "Moctar is only *Profesor* status. He's not a *mestre*, and his *mestre* was Mestre Paulo Boa Vida. At a certain point Moctar wanted to do regional, angola, and Benguela. Why not?" He noted that Boa Vida, strictly an *angoleiro*, wanted to cut ties with Moctar based on the latter's decision to be open to all styles. Africans are often positioned as perpetual apprentices rather than experts, outside of a colonial, anthropological framework of being "local informants" (Biruk 2018; de Sá 2024). Lamine thought through the effects on regular members:

> Now for us, well, if we go somewhere to any capoeira event, the first thing they ask is, "Who is your *mestre*?" And we have to say our teacher is only a *Profesor*, and when they said, "Who is his *mestre*?" then we say Boa Vida. But I've never seen the guy in my life. I've only seen one photo of him, and it was from about ten years prior. He even had gray hair already. If I saw him I wouldn't know him.

The ban demonstrated the unfettered power of whiteness in two distinct ways. The first is the default social status white people are accorded in West Africa that equates the socioeconomic privilege of a profitable businessman with that of a Peace Corps volunteer, collapsing them into an assumed association of whiteness with wealth (Pierre 2012). The second is the way that default white privilege in West Africa coincides with cultural expertise that leaves it unchallenged. The reproduction of colonial dynamics operates not only through assertions of white privilege regarding the right to embody Blackness and claim ownership over Black art forms and cultural institutions but also through postcolonial subjects deferring to the "knowledge and expertise" of white authority *even in Black performance traditions, and even in spaces of their own creative ownership.* Ashley Humphrey (2020, 110)has noted that "mainstream white ideology in North America and Europe [is] still resistant to conceptualizing its role in participating in white supremacy and Black capoeira culture at the same time." Lauren Griffith (2020) does similar work on white Americans' commitment to capoeira practice and apprenticeship pilgrimages in Brazil, which she finds coexists with race and class prejudice toward Brazilians and a lack of understanding about racial inequality in the United States. White Brazilian capoeira experts possess an uncomfortable blind spot in their assumptions about cultural authority and the structures of race. In

African contexts, white Brazilians do not have to directly confront the reality of racial inequality in Brazil. In turn, as experts in this form of Black performance, they feel entitled to represent a practice built on a legacy of Black resistance to oppression, granting themselves license to exercise creative control while ignoring its present social implications. Attending to coloniality in a hyper-transnational contemporary moment requires dislocating our gaze from the usual suspects of whiteness (i.e., "racists") and to think beyond given geographies and predictable sources.

The coloniality of Black performance sits at the transnational intersection of race and gender. Writing about Senegalese wrestling, Irene Peano discusses the topic of intersectional masculinities as requiring more exploration: "The 'global' perspective assumed in wrestling (and in Senegalese culture more generally) implicitly sets the particular masculinities that take shape within it also against an imagined *white* masculinity. . . . The explicit resonances connecting wrestling to African-American masculinities relate to an absent but often very powerfully felt white other, the logic of whose discourses per se is not questioned, but simply appropriated" (Peano 2007, 50). If, as Peano suggests, whiteness is an unspoken standard of masculinity for Senegalese wrestlers and African Americans alike, then white Brazilian experts of a Black cultural form is a phenomenon that evokes deep confusion. Black masculinities in capoeira are similarly formed in relation to an unspoken white standard, yet white and other non-Black experts can represent and provide access to that aspiration toward Black masculinity. Black cultural expertise silences or overrides the fact of whiteness. Brazilian myths—not only of racial democracy but also of the claims of African (cultural) heritage made by white Brazilians—allow whiteness to be a nonfactor in the universe of capoeira.

Becoming "Bush" in the Land of Hospitality

Regardless of who planted the seed for Africa Capoeira, it's more important to ask, what did the trajectory of growth look like during the twenty years of its history? What kind of social and imaginative worlds did Africa Capoeira produce? Senegal is widely characterized as a country relatively devoid of discrimination. This myth has been grounded in historical scholarship that has portrayed Senegal as an example of ethnic tolerance and religious pluralism, and therefore as a beacon of democratic stability in West Africa (M. Diouf 2013; Gellar 2005; Villalón 1995). Scholars are not always in agreement about how this discourse developed, but most locate Senegal's exceptionalism in the unique way its secular government has incorporated religious leaders and institutions, making governance and social development a tripartite system divided between Sufi brotherhoods, the state, and the people by way of democratic associations. The reputation of "moderate Islam" in Senegal comes in part from the historic collaboration between Sufi brotherhoods and the colonial, and now independent, state. Some believe this collaborative system of sharing power between the brotherhoods and the state is responsible for the country's stable democracy, while others are critical of this narrative of the "Senegalese social contract" that assumes the public to be passive followers of religious leaders with political power (Babou 2013; O'Brien 1996; Villalón 1995). In addition to this scholarship, popular and political discourses of Senegalese exceptionalism have also centered around the perception of a precolonial character as represented by the popular Senegalese axiom of *teranga*, or hospitality.

In light of increasing incidents of unrest in West Africa, as well as "ethnic" and religious conflict in the country, some scholars have begun to argue that the notion of Senegal's exceptional stability and tolerance may be under threat. Irene Osemeka (2011) has argued that pluralism and tolerance in Senegal should be more explicitly promoted in national dialogue. While relative democratic stability has translated into a pervasive understanding of Senegal as being religiously plural, as well as socially accepting of minority groups, the self-described experiences of non-Senegalese university students suggest that "Wolofization" in the contemporary Dakar social landscape is not a neutral or inclusive phenomenon. Those outside "Wolof-ness"—in particular, West and Central Africans who have migrated to Senegal—face subtle discrimination at best and sustained social exclusion at worst. Those who experience exclusion are perhaps overrepresented in capoeira, and therefore may not be representative of the general treatment of foreigners. Nevertheless, for them, capoeira has become a space of acceptance, creative self-expression, and reinvention. Another side of this diasporic process relates to the forms of social marginalization migrants experience, and how these experiences are addressed through their participation in capoeira.

The discourse of tolerance and peaceful coexistence does not match the reality of the capoeira training center. Language is one of the key issues through which foreign capoeiristas articulate their exclusion. "Wolofization" is a process by which Wolof language and social norms became hegemonic for minority language and ethnic groups in Senegal (McLaughlin 1995). Speaking Wolof has become synonymous with Senegalese national identity, whereas speaking other languages means that Sereer or Diola ethnic minorities, for example, are considered regionally specific subgroups of the nation (Villalón 1995). A shared language allows for communication and communalism across ethnolinguistic lines in a country as diverse as Senegal. Wolofization, however, poses a threat of homogenization at the expense of a rich texture of histories and identifications that are constantly evolving. As Villalón (1995, 45) put it, "Learning Wolof is thus a two-edged sword." Ultimately, the vast majority of scholarship debating the unique relationship between religion, ethnicity, language, and politics in Senegal has been concerned with the dynamics within the confines of the nation-state (O'Brien 1998). Examining tensions between nationals and non-nationals has remained mostly outside of this purview.

In the past fifteen years, Senegal's first capoeira school has unexpectedly become a sanctuary for educational and labor migrants from other francophone West African countries (primarily university students). This process has led to them seeking refuge in an imagined third space (Bhabha 1994) that is neither their home nor their host "culture." Brazil, a rising economic star and cultural icon around the world, has become increasingly appealing as an alternative to the failed Western promise of opportunity, economic advancement, and modernity. For these migrants, capoeira provides an environment of home and family seldom found elsewhere in a city in which they express feeling socially marginalized by a Wolof cultural and linguistic hegemony they find difficult to penetrate. The repetition of gathering for training on Mondays, Wednesdays, Fridays, and some weekends, creates a rhythm for their daily lives that shapes not only their bodies but also their thoughts, energies, and environments. In preparation for a show at a local Ethiopian restaurant, Elena choreographed a solo and practiced dropping into the splits, an update of her signature move, every day leading up to the show, either on the terrace in her apartment or at the Fann practice space. Dieudonné trained at home too, often taking his berimbau to the beach well into the night to work on his rhythmic technique.

For many of these foreign university students, coming to Senegal was an opportunity to reinvent themselves, and capoeira was one of the main mechanisms of reinvention. Many were driven from their home countries due to lack of opportunity, or out of fear of political violence, which disrupted their sense of national identification. One of the most popular teachers in Afreecapoeira, Sylvèr, came to Senegal after he and his family fled the Congo to settle in Burkina Faso, where he went to high school. Senegal was their original destination, but the cost of the residency card was too high, at 500,000 CFA francs per person (about $1,000). The ongoing conflict in the Congo soured Sylvèr on the idea of befriending other Congolese in Dakar, and he was reluctant to identify with his natal country. When I asked him about his closeness to Souvenir, another Congolese expat in his Afreecapoeira cohort, he told me that they were able to build a friendship because they knew each other through capoeira. Christopher, another Afreecapoeira member, was from the Central African Republic but preferred not to identify himself by nationality, ethnicity, or race: "Those things cause so much division and violence that distracts us from seeing everyone as human."

For others, capoeira was the reason they remain attached to Senegal despite feeling marginalized there. While it was always likely that the market infrastructure would not be able to provide employment to all who came from abroad for education and training, some were already disinclined to even attempt to find a job in Senegal, based on their experience living in Dakar as a student. Aziz had been a committed member of Afreecapoeira since he moved to Dakar from Burkina Faso. Though his free time was limited by his pursuit of a doctorate in physics at the Université Cheikh Anta Diop (UCAD), he still showed up to practice nearly every session to show his dedication to the group—often in a Dutch wax print, button-down shirt and black dress pants—even if he only made the last few minutes of class. Aziz shared with me how capoeira shaped his experience of Dakar:

> If today I'm still in Dakar, I can say that it is 50 percent because of capoeira, because of the capoeira group. . . . At every level, I actually had projects that involved leaving Dakar. But if there is one thing that pushed me to stay here it is capoeira, it is the capoeira group. And I really plan on living capoeira my whole life. I really plan on making my place in the world of capoeira. And I really plan on, I wouldn't say living by capoeira but to have the resources to always come back to capoeira. And I really hope to bring my contribution to this group, to make it grow. I really plan to sacrifice a good amount of my person, of my time in capoeira and in this group.

Not only did Aziz stress the significance of capoeira itself in his life, but he also demonstrated the particular relationship he had to Afreecapoeira. He sacrificed his time, despite his busy teaching and research schedule, to help the organization with performances and events, and to train on his own with friends. This was a testament to how important this group had been to him while living in Senegal. His time there was not always easy, because he was called a *ñak* (African foreigner) and socially excluded for not speaking Wolof. For these reasons, he felt Senegalese were often not receptive to foreign nationals, and on many occasions he considered leaving for better educational opportunities. In the end, it was the "spirit" and the sense of family in Afreecapoeira that guided his decision to stay as long as he had. Almost every non-Senegalese university student I spoke to had a strikingly similar story about how they ended up at Afreecapoeira. They came to Dakar because it houses some of the best universities in Francophone Africa, particularly in the medical field. They all expressed feeling socially isolated as foreigners and non-Wolof speakers. After eight, ten, or sometimes fifteen years of living and studying in Dakar, many had come to enjoy their life there, filled with friends from all over the world except for Senegal.

While the primary barriers to social incorporation seem to relate to language, ideas around belonging in Senegal are often imbued with racialized and nationalist discourse as well; "outsiders" are placed in opposition to Senegalese people on various levels. Once, when I invited an Ivorian woman from the group, Ferelaha, over to conduct an interview, Sokhna, the housemaid where I was staying, pulled me aside and asked me why I was spending time with such an ugly, dark-skinned girl. Because Sokhna had a slightly darker complexion than Ferelaha, I knew she was using skin color as a proxy for Ferelaha's status as a foreigner. In speaking about her experience in Dakar as a foreign national, Ferelaha stated, "I had a hard time integrating here. I didn't have a lot of activities, which actually helped me concentrate and advance in my studies." She moved to Senegal a decade earlier at the advice of a family friend who also went to pursue medical studies.

While diaspora is often a compelling aspiration to West Africans grappling with the colonial legacy of regional hierarchies, regionalism can also be the antidote to diaspora's failed promises. The disappointment or end of diaspora unexpectedly facilitates a new kind of postcolonial regionalism within grassroots, artistic networks. Ferelaha was pleased to tell me she loves all the other Africans she has had the pleasure of getting to know. She loves that they learn about each other's cultures, although she, like others, has not managed to become close with many Senegalese. When I asked how she'd spent eleven years in Dakar without developing many friendships with Senegalese people, she told me it was not her "personal choice":

> The Senegalese are nice but I found that they say *teranga* [Wolof concept of welcoming] but they don't really do *teranga* like they say. They

tell you [they have] *teranga* when you come here but they don't really want to integrate you. Even for speaking Wolof. . . . This is probably why I don't really have many more intimate Senegalese friends. When we are together in a restaurant or somewhere, if the group is two foreigners and everyone else is Senegalese, you two will be next to each other speaking French and everyone else speaks Wolof. They don't try to teach you, they said, "No, you have to figure out yourself how to speak Wolof." Even if you've only been there two or three weeks. Seriously . . . , that doesn't encourage you to learn Wolof! So maybe it's that that discouraged me from learning Wolof.

Ferelaha admitted to feeling connected to a particular capoeira song because of how it helped her understand her experience as an Ivorian migrant who had lived as an isolated expatriate for eleven years at the time. The song, simple and repetitive, is called "Marinheiro Só" (I'm Just a Sailor):

Eu não sou daqui
Marinheiro só
Eu não tenho amor
Marinheiro só
Eu sou da Bahia
Marinheiro só
De São Salvador
Marinheiro só

I am not from here
I'm just a sailor
I don't have love
I'm just a sailor
I'm from Bahia
I'm just a sailor
From São Salvador
I'm just a sailor

She first fell in love with the sound of the song before she understood the Portuguese meaning. The recording was made by Carolina Soares, a Brazilian artist known for popularizing capoeira songs by adding instruments and vocal stylings more characteristic of popular music. The melody of the song itself suggested to her that it had a "very deep meaning." Once she looked up the translation of the lyrics, she thought, "Wow, this represents me so well. It's a little nostalgic." As an ethnomusicologist, Humphrey offers an insightful argument about capoeira's historical trajectory being split into contradictory realities: the marginalization of Black women in its practice and historiography is incongruent with the overwhelming presence of them as subjects of the songs (2020). Nonetheless, music can become the site of reclamation, healing, and political performance for Afro-diasporic women in capoeira (Humphrey 2020). Ferelaha's intersectional identity as a woman and migrant drew her to the song as she read her own experience of regional displacement into the sorrowful musings of an anonymous Brazilian sailor.

Ferelaha was one of many to speak about the years spent in Dakar without being able to crack the Wolof-dominated social scene. Their shared sense of social exclusion was what drew many young West African students to the capoeira school, where they celebrate their diversity through their mutual love of Brazilian culture. In this way, training capoeira, learning Portuguese, and building new intimacies in this unconventional social network of martial artists softened the pangs of perpetual exclusion as an Ivorian female expatriate in Senegal. Relative to migration studies that focus on the masculine "adventure" of dangerous and spectacular treks from West Africa to Europe (Melly 2017), and more optimistic studies on what migrants build rather than lose (Babou 2021), women's experiences such as Ferelaha's turn our attention not only to other circuits of migration but also to how women in particular cope with this displacement through artistic expression.

Discussions of race on the continent have often focused on South Africa, as scholars try to sort out the phenomenon of Afrophobia, or "African national on African migrant" aggression (Mkhize 2017; Nyamnjoh 2006). In this case, Afrophobia reveals a colonial and apartheid-era binary of insider/outsider carried into the twenty-first century, in which the narrative construction of "Africa" is weaponized against a shifting population, anyone deemed an outsider. A country such as Senegal often stands at the other end of the spectrum due to its perceived racial homogeneity and presumed absence of internal racializing structures since the country gained political sovereignty from France. To challenge the narrative of Senegalese exceptionalism means revealing racial logics of hierarchy in the postcolonial context.

In the space of Dakar, various categories of people within the schema of social belonging speak to what Moses Ochonu (2019, 5) calls "a hidden corpus of racial signs and symbols" and "discernible racial or neo-racial tropes capable of structuring lived African experiences" that display continuities with European imperial rule. The Wolof term *ñak* circulates in Dakar today to refer to non-Senegalese Africans, and may have first been used by Senegal's first president, Leopold Senghor, to characterize Guinean migrants to the country. The term carries connotations of "bush people" who lack civility or sophistication, yet ironically may have initially become popularized by Senghor in an effort at regional unity during the period of African decolonization.[7] Senegal's colonial relationship with the French stands out as politically cooperative (Babou 2013) and assimilationist (Conklin 1997), leaving behind a legacy of civilizing rhetoric. Senghor was the exemplar of how African traditional values (and Senegalese national culture) might be combined with the French ideal of civilization to create a proper modern state (Diouf 2013; Harney 2004).

Think of *ñak* now in relation to the term *tubaab* (meaning a white European, now also applied to white Americans, but interestingly not to people identified as "Arabs"), used in contrast to "African." Although resentment toward the presence of whites/Westerners may mean the term is invoked negatively, it is not inherently derogatory, but rather playful or neutrally descriptive. A second binary relates to an African outsider, rather than signaling a local or continental kin: *ñak/senegale*. In comparing these two binaries—African/*tubaab* and *ñak/senegale*—we see that in the first, "African" in relation to *tubaab* (or white person) denotes an anticolonial continental unity within a black/white binary. In the second, *ñak* (read: African) is a racialized outsider, positioned against a civilized Senegalese insider, and also employing historical proximity to French colonial rule and the so-called gifts of its modernity. In other words, the category "African" is at once racialized in opposition to whiteness (*tubaab*), and yet also redeployed to racialize and other non-Senegalese people as "Africans." The ironic figure of the African racialized other is a colonial continuity that can also be found in many other parts of the continent (Nyamnjoh 2006).

Analyzing Senegalese social dynamics in light of this increasing Afrophobia in other parts of the continent, both North and South, might seem useful only as a challenge to an "exceptional" African country's democratic stability and relative absence of xenophobically motivated crime. This variant of anti-Africanness in Senegal is therefore distinct from that of the spectacular violence that accompanies the phenomenon in South Africa. In the Senegalese context, the exclusion manifests itself in subtler (and sometimes not-so-subtle) forms of discrimination in Dakar's social landscapes. It is often displayed in segregated spaces of social life and leisure, as well as the circulation of cautionary tales and insulting remarks about foreign African ways. While the primary barriers to social incorporation could be categorized as issues of language (non-Wolof speakers), ideas around belonging in Senegal are often imbued with racialized meanings disguised by nationalist discourse.

Losing Brazil: Defending Diaspora Without Displacement

Bigue had a telling relationship to Blackness. Almost all of her free time was spent nurturing her deep affinity for Black Atlantic art forms. In addition to capoeira, she trained with several Senegalese dance troupes, drummed in a Brazilian *batucada* group called Sambaobab, and even joined a coveted Alvin Ailey workshop in Dakar. She idolized the Candomblé goddess of the sea, Iemanja, which is also her capoeira nickname (*apelido*), and felt a strong connection to the history of slavery and the plight of Black people around the world. Yet, in Afreecapoeira, Bigue regularly expressed resentments toward the majority non-Senegalese African membership. Frustrated by the fact that most of the trainings were conducted in French, her third language, Bigue complained, "It's normal if you live or work here, you should learn Wolof! They don't want to learn because they don't like Senegalese, and they don't care to integrate themselves." At times, Bigue and other Senegalese capoeiristas referred to the other members as *ñaks*, a derogatory term in Wolof that is used to mean "unsophisticated" or "from the bush." Many in the group who were African migrants to Senegal mentioned they had frequently experienced the insult.

Taking into account her explicit expressions of Atlantic Blackness through her associations, her appearance, and her life's work as an artist within a variety of traditionally Black forms, Bigue's drawing on a xenophobic framework to characterize non-Senegalese Africans might seem out of place. This tension, however, is telling of a particular postcolonial dynamic in which pro-Blackness and anti-African-Otherness can exist side-by-side. In other words, an orientation toward "we Blacks" operates in the same space as "those African foreigners." Bigue pays careful attention to her everyday enactments of Black self-fashioning, such as donning a hair wrap to conceal her dreadlocks that she said would otherwise garner judgment from other Senegalese who might associate them with a wayward lifestyle.

The global reputation of certain forms of Black aesthetics and artistic production have been somewhat racially sanitized and packaged. This allows Black performance to be globally marketable, particularly for idle-class Western consumers (Robitaille 2014). The fact that other forms of Blackness are still considered unpalatable or shameful (e.g., dreadlocks), speaks to an environment in Dakar that is simultaneously a bastion of eclectic Black cultural innovation as well as pervasive anti-Blackness.

There is thus a danger in essentializing Black performance, histories of racialization, and political subjectivities. To view Blackness as either present or absent, as either relevant or irrelevant (even if its irrelevance is argued through a rhetoric of "Blackness as default" in an "already all-Black country" such as Senegal) not only obliterates the multiplicity of its raciontologies (Rosa and Díaz 2019; Shankar 2019). It also obscures the possibility of seeing the ways that white supremacy operates insidiously through the discursive celebration of global Blackness that distracts from myriad forms of racialization on the ground, in the context-specific every day—two forms of Blackness in apposition, but ultimately at odds.

Arnaud is a former member of Afreecapoeira who grew up in the densely populated suburb of Parcelles where he learned under the instruction of a Franco-Senegalese woman who taught capoeira to working-class Senegalese youth on her trips to Dakar. Yet Arnaud's attachment to his days as an active capoeirista was illuminating: He still carried his membership card in his wallet since he quit his training in 2005 (figure 2.5). The card is his physical link to this diasporic practice, particularly as it demonstrated a link to one of the prominent Brazilian capoeira schools, Grupo Senzala. He grew up on the outskirts of Dakar, discovered capoeira there, and acquired his *apelido* "Ndong" (a surname in Wolof, but in this case a term teasing him about the size of his head). He still lives on the outskirts, and has only the card left as a remnant of his diasporic passion. For Arnaud, his status as being from the *quartiers populaires* or "populous neighborhoods" such as Guediawaye and Parcelles—marginal (geographically and otherwise) working-class areas of Dakar—was meaningful in regards to how he might have been perceived by the foreigners, a deficiency rendered irrelevant in the face of superior capoeira skills.

I met Arnaud accidentally when I went to the major electricity company Senelec to pay my bill. Arnaud was working there as a clerk, and he overheard me chatting in English. He interjected in English to say, "Are you talking about Afreecapoeira? I used to train with them." I proceeded with a host of questions, and Arnaud, seated still with a calm grin on his face that

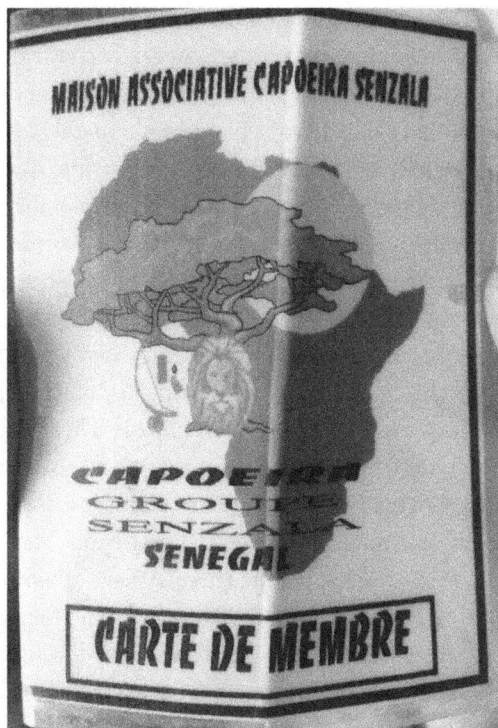

2.5 The front of Arnaud's capoeira ID. Photograph by the author.

countered my unfettered excitement, explained to me the events of a particular show from years before. He believed this event to be the climax of building tensions between Senegalese members and the new population of foreign Africans in the capoeira group:

> We rebelled. We stopped. Because they [other members] said we are indispensable, without us the shows would be less interesting. That's why we stopped. We went to a show at Petersene [market area]. There's a cultural center. There are guys doing art there, not far from the Grande Mosque. We left to do a show there, there were some differences between us and the foreigners, then Ndiaye [Moctar] took to their defense. So, seeing that things were like that, we decided not to do the show. I don't exactly remember [what the problem was] anymore. It was an issue with that one guy [name redacted], he wanted to organize everything "Yeah, we're doing this and that," you see. And we didn't want to. So . . . Ndiaye didn't defend us. We weren't discouraged, we were just mad. We left. We said if it's going to be like this we won't come anymore. And they didn't try to stop us. They really didn't give a shit.

The ultimate betrayal for Arnaud was that Moctar seemed to favor the African foreigners over the Senegalese crew from Parcelles. Curious about the state of the group now, he inquired about the current members, so we went through Facebook pictures, alternating between him showing me the Senegalese who were there before my time, and me showing him the new generation. As I pointed out the active members, his assessment of Afreecapoeira was expressed in the rhythm of a single repeated phrase: "Nothing but foreigners (*étrangers*). Nothing. But. Foreigners. *Nothing* but foreigners, you see? *Nothing* but foreigners. You see, no? Nothing. But. Foreigners." In order to get more information about who he meant by "foreigners," I asked his opinion about the frequency of white participation when he was in the group, to which he responded: "Diversity." Arnaud then elaborated: "It's cool. In our time it was cool. We all got along; we didn't have a problem with the Europeans." His resentment toward the foreign majority in the group was thus solely directed toward non–Senegalese Africans. More than ten years after leaving the group, Arnaud still displayed bitterness about the perceived mistreatment of him and other Senegalese *distinctly in relationship to other Africans,* whom he believed were less skillful in capoeira. He was still upset not only about the events of the 2005 show that resulted in the demise of his capoeira career but also about the negligible Senegalese representation in the group during my period of research.

The weight of what is at stake has something to do with the ephemerality and intangibility of spaces of Black cultural production in Dakar. Since the exodus that Arnaud spoke of in 2005, Afreecapoeira has seen dwindling numbers of Senegalese participants. The group has since been overwhelmingly composed of non-Senegalese Africans, typically university students at UCAD and young professionals. The narrative as to why the group lacks Senegalese members is also shaped by racial colonial discourse: synchronic explanations that rely on culturalist frameworks (Mudimbe 1988; Trouillot 2003). As Moctar, the founder, offered (as did many other Senegalese and non-Senegalese practitioners alike), the Senegalese are "very religious," "they don't know capoeira," and "they don't like it." Despite the fact that for much of the group's history there was strong Senegalese representation, the default argument for explaining their absence relies on tropes of cultural alterity, narrow-mindedness about worldly things, and an ignorance or aversion to nonlocal culture attributed to "the Senegalese" (Diawara 1998). Arnaud's affective reaction to the Facebook photos speaks to the difficulty he has in seeing foreigners at the center of something precious to him, as someone who was there in the early years, and as a Senegalese from the working-class neighborhood of Parcelles with a crew of peers he framed as highly talented renegade acrobats.

Drawing on Manthia Diawara, Xavier Livermon writes:

> Therefore, in a society still structured unevenly by racialized class, those moments where the individual can operate or fashion a technology of the self (even if only temporarily—let's say at a party) remain of utmost importance. This self-fashioning is, as many scholars point out, an important facet of the "black good life," . . . It is about an unapologetic celebration of life. In the midst of unequal life chances, the insistence on the black good life marks a refusal to reduce one's life experience to the real challenges faced by unequal access to capital in all its guises. (2014, 293–94)

In this case, the working-class Senegalese capoeiristas fought for ownership and representation of the capoeira group as a technology of self-fashioning in which they were "the best at acrobatics." It was a mode not only of being seen but also of being sought after, distinctive, and possessing expertise. This could easily be misread non-intersectionally in terms of "class" distinctions, precisely because the culprit of their perceived marginalization is a fellow working-class Senegalese (the founder) and fellow African martial artists. Arnaud's claims could even be misread as a crude expression of Senegalese nationalism. However, the legibility he sought, and the way he presented the problem itself, was in a fundamentally racial colonial grammar that demonstrated a racial affect (Kondo 2018), and a paradoxical kind of pain over the loss of a space of Black joy and talent at the hands of *ñaks*.

To refer back to the twentieth anniversary event, Boa Vida, a conduit of Brazilian capoeira schools via France, acts as gatekeeper of a foundationally Black form of cultural production in a way that partially dispossesses Senegalese and other West Africans of full ownership over their own practice, in an ironic attempt to introduce an Afro-diasporic practice "back" to Africans on the continent. It is no wonder, then, that the first autonomous African-founded capoeira school in Senegal has a contentious history with respect to issues of ownership and belonging among shifting waves of new members. The fight for cultural and symbolic ownership of the capoeira school (a representation of Black triumph over enslavement, but also of the freedom of individual expression and the right to build community in Dakar) is a debate that extends the discussion of white supremacy into the political space of intra-African interpersonal interactions and worldviews.

Tubaab Pride: Racializing Regionalism and Depoliticizing Whiteness

Jemima Pierre and Laura Chrisman have demonstrated how the African diaspora (predominantly in the United States) is privileged with tacit ownership of race and slavery as cultural and political subject positions (Chrisman 2003; Pierre 2012, 2020). What's more, Africans are often portrayed as either passive imitators of Black diasporic culture or opportunistic in identifying as Black in order to have proximity to Western modernity via the Black diaspora (Chrisman 2003). In addition to the centering of diasporic experiences in sighting/citing/site-ing race, Latin American contexts such as Brazil are automatically celebrated for their African "cultural survivals," which are often confused for Black political consciousness and can even be at odds with it (Smith 2016a). The emphasis on the continuation of "African culture" in the Brazilian national imaginary tends to depoliticize the racial hierarchy that structures Brazilian society. This self-image is then reinforced through the global export of performance traditions such as capoeira. Black/African bodily practices are further depoliticized once they are considered up for grabs by any Westerner who can afford to join a capoeira school or take a dance class (Robitaille 2014; Sawyer 2006). The lived reality of race for Africans recedes even farther into invisibility.

Combat forms are classed and spatialized as extensions of colonial logics of racial hierarchy. Take, for example, the discussion of modernity with regard to Senegalese wrestling, the Wolof practice that is institutionalized vis-à-vis stadium infrastructure and mediatization. However, there are other wrestling traditions in the region—for example, among Diola women in the Casamance region of southern Senegal and other parts of West Africa. On the surface, the central concern seems to be the "neoliberal commodification" of a combat game that was considered traditional and therefore romanticized as a marker of Senegalese cultural autochthony before colonial rule. Wrestlers are characterized by a linguistic style, *français mbër*, which, in fact, is not particular to wrestlers. It is often associated with working-class, rural, and marginalized people, particularly in urban populations such as Dakar that prize the linguistic mastery of French. "You All Will Die of Laughter," an interview on YouTube with Gouye Gui, highlights the wrestler's *français mbër* accent and grammatical deviations from metropolitan French.[8] Some have described the phenomenon of *français mbër* as "class snobbery" that privileges the colonial language, without explicit mention of race (Hann et al. 2021). Yet peripheral, poor neighborhoods from which many wrestlers emerge in Dakar are called ghettos in English (Hann et al. 2021). I read this terminology, alongside the mockery of French language skill, as a constellation of ways in which racialization is both transnational, and directly linked to the production of ethnicity through performance (wrestling) and performativity (modern subjects). The reference to ghettos is not an importation of racialized spatial frames that are foreign to Dakar's historical processes but, rather, a borrowed lexicon that provides a short-cut for speaking about the similar dynamics of poor Black masses marginalized in the once-colonial headquarters of the region.

Why does it matter that it is wrestlers in particular who are mocked? Framed another way, why have wrestlers come to embody the trope of a Senegalese failed modern subject? In part, wrestlers are expected to embody tradition, which is both revered and romanticized as an example of Senegalese precolonial history, spirituality, and ethnic origins through the recitation of Wolof poetry. Yet the failed Senegalese modern subject from the "popular neighborhoods" of Dakar—a racialized colonial trope—and the paragon of Senegalese Wolof ethnic tradition are one and the same (body). The idea that Africans become racialized as Black when they migrate or travel to the West is colloquially established as social fact. How African bodies are racialized in African contexts is an underexplored aspect of the processes of colonial continuity in the contemporary moment.

Senegal enjoys a "special" status as the crown jewel of French colonial assimilationism. As the administrative headquarters for French West Africa, it served as the site of the civilizing mission's racial hierarchical construction of the region. The postcolonial legacy of this is evident in common phrases, such as the description of colonial Dakar as the "Paris of West Africa."[9] We can also extend Senegal's special status to the "peaceful" reputation of the country's Islamic and decolonial movements. While the postindependence Négritude movement centered on a celebratory rhetoric of Blackness, discussions of *whiteness* as a currency of social power after decolonization remained largely absent.

Jemima Pierre (2012) has written about how West Africans approach Blackness with a complex set of distinctions and considerations, while whiteness is far less interrogated for its relationship to wealth and un-doubted social status. One of the few and earliest studies of whiteness in Senegal was Rita Cruise O'Brien's sociological study of French expatriates in Senegal directly before and after independence in 1960. O'Brien (1972) argued that in the context of the newly independent West African nation, regional and class differences that would be meaningful in the French context disappeared in the production of a cohesive white identity in Senegal for the expatriates. Social distinctions that were meaningful in France dissolved in Senegal. Whiteness was consolidated in large part through the construction of a racialized Senegalese Wolof other while pitting the trope against other ethnic groups, such as the Sereer, who were considered more civilized. She reports, "They regarded certain aspects of Senegalese behavior as a manifestation of the inferior or 'uncivilized' nature of African society . . . considered to be a clear indication of cultural backwardness," which they explained through "ethnic or tribal differences" that were attributable to "Wolof society, for example" (O'Brien 1972, 144–45). O'Brien continues, "Paradoxically, however, expatriates interviewed in the Casamance . . . said that Diola or Manjack characteristics were inferior to those of the Wolof who, it was said, worked hard. Others tried to explain Senegalese behavior on the basis of national characteristics: 'The Senegalese have more of an inferiority complex (*complexé*) than the Ivorians, who are not ashamed to admit that the French still run their country'" (O'Brien 1972, 145). These distinctions demonstrate how categories of West Africanness were not only differently positioned but also used to create degrees of proximity and distance between the poles of whiteness and Blackness or "natives" (Pierre 2012, 2020).

In an updated version of O'Brien's study, Hélène Quashie (2015) argued that whiteness in Senegal is a double-edged sword: It both provokes "repulsion" about straying too far from "African origins" and constitutes a marker of sophistication, efficiency, and productivity. *Tubaab*, therefore, circulates as a way to describe Senegalese who are perceived as acting bourgeois, having an affinity for Western-ness, or spending time away from Senegal and therefore abandoning their cultural roots. Ousmane shared that he was known as "the *tubaab* of [his] family" even before he migrated to France because his passion for education was perceived as acting white. "Modernity is racial," and whiteness is therefore not bound to corporeality (Hesse 2007). This shifting aspect of whiteness reveals it as a discourse of power rather than something that is contained in certain bodies. Yet the consistency regarding who is considered "white" shows that whiteness equals power for white subjects but shame for Black subjects—either because they are seen as inappropriately embodying it or because it is used as a compliment about those who have achieved white proximity, therefore reinforcing disregard for those who have not. Whiteness is used as a rhetorical weapon that attempts to explain the structural inequality in Senegal.

While studies of whiteness in Senegal bring attention to colonial attitudes and interactions from French and American interlocutors, they also serve in part to individualize the phenomenon of whiteness and racism as an "attitude" rather than an "ideology" (Fields 1990). We need to return to the decolonial approaches of midcentury thinkers such as Aimé Césaire, Frantz Fanon, and Cheikh Anta Diop to analyze the embeddedness of whiteness as a social structure in post–structural adjustment Senegal. This is crucial because of the evidence of white supremacy morphing from an explicit, political, social, and economic project of colonial rule to normalized, everyday forms of Afrophobia and anti-Blackness targeting so-called others and "foreigners." Hamidou Anne (2021) has even argued that the Senegalese tendency to privilege a narrow ethnic lens through which to envision the country's political future, thus excluding the country's historical Lebanese and Guinean populations, suggests a type of protofascism. While anti-foreign African sentiment is an ostensibly pro-Senegalese nationalist stance, it reinforces xenophobic hierarchies that are continuations of French colonial logics that distinguished certain groups as more assimilable into a white, French civilizational standard (Wilder 2005).

Popular culture's depictions of whiteness contribute to the depoliticization of the *tubaab* figure, which is often harmless or silly and can be teased but is ultimately incorporated into and even centered in national identity. For instance, *Toubab du Woujj* (White People Aren't Polygamous), a film directed and starring Lamine Mbengue, tells the story of a Senegalese man living in France with his white French girlfriend. On his trip home, the French girlfriend pays him a surprise visit in Dakar and discovers he has three Senegalese wives. The ensuing antics involve the wives dressing up as white women to combat the French girlfriend's embodiment of a Senegalese woman, which she performs by wearing local outfits and conducting household chores. While the Senegalese wives are made to appear ridiculous in their failure to mimic whiteness, the white woman manages a "successful" racial embodiment of Black womanhood by cooking a delicious couscous dinner. The love story ends with the man and his French girlfriend returning to Paris and strolling amorously under the Eiffel Tower.

A musical group called Toubab Krewe, based in Asheville, North Carolina, provides another example of the way white people feel free to coopt West African cultural traditions. The band members (all white except for one Black member) play with whiteness ("Toubab") and New Orleans carnival lingo ("Krewe") while centering the kora, a West African instrument linked to a tradition that requires family lineage for apprenticeship. Reviews on the group's website feature a *New Yorker* blurb that states, "Their music avoids cliché with authentic extrapolations of traditional Manding beats, percussion, and jam-band flare," while another blurb from *Blurt* declares, "This is the sound of liberation."[10] The figure of the *tubaab* is ultimately a portrayal of whiteness and the ability to take on and off Black West African cultural forms, bodies, and political subjectivities in a playful spirit, divorced from the structures of white dispossession through coloniality.

Ideologies of assimilation and assimilability structured policy and action for the French colonial project and therefore took center stage during various phases of decolonization. Speaking to the structural divide between the citizens of the Four Communes—Senegalese cities that were sites of relative privilege for French West African colonial subjects (Diouf 1998)—and the rest of the colonial subjects in Senegal, Paul Mercier (1960, 6) states: "In Senegal, historical factors account for the sharp division between city and countryside. In the old coastal cities, a separatistic history and a particular juridical status have contributed to their marginal position in Senegalese life. The consequences of the separation between the former 'citizens' of 'the four communes' and the former 'subjects' of the interior have not been entirely wiped out, even in recent years." Political rights were also phased in on a racial spectrum of white supremacy, from Europeans to (elite) mixed-race populations, and then to Africans (Mercier 1960, 7).

By scaling out to a regional level, we see everyday discourses of comparative status in the context of a hierarchy constructed by a white supremacist civilizing mission (Conklin 1997; Wilder 2005). For example, Dakar and Abidjan have both carried the (externally originated) title "Paris of West Africa" (Petrocelli 2024). The notion of an African Paris or Parisian Africa is also significant in the fact that it is a shifting location, a reputation "lost" in different moments of the Ivorian Civil Wars and the Senegalese Casamance conflict, moments that produce nostalgia among Ivorians and Senegalese. In other words, the title also carries a threat of the country losing its status as modern and worldly should there be a backward descent into "ethnic" or "civil" conflicts, which, in fact, are colonial, regional, and international (Tandia 2013). The "Paris of West Africa" title also attests to a white colonial construction of civilization and modernity, not just within groups with respect to their degrees of assimilation and assimilability, but between former colonies and the (imagined) groups they represent (i.e., Senegalese, Ivorians).

Racialized logics of white supremacy structure the ways that disenfranchised and marginal groups are discussed even within the Senegalese population. Ousseynou Faye and Ibrahima Thioub (2003) argue that throughout the century of colonial history, marginalized groups were referred to as "beasts" and confined through urban infrastructure. Again, we see a public reluctance to acknowledge the continued effects of the slave trade, coloniality, and racial trauma, which revealed themselves in moments of political turmoil, such as the "Sonko-Adji Sarr affair" and its ensuing protests targeting Auchan and Total (Anne 2021).[11] This dynamic is also evident in how the state systematically harasses marginalized citizens during diplomatic visits by presidents of the United States, as I witnessed when a gendarme patted down a Baye Fall friend of mine but did not even ask me for identification. Within Senegalese society, the underclasses are racialized by the same colonial categorization, particularly in the language referencing their status and deservedness; their disruptive presence; and their inability to be civilized, behave properly, be urbanized, assimilate, or speak French. This trickles down to everyday interpersonal interactions in the city.

In Senegal, regionalism *within* the country is a central issue, and often one that is classed. Social categories that originate in Senegal—tropes that are not all-encompassing but, of course, contextual and situational—also migrate globally and are in dialogue with other ideologies of social categorization, including race (Hannaford 2017; Ndiaye 2020). For example, *kaw kaw* is a Senegalese term that carries connotations of a country bumpkin. In Dakar in particular, it operates as an insult directed at unassimilated rural migrants based on how they speak, act, or dress. Interestingly, there are also terms that connote ingenuity and pride in someone who possesses rural origins and translates them into global entrepreneurialism and resourcefulness, such as *bana bana, baol baol,* and *modou modou.* However, even these terms are entangled with coloniality. In her study of transnational Senegalese families, Dinah Hannaford (2017, 29; see also Bourdieu 1984) offers a telling ethnographic moment:

> The women I interviewed who were courted by migrant suitors said the courtship was punctuated by gifts from abroad, either cash or commercial goods that were also clearly marked as foreign—such as ready-to-wear clothes, handbags, shoes, and perfumes. Parodies of *modou modous* home on visits conspicuously interject Italian or English words into their Wolof conversation. I should note that this satire is meant to poke fun not only at the showiness of this linguistic tick, but also to mock the stereotypical rural-born *modou modou*'s ignorance of French due to a lack of formal schooling—and thus a lack of "linguistic capital" and "educational capital."

French continues to symbolize superiority in Senegal, even in a nation-state that has institutionalized and takes pride in a native African language (Wolof).

Not all Black African populations experience the same form of social exclusion, which is why a finely tuned understanding of how Blackness operates explicitly or implicitly as a racial tool of social exclusion is required to track which specific groups are targeted, such as migrants and internal "others"; at which historical moments; and through which types of exclusion. In the colonial period, those from the minority Christian Sereer and Diola groups were referred to as *gourmet*, a term designating high taste and signaling their proximity to whiteness in relation to the majority Muslim Wolof (Quashie 2015). The legacy of the Four Communes resulted in privileging those who lived in urban areas at the expense of "the masses," such that Dakaroise and Saint-Louisians have exhibited a paternalistic attitude toward people from rural areas since at least the period of independence, using designations such as *kaw kaw* and *Bawol Bawol* (Labrune-Badiane 2013).

The circulation of the term *ñak* (non-Senegalese African) suggests the ways in which racialized nativist thinking emerges in the contemporary moment.[12] However, Mame Cisse, a Dakaroise woman in her seventies and the dear grandmother of a friend of mine, shared with me that *ñak* did not always have derogatory connotations. Instead, it used to mean "border" or "fence" and was used as a way to describe neighbors from bordering nation-states.[13] Indeed, the earliest documented use of the term comes from an 1858 Wolof grammar book by M. David L'Abbé Boilat, a famous métis in nineteenth-century Senegalese history (Jones 2013), who defined *gnak* as *"(la) haie,"* French for hedge, hurdle, or fence.

Many Senegalese groups are seen and see themselves as a people who have always migrated at various geographic scales (Melly 2017) and hold accompanying ideologies of geographical mobility that are rewarded with social mobility. Nonetheless, other Africans who migrate to Senegal are often (recently) perceived as particularly unassimilable Africans with strange ways. While the term *ñak* has been defined as referring to "other sub-Saharan Africans" (Diouf 2017, 33), it is used most often for other Francophone West Africans, paradoxically suggesting a certain intimacy, regional proximity, and shared history with those considered outsiders to the Senegalese national imaginary. If we take the descriptive "other" in the social context of power as "Others," similar terms arise elsewhere in the continent, such as *makwerekwere*, a derogatory South African term for African immigrants (Livermon 2020). When I asked Senegalese people who *ñak* does and, equally important, does *not* refer to, I often heard a sentence beginning with

"*Tu sais*" (You know), followed by a list of Francophone African countries: Ivory Coast, Togo, Benin, Gabon, Cameroon, and so on. I understand this seemingly minor phrase "*Tu sais*" as another instantiation of the common sense of social difference (invisibly) inflected with racial implications, as if this grouping of other Africans/African others, but only *certain* Africans—those with a shared imperial history under French rule—was self-evident. While Anglophone Africans are most often referred to by their nation-specific designations (e.g., Nigerians), which still hold their own derogatory connotations in Senegal, it is not the same type of metadiscursive categorization. In other words, there is a relational way that *Senegaleseness is constructed against these other former French colonial subjects.*

While social difference is evoked through regional metaphors (i.e., "bush people") and the urban segregation of marginalized groups (Faye and Thioub 2003), the imaginary of outsiderism is not spatially fixed. The "bush" is not just rural Senegal; it extends to the larger region of French West Africa. This racialized regional imaginary (which supposes a hierarchy of civilization, phenotype, appearance, and entitlement) traffics in notions of difference that may have epistemological roots outside European colonial conceptions of race. Still, nineteenth-century colonial grammars of race are in inescapable dialogue with local and other global and regional ideologies of difference. West African regionalism and the ethnicization of regions within the country play a central part in how racialization occurred historically, which results in a coloniality that shapes ideas of belonging, entitlement, and difference in twenty-first-century postcolonial urban spaces (Dakar). Colonial categories of (white) human/political subjects, assimilated Africans, and natives are racialized categories that persist in postcolonial political subjecthood (Garuba 2008; Pierre 2012). Regionalism and ethnic localism are not at odds but, rather, inextricably linked and overlapping, impossible to disentangle but perceived as distinct because of how nationality—often based in ethnic oversimplifications—is taken for granted. Discussing the effects of the French colonial policy of *assimilation*, which aimed to transform their African colonial subjects into Frenchmen with access to civil rights, Michael Crowder (1962, 5) writes:

> The French never really faced the full implications of assimilation. . . . Thus in 1921, twenty years after France had established the French West African Federation, the vast mass of the population still had the inferior status of *sujet*, that is they were subject to summary administrative justice and the *corvée* or forced labor and had no political rights. [Ivory

Coast] had only 308 inhabitants with the privileges of French citizens; Dahomey, 121; Upper Volta, 17; Niger, 9. As late as 1936 out of a total population of fifteen million in French West Africa there were only 2,136 French citizens, with the exception of the citizens of the Four Towns or *Quatre Communes* of Senegal.

In other words, under colonial rule, citizenship and political rights were granted to a select few under the condition that they assimilate to French systems of identification and education and remain subject to French law. Despite these conditions, West Africans were still denied access to political power and rights on the basis of a racialized hierarchy that effectively rendered their Africanness a failed project of civilization. Political rights were explicitly linked to the "civilization" and de-Africanizing of colonial subjects, a quintessential project of enacting racial hierarchies of human worth, cultural value, and political rights. In many ways, Senegal was an exceptional space (Crowder 1962; Diouf 1998; Villalón 1995). Not only did it contain the primary sites of exceptional political access, but it was also a site in which the anthropologically informed governor-generals of French West Africa propped up "local" and "ethnic" expressive cultural practices as central to colonial education and the construction of a model colonized subject (Castaldi 2006; Kringelbach 2013).

Conclusion

White supremacy manifests not only in the presence of white bodies but also in urban and political infrastructure. In March 2021, scores of Senegalese young people in pockets across the country took to the streets in massive protest. In moments of political turmoil in the past, we have seen discussions emerge around the transnational idioms that become mechanisms for political expression. The controversy concerned the arrest of Ousmane Sonko, an opposition leader to President Macky Sall. Sonko presents a threat not only to the potentially dictatorial establishment but also to the coloniality of power relations that the country's leadership has maintained with France and other Western actors. Pro-Sonko protestors were emboldened by his rhetoric and expressed their anticolonial sentiment through the destruction of French supermarkets and gas stations (Anne 2021; Thomas-Johnson 2021), not unlike protesters in the United States targeting the Arby's fast-food restaurant in Minneapolis or the Apple Store in Philadelphia that symbolized gentrification, unequal access, and America's prioritization of accumulating capital over the well-being of local, marginalized communities. In fact, Senegal has a long love affair with hip hop as a tool of political mobilization (Appert 2015; Fredericks 2014), and Dakar residents engaged in public demonstrations in solidarity with the US uprisings over the state killing of George Floyd. The unfolding drama of this latest challenge to the presidential stronghold in Senegal begs the questions: What is coloniality, and what does it look like in the context of a country touted for its "relative democracy" and stable society? And what, if any, is the role of diaspora in the way young West Africans envision themselves and their future?

Without the significant presence of white bodies, and with the powerful social reality of social norms around frameworks such as caste, why even bring race into the conversation about Senegalese society? I argue that forms of racialization rooted in coloniality and other ideologies of social stratification in Senegal, such as nationality, are inextricably linked, sometimes operating simultaneously within the same interaction. I take seriously the wise caution of some Senegalese scholars not to collapse the complex schemas of social difference (e.g., ethnicity, nationality, caste) that are perceived as "parallel" to race but are ultimately distinct.[14] However, I also take seriously that the Senegalese capoeiristas' confusion; their tendency to conflate West African and Black diasporic concepts; and their belief in a geographical distinction between ethnicity as an African concern and race as a concern elsewhere and the ways they are entangled require scholarly attention. Focusing on the distinctions and making room for the possibility of their historical connection is also of great urgency as we enter a new moment in which there is tremendous energy building around solidarity movements on the continent with US organizations such as Black Lives Matter. How can these transnational solidarity movements be generative in their dialogue around global white supremacy while also potentially further confusing the specificities of racial categories (i.e., Blackness or whiteness) in different contexts, especially given how they interact with other localized conceptualizations of difference? In addition, contemporary African migrants are increasingly racialized or privileged in ways that suggest we can no longer hold racial ideologies separate from social categories and hierarchies relevant to African contexts (e.g., Andersson 2014; Hannaford 2017; Ndiaye 2020; Pierre 2004).

We need to examine autochthonous definitions of Blackness in dialogue with global notions of Blackness. We also need to attend to the ways that discourses and instantiations of whiteness elucidate how coloniality operates. By looking at the coloniality of Black performance, we see that discussions of Blackness, slavery, freedom, oppression, and expression are conventional, though imported from a diasporic context. What does not get imported, however, is an appropriate framework for understanding whiteness and Blackness(es) specific to Senegal.

In contemporary Dakar, white supremacy manifests as the upholding of whiteness as an aspiration, the protection of whiteness from political scrutiny, and the infiltration of language and ways of perceiving social difference located in the body. The global nature of whiteness is not to be ignored. If we only look to former or contemporary empires for the production of whiteness, we miss how racial ideologies have local specificities but also operate through global mythologies about how the world is racialized. Brazil's rather successful propaganda campaign of projecting racial mixture and racial harmony to a global audience is as popularly consumed in West Africa as it is in the United States. Black performance in Dakar is at the intersection of three key contexts: (1) Brazil's so-called racial democracy; (2) diasporic Blackness as central to discussions about race and slavery; and (3) Senegal's dual legacy of racial empowerment along with a denial of the continuity of colonial logics. In the celebration of Black arts, the collision of these intersecting colonialities is on full display.

CHAPTER THREE

IN PURSUIT OF HERITAGE
UNPACKING THE MATERIALITY OF EVERYDAY OBJECTS

The group was in the last days of preparation for the event: We had to sweep the performance space, work out the budget to feed and lodge the invited capoeiristas, and collect the newly tailored uniforms. A few showed up early to the École Franco-Sénégalaise, a private French elementary school, where the outdoor activity space served most weekday evenings as training grounds for Africa Capoeira–Ilha de Gorée (Afreecapoeira). Moctar, the founder of the group, was recounting to me the story of how he first learned about capoeira and took a phone call mid-sentence. It was the man bringing the wood for the berimbaus—capoeira's central object, a long, single-stringed bow instrument. When a bunch of smoked kinkeliba trees arrived, the group's instructor, Souvenir (*apelido* Lembraço), worried: "Ah, there's not a lot." He crouched down, laying both hands on the bundle of sticks while he described how they would be turned into musical instruments. The cement floor the sticks rested on was an addition to the elementary school playground that Moctar had installed as a replacement for the rough gravel that could tear up the bare hands and feet of capoeiristas performing acrobatics. Souvenir shared that the group orders the sticks from a man who retrieves them in forests near the Tambacounda region, in Senegal's interior. After collecting the sticks, he smokes them until they are dry enough to withstand being bent into a firm arch without snapping.

"See," he said, showing me. "They give the impression of being burned, but it's just the skin."

Souvenir is one of the strongest singers in the Dakar capoeira community. He is known for the beauty of his voice and his impressive repertoire of songs in Brazilian Portuguese. While all capoeiristas in the group learn to sing and play instruments, more knowledgeable members such as Souvenir take responsibility for the energy, pace, content, and emotional tone of many *rodas*. When I initially asked him what had attracted him to capoeira, Souvenir said it provided him with "the possibility to know my own culture," "to know Angola," and "to know Lusophone culture." I knew his father was Angolan but that he had spent little time there since his birth to a Congolese mother in Ivory Coast and a childhood spent between the Congo and Senegal. Still, he insisted on Angola's centrality to his sense of self:

> It's the only place that I don't know from my origins. I already went to Congo. . . . I went there to work to understand how things work. Côte d'Ivoire I know because I was born there and I still have friends there. Senegal, OK, there's no problem. But I didn't know Angola. We never set foot there . . . , so that means that even our grandparents, all the family on the other side, never saw us. So now what I'm trying to do, and the reason why I got into capoeira, is because it allows me, bit by bit, to re-learn the culture, to learn Portuguese, to see how that goes before going back [to Angola].

For Souvenir, Afro-Brazilian capoeira and "Angola" were synonymous, symbols of the larger Lusophone world. Having grown up primarily in Francophone African sites, Souvenir aspired to become more Angolan, like his paternal family—to become fully Lusophone in language and cultural proficiency. He has devoted his life to the study of capoeira as a way to fill a void in his background.

Looking locally to create Afro-Brazilian things is also a process of African self-discovery. The effort to reproduce Afro-Brazilian capoeira's standard objects through what is common and accessible in Senegal (trees and timber workers, fabric and tailors, yarn and braiders) ends up cultivating a deeper intimacy with what is Senegalese heritage, what is West African heritage, and what is Afro-Lusophone heritage. Learning more about the local by way of pursuing the diasporic is circuitous. So, too, is the route to deeper intimacy and knowledge about what constitutes African heritage. Capoeiristas from the Central African Republic who have spent years in Senegal discover that Guinea-Bissauan craftsman also share a connection to Dakar and to Brazil. Senegalese capoeiristas looking to reproduce the West Central African–based Afro-Brazilian berimbau learn the forested regions of Senegal in pursuit of the closest styles of wood. In other words, through a pursuit of diaspora, African heritage on the continent becomes more expansive.

In this chapter I focus on the minority of capoeiristas in Dakar who have grown up in Francophone countries but whose families migrated from Luso-African countries, primarily Guinea-Bissau, Angola, and Cape Verde. Their stories reveal a unique interaction with Brazilian capoeira traditions as an avenue of self-discovery. These Franco/Luso-African practitioners often identify as possessing distinct "Lusophone" qualities, despite varying degrees of familiarity with their parents' country of origin. For the most part, they are Christian in a predominantly Muslim setting in Senegal, which may also contribute to their sense of social distinction and desire to connect with their origins.

This chapter explores how diaspora is not the sole source of racial self-making and Black belonging in West Africa. Although rendered visible through the process of gathering the necessary elements to create a capoeira school (instruments, belts, uniforms), cultural forms originating from the African diaspora are not solely responsible for the importation of ideas about Blackness; nor are diasporic geographies the privileged sites of Blackness. Here, a diasporic form (i.e., capoeira) is the site of *overt discourse* around Blackness and Black tropes (slavery, liberation, return). However, the racial subjectivity stemming from West African contexts and participants is articulated through nonracialized frameworks, located instead in the coloniality of postindependence life that is linked to issues such as civil war and related migration and displacement. Frameworks for racial empowerment also arise in the way that West Africans attach to what is regional or continental and oppose it to what is Western or European, which is also a racial binary rooted in the history of racialization under European colonial domination in West Africa (Ochonu 2019; Pierre 2012). Souvenir, for example, discussed his aspiration to know Angola better. The option to move to Europe was always looming, but he felt strongly that he didn't plan to "end up" there. These postcolonial predicaments push young people to seek out alternative forms of expression and self-identification that are rooted in Black tropes of slavery and liberation, which provide a sense of belonging and the discovery of disrupted family histories and cultural knowledge. In the landscape of coloniality, colonial categories are reproduced, and the search for heritage is itself entangled in a resignification of colonial languages (Portuguese and French).

The Object of Heritage

Afreecapoeira has worked to establish capoeira in Senegal since the mid-1990s, which has proved particularly challenging as compared with the century-long tradition of capoeira institutions in Brazil. Members grapple with financial barriers to importing pricey instruments and fabric for uniforms from Brazil and have to navigate the differences between Senegalese and Brazilian ecology for making instruments, drawing on available resources as substitutes. However, sometimes local substitutes happen to come in the form of material culture from Luso-African traditions of the region. For those with heritage from these cultures, Afro-Brazilian capoeira has become a proxy for the gaps or silences they perceive in their Luso-African cultural education from having grown up in Dakar with insufficient knowledge about their parents' backgrounds. In the analysis that follows, I ask the following questions: Which objects are part of the social fabric of the everyday in Dakar, a representation of heritage for a range of West Africans, and which are foreign or imported? How have historical diaspora and regional migration always been a part of the construction or disruption of what is considered ordinary in urban West Africa?

West African capoeiristas' relationship to material culture offers alternative readings on how Africans "make do," beyond the trope of African resourcefulness, a category inflected through colonial frameworks of lack. In the context of postcolonial West Africa, where "a civilizational narrative [portrayed] the consumption of foreign goods as Africans' path up the gilded evolutionary staircase," cherishing these coveted capoeira objects means turning attention away from modernity's capitalist standards to valorize a Black diasporic good (Matlon 2022, 4). Moving beyond the spectacular violence of slavery as informing the ways in which West Africans are putting capoeira to work, I explore ordinary objects and strategies as holding potentiality (Berlant 2011; Stewart 2007). As a crucial part of their practice, capoeiristas must construct special objects such as instruments and uniforms out of the everyday objects available to them. In doing so, they also construct a dialogue with the conditions of possibility for heritage and Blackness, among other intersecting forms of postcolonial belonging. What's more, Blackness itself is located in the "making do" of identity and community and the patching together of heritage through the rubble of coloniality's destruction of one's sense of belonging—whether it is from the political conflicts endemic to nation building or the narrowness of national imaginaries, both of which trigger physical and figurative displacement. In this case, Brazil is appealing as a stand-in for diaspora (as we saw in previous chapters), because for most West African practitioners, it symbolizes a triumphant will of Blackness over oppressive forces. Furthermore, I am using heritage as an extension of scholarship that troubles linear narratives of Black origins (Wright 2015) and uses the concept of Atlantic world creativity to do so (Feld 2012).

Migrations both disrupt and produce the ordinary through the circulation of objects, people, and ideas. The process of searching for one's heritage, and therefore one's sense of place and belonging, is an active and ongoing one, as is making do, or "the art of being in between" in which one "draws unexpected results" (Certeau 1984, 30). Young capoeiristas often identify as having a kind of Lusophone character despite having grown up in Dakar, as they feel out of place as Christians and as minority ethnicities and nationalities. Just as many diasporic Black people look to Africa to fill a void in their personal and collective history, these African youths look in part to the diaspora, and in particular to Afro-Brazilian expressive arts such as capoeira, as a kind of pedagogical tool. For many, capoeira, a martial art developed by Afro-Brazilians under conditions of enslavement, is a vehicle to redefine (and sometimes discover anew) their own sense of "Africanness." The background they aspire to "relearn" (as Souvenir put it), or to discover for the first time, is a sense of being culturally, nationally, linguistically, and historically situated. They do so not out of a romantic notion of substitutions void of contextual nuance but, rather, with the dual strategies of improvisation and practicality through which they claim authority over their understandings of—and aspirations for—heritage.

Eric Gable (2006) has written about how the word *reality* (*realidade* in Portuguese) in Guinea-Bissau circulates as a denigration of village life, a concept that, he argues, is mired in development discourse. Gable sees the framework of "reality" deployed by young Manjaco emigrants in Dakar or Paris as evidence of their frustration with the experiment of a postcolonial nation-state that is still disentangling itself from the violent legacy of Portuguese imperialism. Capoeiristas from Senegal, from Luso-African countries, and from other African countries encounter new realities in Dakar. In the process of finding the resources to create an "ordinary" (or typical) capoeira practice in a new place, they encounter objects whose everyday use in the context of Senegal is unfamiliar. Through their repurposing of these everyday objects to replicate what is standard in longer-standing capoeira communities elsewhere, they encounter other daily realities of migrants in Dakar that, through entirely different trajectories, reflect a similar constellation of overlapping Luso-Franco-Wolophone interactions and cultural practices.

This engagement with Brazil as an entity imagined as racially, linguistically, and historically familiar—albeit geographically foreign—allows capoeiristas a kind of abstraction from their differences as West Africans from various countries, ethnicities, and linguistic backgrounds. In chapter 1, I discussed coloniality in the form of diaspora embodied by white Brazilians, as well as the racial grammars used to create forms of social difference or to discipline the body. Here we see how social practices produced through capoeira are not only brokered through whiteness; they also rely on and draw from other Black forms, histories, materials, and networks.[1] Combing through the landscape of everyday objects, linguistic communities, and even popular culture allows us to see that.

It is necessary, therefore, to examine the paradoxes of regionalism. For example, those born and raised in Dakar who are fluent Wolophones describe being regularly questioned when they claim to be Senegalese because they are of Guinea-Bissauan background. Diasporic forms such as capoeira provide one way around the coloniality that disrupts a more coherent regionalism. Whereas language, citizenship, and cultural practices constitute key ways of analyzing subjectivity, the consumption and circulation of meaningful objects illuminates how people creatively craft their selves. In the subtlety of the everyday, we see how capoeiristas in Dakar navigate postcolonial belonging through interactions with the ecological, commercial, and social resources that resist any singular framework of heritage for Black West Africans. Historical diaspora and regional migration are in explicit dialogue with how they are and aspire to be situated.

I draw from examples such as the students choosing to learn Portuguese through capoeira songs or the borrowing of Guinea-Bissauan braiding techniques to braid the capoeira *cordas*, or belts that define levels of skill and experience. From uniforms to ordinary dress, practices of adorning the body have been considered "primary symbols in the performances through which modernity—and therefore history—have been conceived, constructed, and challenged in Africa" (Hendrickson 1996, 13). In an effort to look beyond African contexts as bounded, I argue that the circuitous practice of martial artists in urban West Africa borrowing and substituting diasporic traditions for local ones, and vice versa, demonstrates the everyday practice of constructing Black heritage in West Africa.

Lusophone and Francophone
West African Regionalism

Scholarship on diaspora and regionalism tends to focus on intellectual movements and political elites. The ways that these imperial histories are actually lived, experimented with, and negotiated by middle- and working-class people has received less attention. Similarly, migration studies have contributed to the overemphasis on extreme iterations of migration, mostly from West Africa to Europe, rather than on intraregional migrations within Africa. We see even less scholarship engaging with first and second generations in the host country to which people have migrated, in large part because mobility is so common in African contexts. Still, there is much left to be explored ethnographically about how people's everyday practices reveal emerging forms of regionalism.

A key example of what we miss is how coloniality arises in unexpected ways, as do its antidotes and responses. Portuguese is a colonial language that acts as an instantiation of origins and heritage for Lusophone African migrants to a Francophone country. Scholars of Senegal have often discussed Wolofization—the process of Wolof becoming a hegemonic language and flattening linguistic diversity in the region (Appert 2018; McLaughlin 1995; O'Brien 1998). Beyond simply a linguistic mandate, however, Wolofization is also a tool of social exclusion, making it difficult for other African foreigners to learn the language (or be motivated to do so). The colonial language of Portuguese, then, has become a refuge and provided a sense of belonging for those of African Lusophone heritage, in part due to the centrality of Wolof as both mandatory and exclusive.

Intersecting histories of Lusophone and Francophone regionalism show a web of relations between the colonial history and the postcolonial legacy of competing and overlapping European imperial systems in West Africa that influence migration and diaspora. There are many related angles through which to think about the history and legacy of Francophone and Lusophone worlds beyond the direct history of Portuguese imperialism in West and Central Africa (Bennett 2018; Desch-Obi 2008; Heywood and Thornton 2007; Sweet 2011). We can also consider the less visible history of repatriation of formerly enslaved Afro-Brazilians to Francophone sites on the West African coast in the nineteenth century (Amos 2001). The twentieth century offers an understanding of the political and diplomatic alliances and decolonization efforts among Senegal, Brazil, and Guinea-Bissau (Dávila 2010). Finally, we can also consider contemporary

Senegalese migration to Lusophone sites such as Brazil and how this relatively recent wave of migrants read their own backgrounds in relation to Brazilian racial ideology (Ndiaye 2020).

The question of the coloniality of postcolonial West Africa explored throughout this book also resides in the materiality of borders themselves and their implications for political and social belonging. The way political territories are taken for granted shapes what we view to be our own history, origins, and heritage. Senegal has been a central destination for West African migrants in pursuit of educational and labor opportunities since well before independence. While Senegal is a predominantly Muslim nation-state, there is a small subset of Christians, in large part from the Southern Diola region of Casamance that also borders countries with higher numbers of Christians.[2] Therefore, many migrants find themselves doubly distinct from the majority of the Senegalese population due to both their nationality and religion. Dakar specifically boasts a vibrant Luso-African cosmopolitanism that exists in and around the dominant Wolof Francophone social scene, influencing church culture (Samson 2016), as well as young people's musical tastes and extracurricular activities (e.g., the popularity of Angolan *kizomba* dancing). Bissau, Senegal's Lusophone neighbor, is responsible for 11 percent of the migrants to the country. A vast majority of refugees during the Bissauan Civil War of 1998–99 sought asylum in Senegal, and Guinea-Bissau took in roughly half the population of displaced Senegalese during the secessionist conflict in Casamance, bordering Guinea-Bissau, in the 1980s and early 1990s (Evans 2007; Tandia 2013).

"The Lusophone"

In some iterations of the everyday in Dakar, we see how notions of race, diaspora, and migration are used by people to relate to one another, understand the world, and make meaning. Those who migrate to Senegal from the southern coast or West Central Africa are typically educational or higher-skilled migrants, while those in bordering countries such as Mali and Guinea-Conakry are in agricultural and merchant trades, among other working-class industries. Those considered outsiders to the national Senegalese imaginary nonetheless share intimacy with their host country due to regional proximity and historical relations. Many are Christian and grew up speaking French and Wolof. Some speak limited Bissauan Creole, but few speak much Portuguese. The durability of colonial subjectivities (i.e., pride in being a Lusophone) is not that distinct from ethnic pride, and an emotional attachment to both is heightened or even brought about by the intergenerational distance produced by migration. This kind of postcolonial urban West African "double consciousness"—of identifying with the culture of one's colonizer and feeling inherently distinct from it—also speaks to a distinctly African epistemology of adaptation and accommodation and an expansive multiplicity of being (Apter 2017; Matory 2005).

Among a number of capoeiristas with whom I conducted research, the category Lusophone came to mean much more than being a Portuguese speaker. They discussed the demarcation as a personality type, someone with distinct characteristics inherited from their cultural background, and it served as a trope in their anecdotes, an evaluative narration about behavior. Despite the prevalence of Lusophone expressive cultures in Dakar, the trope of "the Lusophone" was characterized as out of place in the city's social landscape. Two members of Afreecapoeira—Souvenir, of Congolese and Angolan heritage, and Alexandra, of Cape Verdean background—both described Lusophones as sexually impulsive, especially in juxtaposition with the stereotype of the overly conservative Senegalese Muslim whose moralizing, they argued, limited "freedom" for all those living in Senegalese society.

The divide between Lusophone and Francophone Africa seems to be larger today than in previous historical moments. Historiographies of former imperial powers tend to reinforce the nationalistic narrative—namely, the inevitability of the present political formation (the nation-state), as well as the downplaying of colonial conquest and exploitation as foundational to that history (Wilder 2005). Racial formation was in fact a bigger determining factor for the expression and construction of belonging through cultural practices than which specific European empire colonized the country. For example, in the nineteenth century, when Luso-Africans in Senegambia worked to hold on to their waning group identity, those residing in the Joal region aligned their identities with the Franco-Africans of Gorée to distinguish themselves from the Sereer. Some described "the Luso-African" and "the Franco-African" as the same class of people, with similar habits, customs, and even beverage preferences (Boulègue 1989). The second half of the twentieth century revealed a different geography of connection for racial politics that stretched between West Africa and Brazil in the form of anticolonial resistance movements (Dávila 2010). Women such as Carmen Pereira (known respectfully as "Tia Carmen") organized Senegalese women and others in the region across Francophone and Lusophone divides to rid Guinea-Bissau and Cape Verde of white settler colonial rule, despite the male leaders of the African Party for the Independence of Guinea and Cape Verde (PAIGC) reinforcing the Portuguese colonial strategy of creating a class of light-skinned Cape Verdean elites in the region (Ly 2014). Yet in contemporary everyday life in Dakar, decolonial solidarities seem to have been forgotten, and colonial divides have been revived. To be Senegalese or Guinean (Bissau) is to inherit the colonial reputations of the erotic Lusophone and the respectable Francophone.

The Everyday Materiality of Capoeira Music in Dakar

For Dieudonné, a longtime member of Afreecapoeira, having Lusophone origins sometimes worked against him. He was born and raised in Dakar, in communities speaking Wolof and French. Yet his parents were from the Manjaco ethnic group in Guinea-Bissau. They raised him in a Christian household where Bissauan Portuguese-based Creole was the family language. Dieudonné often defended his right to claim a Senegalese identity to other Senegalese, who believed his Portuguese last name and Bissauan heritage undermined his upbringing in Dakar. Yet these same Lusophone origins gave him a significant advantage in the context of capoeira, a kind of cultural cachet that provided a richer texture and sense of authenticity to the group. Dieudonné's ability to speak Portuguese meant that he could not only pick up capoeira songs much more quickly than most but could also learn songs that were longer and more complex. In fact, his love and mastery of capoeira music helped him improve the Portuguese skills he inherited from his parents. Dieudonné's mastery of the berimbau and seemingly endless repertoire of songs made him a figure peers relied on to carry the *rodas* that are so crucial to sustaining the energy and structure of the capoeira ceremonies. Despite the constant, subtle reminders of his outsider status in the Senegalese society he called his own, Dieudonné's life as a capoeirista provided him with a space in which he could express the complexity of his fullest self—and be celebrated for it. He is at once Senegalese—in fact, one of the few native Wolof speakers in a group made up primarily of African foreigners—and Bissau-Guinean.

Some of the capoeiristas were hesitant to disclose their Luso-African background. Their dedication to capoeira, however, suggested a possible connection between their origins and their attraction to the art form. Didier, for example, was one of the more advanced and longtime students at Afreecapoeira; he was known to surprise spectators by executing complicated acrobatic moves while upside down, despite a deceptively hefty figure. However, he rarely spoke about his family. It was only when his mother passed away and members of the group attended the church funeral proceedings that members of the group learned his mother was from Cape Verde. The pastor spoke glowingly of his mother's character, remarking that she worked diligently not only for the church but also to support other Cape Verdean women in Dakar. In Afreecapoeira, the figure of "the Lusophone" was not the only discourse about heritage and belonging that took root. As a musical martial art, song lyrics and the materiality of instruments revealed the production and the productive misrecognitions of Black heritage in Dakar.

Everyday and symbolic objects often have unlikely origins, and without access to the Brazilian biriba tree from which berimbaus traditionally have been made, Afreecapoeira members build their instruments from regional shrubs of kel and kinkeliba trees. Kinkeliba is known in Senegal for producing a local tea and is a national symbol for its wide range of uses as a treatment for inflammation, hypertension, and diabetes, as well as being a centerpiece of breaking fast during Ramadan. Scholarship on Senegal's contemporary political economy has pointed to *attaya* (Chinese green tea enjoyed with high quantities of sugar and sometimes fresh mint leaves) not only as an everyday ritual but also as a symbol of the stagnation of the youth, who are crippled by the lack of structural support that is directed instead to multinationals and political elites (Buggenhagen 2012; Melly 2017). Baye Falls—a subgroup of Murid disciples—similarly drink Café Tuba to pay tribute to Cheikh Ibrahim Fall, disciple of the Senegalese Murid Saint known as Seriñ Tuba, even though coffee is not a locally grown product.[3] The ensuing discussion explores how Senegalese youth "make do" (*góorgóorlu* in Wolof; *se débrouiller* in French), or the notion of a particular propensity to hustle, when confronted with difficult circumstances. But without careful analysis of the structural context in which people respond with resiliency, discussions of "making do" can reinforce an essentialized view of African resourcefulness or an overused trope of Black hustle.

Language—through music—is one of the motors of capoeira's driving energy. Both improvisational commentary and collective singing of rehearsed songs shape the atmosphere and provide inspiration and directives for those actively playing. Songs (written and sung), and the instruments that accompany them in the capoeira *roda*, circulate and get resignified. Through misinterpretation, these practices reveal a flexibility that is productive in the pursuit and construction of heritage.

In 2015, Souvenir opened a *batizado* (graduation ceremony) in the central plaza on Gorée Island with this *ladainha* (*roda* opening song):

Eu nasci no Senegal
Cidade de Cidadão
Terra boa hospitaleira
Tudo mundo dá valor
E criei na Capoeira
Escutando o berimbau
Que gemeando bem tocando
Que fundo meu coração
Samba foi meu professor
Na la ilha de Gorée
Que me ensinou Malandragem
Como um faço de viver
Iê viva meu deus.

"Samba foi meu professor / Na la ilha de Gorée / Que me ensinou Malandragem / Como um faço de viver."

Samba was my teacher / on Gorée Island / who taught me *malandragem* / as a way of life.[4]

Apollo, the Senegalese author of this song, modeled it after an existing Brazilian *ladainha*, changing the words to tell the story of an adopted Senegalese child who learned capoeira in France and then introduced it to Moctar, who later founded Afreecapoeira. The line *"terra boa hospitaleira"* in Portuguese refers to the Wolof concept (and a core motto and social value in Senegal) as the country of *teranga* (hospitality), as discussed in chapter 2.

Souvenir, a former student of Apollo's who chose to sing what is a staple of Afreecapoeira's repertoire, has developed an understanding of Portuguese through capoeira and Cape Verdean music and his attempts to connect to the heritage of his Angolan father and love for the city of Lisbon. He had sung this *ladainha* for years, but when I asked for the lyrics, he hesitated to write them down for me. He eventually agreed and sent them to me in a WhatsApp message, with a comment accompanying the second line: "On this phrase even I don't really understand its meaning. As in, he wanted to say the city of all cities." (*Sur cette phrase mme moi jy comprends pas vraiment le sens. Genre il voulait dire ville des ville.*)

As Gaurav Desai (2001, 5) wrote, "The question to ask of a discourse is not so much what it says but what it does." Kevin Dettmar (2014) notes that there is sense to be made from how we mishear musical lyrics. This song, only partially understood by the members, is a crowd favorite that has become one of the group's anthems. That Souvenir sang it in the context of one of Afreecapoeira's summits targeted at building up the West African capoeira network is particularly significant. He modeled the standard structure of Brazilian capoeira: using the opening *ladainha* to set the tone and even comment on the event. His choice to sing this song at the first *roda* on Gorée Island was no accident: He positioned those present in a specific time and place, as well as in the center of capoeira history. Souvenir has moved around looking for his place in the world, living in four different West and Central African countries. Capoeira, he explained, provided him with a closer link to his heritage, and a family—wherever he finds other capoeiristas.

Souvenir's heritage is multiply situated. Capoeira is a method to reclaim heritage as the son of an Angolan father alienated from his Lusophone culture. Gorée is the heritage of a capoeirista developing the institutional practice in Senegal. As he embodied Gorée through the song, Souvenir positioned himself in an imagined origin that created the conditions for capoeira's possibility. Each of these levels is rife with the uneven, patchy work that the pursuit of heritage entails, which involves mystery and misunderstanding, partial knowledge, and creating new narratives that are laminated onto older ones. With the circulation of a song created for a Dakar-based capoeira group, there are multiple layers of productive misunderstanding operating at once. Apollo's interpretation was based on his understanding of Portuguese, a process that is still incomplete. He is one of the few Afreecapoeira members who developed a baseline level of proficiency in Portuguese almost entirely through his efforts to master capoeira songs. He then taught the song to Souvenir's generation of *gradés* (advanced students), who then shared it with the larger group. Although most of the members understand little to no Portuguese, they are expertly trained in how capoeira songs are structured: when the chorus should join in and how to follow the improvisation of the lead singer when, for instance, he or she offers praise to his or her *mestre*, to God, and to new generations (*Ieee viva meu mestre, Ieee viva meu Deus*, or *Ieee menino é bom*).

Souvenir is also a key berimbau player in the group. He was the first to attend to the freshly arrived bundle of sticks ready to be transformed into berimbaus for the event. He takes the instruments seriously as central to the bodies of knowledge it takes to become a capoeirista. His berimbaus and those he crafts for other, less experienced players who want an instrument of their own to develop their own bodies of knowledge and skill are often made from kinkeliba trees. In this way, kinkeliba has become ordinary in the capoeira world in Senegal, yet in a remarkable way. Senegal's ecological resources are central to the "making do" of creating capoeira in Dakar. "Making do," the notion of a particular propensity to hustle, is a popular analytical concept for scholars of Senegal. How can we decolonize the exceptionalism of "African resourcefulness" and think instead of the ways West African practices render the everyday unexceptional? How do postcolonial Black subjects make do with systems not built for them to thrive as ordinary people by constantly and creatively rethinking what is ordinary?

In the early history of Afreecapoeira, founding members constructed a capoeira school in Senegal from scratch, and in that construction we saw an everyday "making do" of Black heritage—a resourcefulness that was both ordinary and remarkable in its process of becoming ordinary. When speaking to the source of the berimbaus provided to the group, Moctar shared that they come from the woods near Mbour:

CELINA: Where do the *tiges* [stems] come from?

MOCTAR: They come from kinkeliba trees. Before it was kel, which was the best. It's the closest to biriba. But there aren't any more. People cut them so much that it's really difficult to find. The ones that I do have here that are kel are really fine. Before, there were thicker ones. But it's been a dozen years since I could find those. For a while, they sent me *tiges* of Nîmes. But the advantage of kinkeliba over Nîmes is that they have fewer stops [knots]. Nîmes dries faster, though, in four or five months, bending and straightening it will loosen up—but kinkeliba takes a year.

CELINA: How did you learn how to make berimbaus?

MOCTAR: Paulo (Mestre Boa Vida) showed me. It was very quick. When he came the first time, he made a berimbau in front of us. He took us to find the *tiges* and showed us how to prepare it.

CELINA: How did he know how to find the right tree?

MOCTAR: He didn't know. He just said we have to find a wooded area like Parc de Hanne [Dakar's zoo] or certain zones in the countryside.

We took almost a full day looking. We had a car with a driver that the ambassador made available to us. And we went very far and we finished at Parc de Hanne and that's where we found the closest thing. It was a variety of acacia. Nîmes is also a variety of acacia, and it was better, but then we couldn't cut trees there anymore because it's a protected area. I went there a few times around that time and talked to the director, and he let me cut some trees—four or five, but no more.

What has become an ordinary landscape of the objects of capoeira, informed by knowledge constructed within the local geography, was a process with differently positioned actors: a white Brazilian *mestre* in Senegal for the first time and therefore unfamiliar with the terrain, Senegalese preservationists looking to protect the local habitats, and a Goréean man dedicated to starting the country's first capoeira school from scratch. Senegal's ecological resources were central to the creation of a regular capoeira school, and to the continuation of a Black legacy.

In his memoir about growing up with mixed national heritage in East Africa, Binyavanga Wainaina (2012, 25) leans on the invention of language to make sense of the multitudes of sources that converged to make him and his world:

This is my new word, my secret. *Ki. Maay.* I let my jaw fall slack, with the second syllable, like a cartoon man with a cash register jaw. *Ki-maaay.* It calls at the most unexpected moment. Certainty loses its spine, and starts to accordion. My jaw moves side to side, like a mouth organ. Once the word lives, *kima-aay*, it makes its own reality. . . . *Kimay* is the talking jazz trumpet: sneering skewing sounds, squeaks and strains, heavy sweat, and giant puffed-up cheeks, hot and sweating; bursting to say something, and then not saying anything at all; the hemming and hawing clarinet. *Kimay* is yodeling Gikuyu women, Scottish square dancing to the accordion-playing man who wears a hat with a feather. It is a neon man called Jimmy, who has a screaming guitar and a giant Afro. It is ululating Gikuyu women crying around Kenyatta's body on television.

Postcolonial realities are patchworks of fraught and inspirational influences. Related (diasporic racial kin) and seemingly unrelated (friction of white colonial difference) are manifested in images, objects, popular figures, and representatives of the ordinary. Wainaina captures brilliantly the interplay of language, sound, music, and the body, as well as how objects communicate all these intangibles.

My presence in the group—colored by the expectations of me as an Afro-Brazilian American daughter of a capoeira *mestre*—revealed some productive misrecognitions and assumptions around race and nation and spoke to the dynamics of Lusophone skills, knowledge, and belonging. My expertise about Portuguese and capoeira somewhat crumbled when I was asked to translate, explain, or provide context for certain words or movements. I trained capoeira as a child, growing up in the San Francisco Bay Area in a household in which *mestres* and students circulated through our house. Weekends were often devoted to cultural events (*batizados*, Brazilian music jam sessions, performances, and rehearsals for the annual Carnival parade in San Francisco). However, my Portuguese suffered due to the dominance of English in our household, compounded with my shyness to speak. I studied French in high school and college and attained a better grasp of the language once I started traveling to Senegal; my second language thus became French, dwarfing the ebb and flow of my Portuguese skills. The assumptions about my identity as a Brazilian capoeira *mestre*'s daughter being projected onto me at any moment often led to unexpected insights. In many ways, through the practice of capoeira, the members of Afreecapoeira and I were discovering heritage together, as my Portuguese improved during my time in Dakar. We leaned on one another's patchwork skills, drawing from whatever made the most sense in the moment.

One afternoon, as I walked to practice holding a berimbau, I passed a yellow boutique close to the main boulevard. A group of older men sitting together stopped me to ask what type of wood I was carrying. When I said it was kinkeliba, one of them said, "Tu ne sais rien. Moi j'habite ici" (You know nothing. I live here), then asserted he was a Baye Fall. He inspected the knots in the stick, insisting, "Du kinkeliba. Kel la" (It's not kinkeliba. It's kel), sharing that he used to grow kinkeliba. After asking what I used it for, he became curious about "capoeira" and asked for a demonstration, which I awkwardly declined in a hurry to get to training. Within the group, my identity as a capoeirista was a foundation for being considered an insider. However, in this interaction my foreign status was not only obvious but also likely elevated by the fact that I was carrying a local tree, displaying what the man perceived to be false knowledge about it and transforming it into an object of ostensibly foreign use (i.e., a musical instrument). This process of misunderstanding and misrecognition illuminated what is considered ordinary or out-of-the-ordinary materiality, how ordinariness gets put to use or literally reshaped, and what sense people make of it for claims of cultural heritage.

3.1 Marianne seated in the training space at a decorated atabaque, an instrument common in Brazil but uncommon in Senegal. Photograph by the author.

Marianne's Practical Connections: A Circuitous Search for Heritage

Losing her mother sparked Marianne, who began training capoeira with Afreecapoeira in 2014, to explore her sense of Luso-African personhood. Her parents had migrated from Guinea-Bissau to Dakar in the late 1960s but never took Marianne and her sisters back to their home country. As a child, Marianne often asked why they never visited their country of origin just to the south, but her mother refused to reply or gave cryptic answers. After her mother's passing, and trying to distract herself from grief, Marianne was told by a friend about capoeira. Initially, she trained just to get out of the house and away from her feelings of loss (figure 3.1).

Two years later, Marianne was on her way to earning a second-level belt from Afreecapoeira. The scramble to find all of the materials necessary for the *batizado* graduation ceremony was well underway, but the logistics for crafting the belts needed for the graduates caused concern. The centerpiece of the event—when students advance to the next level in their training— had to be marked by tying a brightly colored braided belt around the students' waists. However, few of the members knew how to braid the colored yarn into *cordes* (belts in French), and there was neither enough time nor funds to import them from Brazil or elsewhere. Marianne offered a solution: Through family connections she knew a Bissauan man, Carlos, from her family's neighborhood in Dakar who was an expert braider. Belts (*cordas* in Portuguese) are part of the repertoire of special objects that are essential to the process of identifying as a capoeirista, along with a uniform of typically white pants and a T-shirt identifying one's capoeira school, as well as a collection of musical instruments—berimbau, atabaque (standing drum), pandeiro (tambourine), and agogô (two-tone bell). Practitioners also generally possess books and other texts about capoeira history and mine the digital space for YouTube videos, photographs, and Instagram links that instruct, depict challenging acrobatics, and showcase players they admire around the world. Dieudonné kept all the belts he ever received together in the same duffel bag that held all his capoeira paraphernalia. In Dakar, capoeiristas also debate how to carry a berimbau and how to hide the part of the capoeira belt that hangs down on one side to avoid the spectrum of public reactions, which can range from curiosity to mockery.

Ordinary objects and self-presentation within a capoeira-familiar context are considered abnormal in Dakar, but the rich history and diverse infrastructure of African innovation there becomes an invaluable resource to the emerging local capoeira community. The production of capoeira aesthetic norms also relies on the tailoring expertise in the city, which is known for "techniques of accumulation and refinement of textiles in the vibrant capital of Dakar, celebrated as one of the main fashion cities on the continent" (Kastner 2024, 91) (figure 3.2).

The braided belt system was introduced to capoeira by Mestre Bimba, a legendary figure in the art form's history who was the first to standardize its movements, instrumental ensemble, and song repertoire, bringing it out of the shadows of legal prohibition. The system was modeled by Mestre Bimba to rival national martial arts forms elsewhere in the world, such as karate, but the idea of the braided belt has unclear origins. As the capoeira scholar Greg Downey (2005, 104–5) stated: "Colored cords used to mark a student's progress in some groups were said to be a reminder of some of the colored scarves given by Mestre Bimba upon a student's 'graduation.' The scarves commemorated similar silk ones worn by turn-of-the-century *capoeiras* to protect their necks; silk was thought to resist slashing with a razor." Due to the ambiguous origins of Mestre Bimba's decision to include braided belts, this Lusophone proximity of belt construction is, on the one

3.2 Lamine working with a tailor to explain the group's vision for capoeira pants for the 2016 *batizado* event. Photograph by the author.

hand, imagined and yet, in the postcolonial urban context of Dakar, on the other, it provides powerful cultural cachet, making the Bissauan community a cultural authority where capoeira is concerned.

For centuries, West Africa has participated not only in trade but also in the exchanging and borrowing of aesthetics within and outside the region, offering a rich landscape in which to theorize the circulation of material objects and their shifting relationship to the special, the ordinary, or the symbolic. For instance, textiles—and, more important, the way people both wear and "rework" them through various alteration techniques in Senegal—embody the layered circulations of "physical, social, virtual, or imagined" movement (Kastner 2024, 91). In the case of Senegal and Guinea-Bissau, Murid Senegalese women prefer the sophistication of Manjaco weaving techniques, using *sër-u-njaago* (in Wolof, *sër* is wrap and *njaago* is the term for Manjaco people) textiles for significant life events such as the birth of a child, a death, or a wedding, as well as in other family ceremonies (Buggenhagen 2012; Kastner 2024).

Manjaco textile expertise tells a story of African innovation across geographies and with imperial overlaps—an arc that does not require a fixed African origin or claim to origins. The *sër-u-njaago* technique was first brought to Africa by the Portuguese empire, which introduced a weaving technique to Cape Verde in the fifteenth century that then spread to its continental colony Guinea-Bissau (Diop 2008; Kastner 2024). Manjaco weavers uphold the position as experts, and the textile has "continually experienced modifications in motives and materials" (Kastner 2024, 93). The newest iteration of Manjaco weaving expertise circuitously ended up being put to use in Dakar for the construction of an object from another former Portuguese colony: Afro-Brazilian capoeira *cordas*.

Christopher, a Central African member of Afreecapoeira who migrated to Dakar to pursue higher education, encountered the Manjaco process of braiding for the first time when he volunteered to pick up the belts for an upcoming Afreecapoeira *batizado*. He and I made our way to the neighborhood of Grand-Dakar to sort out the order for our event. We arrived at a compound and greeted the first person we saw with "Salaamaleekum" (a Muslim greeting meaning "Peace be unto you"). When we asked for "the woman who makes the belts," we realized—after considerable trial and error—that she did not speak Wolof, French, or Portuguese. "Creole," she whispered. Christopher took out his smartphone to verify the name of the woman Marianne told us to meet, Carmen, so we could be more precise in our request. Then we were led further into the compound. There she was, sitting on a stool. Without getting up, she turned in our direction to ask in French what we wanted. Christopher said, "Nous sommes des amis de Marianne qui viennent pour les cords" (We are Marianne's friends who have come for the belts). "Oui, oui," she said, standing up. "Je vais vous emmener là-bas" (I will take you over there). As we followed her down a few streets, I started to realize we were in a Bissauan enclave of Dakar. She greeted people along the way, sometimes in Creole and sometimes in Wolof. We arrived at another compound that seemed to double as a living space and a craft factory (figure 3.3).

As she took us through the neighborhood, Carmen burst into righteous laughter. "If we go back to our country for good, you guys will be screwed because the Senegalese don't know anything about this!" she boasted, recognizing the cultural cachet of their skill. I asked whether I could take pictures when she emerged with her arms full of braided belts, a message underscored by Christopher, who added that we wanted to document the belt-making process to learn from it. We followed Carmen back to the front yard to watch Carlos, the expert braider, in action. He was in the middle of crafting one of our blue-and-yellow belts, which corresponds to the level just

3.3 The author (*left*) posing with the Bissauan braiders and the cache of event belts. Photograph by the author.

below the solid blue *gradé* (advanced). Christopher was deeply impressed with Carlos's skill and peppered him with questions. Carlos graciously answered (figure 3.4). He taught us how the Manjaco in Bissau have a traditional method of square braiding that is used to make belts, which are often worn for ceremonial funerary dances. Christopher filmed the braiding on his cell phone, illuminating the fact that documentation is not the sole privilege of the anthropologist (Jackson 2013) (figure 3.5). For our benefit, Carlos attached the belt to his waist to demonstrate the sartorial styling of Manjaco funeral dancers for his audience of two representatives of a martial arts group making do as we learned from new Black Atlantic inspirations.

The line between material culture and discourse about it is not a hardened divide but, rather, a dialogical relationship between how cultural objects are used and understood and the linguistic context of their meaning making. On the visit to pick up the belts, I spoke in Wolof with Antonio, Carmen's younger brother. He explained the difference between Portuguese from Cape Verde and from Guinea-Bissau, giving as an example that *agua* (water) is pronounced "yaagua" (I believe by the Cape Verdeans). He said, "Sunu creole ci Guinea-Bissau mo gënn set bu Cap Vert" (Our Creole

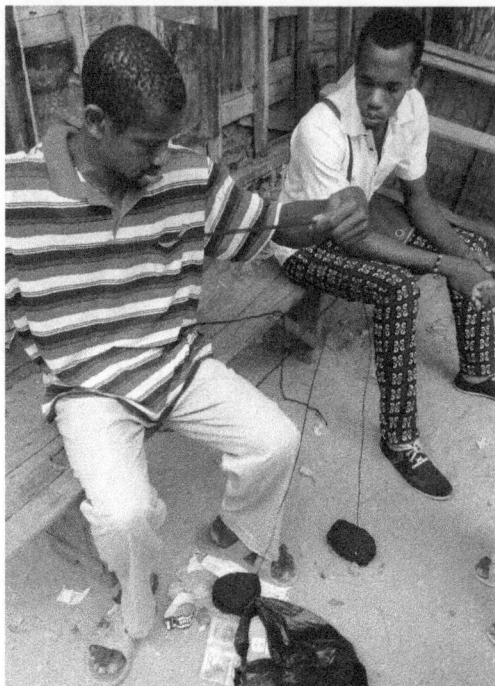

3.4 Christopher learning from the expert braider. Photograph by the author.

3.5 Christopher documenting the eight-strand square braiding process. Photograph by the author.

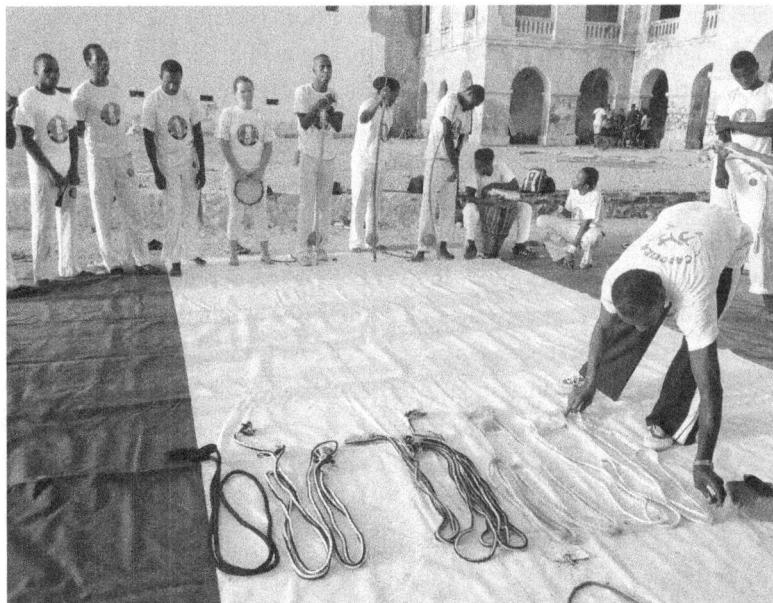

3.6 Moctar laying out the belts by level on the *batizado* event tarp in the fireman's quarters on Gorée Island. Photograph by the author.

in Guinea-Bissau is cleaner than that of Cape Verde). He then asked where I was from, and when I said I was from Brazil and the United States, he claimed that the Brazilian side was apparent. In fact, he shared that Brazil's soccer team was his favorite, despite the upset of the recent World Cup and Brazil's brutal 7–1 loss to Germany in 2014. I invited him to our event so he could see what we were doing with the belts. He sounded excited and then, in Wolof, told the man making the belts that they should go to the event and use it as a promotional opportunity.

Christopher invited all of our new friends to attend the Afreecapoeira graduation ceremony (figure 3.6). Antonio mentioned that he had a friend who could take him to Gorée Island for free, so it wouldn't be a problem for him, although he hadn't been there in fifteen years. I asked when he had migrated to Senegal, and he said that it was a long time ago but that he always goes back and forth between the two countries for vacation. I asked Antonio whether he was familiar with capoeira, as most residents of Dakar were not likely to be. "Yes! Of course! We even have it in Guinea-Bissau. It's in Brazil, too," he said. "Yes," I responded. "Capoeira is considered to be from Brazil." "Exactly," he said. "Capoeira dafa neex" (Capoeira is great, in Wolof). From his perspective, Guinea-Bissau was not the site of origin of capoeira, but it was a horizontal site, alongside Brazil and Senegal, a key location for the practice of capoeira. Displaying the ease with which he moved through and made connections with these overlapping spaces (Brazil, Guinea-Bissau, Senegal), he revealed them all to be not only familiar but also seamlessly related in his daily life constructed by West African and Black Atlantic regionalisms.

Without enough members in the group who knew how to reproduce the standard Brazilian method and aesthetic for braided yarn belts, capoeiristas turned to local Bissauan braiders to provide the closest substitute. In what was regarded by the group as a practical decision, the so-called lack of knowledge to accurately mimic Brazilian traditions led to a reliance on the group's diverse African resources, which produced a new aesthetic—a belt unique to the group that would not be found in any other site of capoeira practice. These Bissauan braiders helped shape what ultimately became the Senegalese school's representation of an Afro-Brazilian practice that "returned to Africa" in a place it never before existed.

On our way out, Christopher and I passed a small market with a calabash vendor to find gourds for *cabaças*, the open, polished gourds that make up the base of the berimbau. Gourds transformed into *cabaças* project and distort the sound emanating from the berimbau to create the texture of its sonic voice. We were supposed to grab a bunch to go along with the freshly smoked kinkeliba trunks that had just arrived from Mbour for the upcoming *batizado*. The calabash is a capoeira object with one of the strongest associations with West Africa. Although it is found around the world, West Africa has made particular and legendary use of dried gourds for everything from the transport of consumer goods atop the heads of market women to the dozen or so percussive and stringed instruments that originate in the region (e.g., the *kora*). Despite this diversity of use for the calabash, the merchant was not familiar with what we planned to do with them. We found only a few that were of the small size we needed for the berimbaus in a large bin next to everyday household items such as brooms and colored plastic water scoops.

Through grappling with her grief and searching for her cultural past, Marianne brought a form of cultural capital to Afreecapoeira: her ties to the Bissauan enclave, where the group has had its belts produced ever since they were made for the capoeira *batizado* ceremony. The fact that the braiders are from Guinea-Bissau is partly just a coincidence; they are the people with the best yarn-braiding abilities. However, this process also reflects the importance of Senegalese proximity to Luso-African cultural practices that can be viewed as unrelated and yet function as a fitting substitute. Tracing the source, circulation, and production of cultural objects disrupts our simplistic understandings and claims of origins, heritage, authenticity, migration, and diaspora. An item can go from being a ritual item to an everyday item to having a new kind of significance as a coveted item. In this case, the belts serve as both a substitute for a diasporic object *and* as a way for some capoeiristas to connect to their heritage, even if those items are not otherwise significant. Marianne might not have been particularly drawn to Manjaco ceremonial objects such as these had it not been for her participation in capoeira, yet a poetic irony is contained in the fact that she rediscovered an object used for funeral rituals in the country of her heritage due to an Afro-Brazilian martial art she engaged in not necessarily for its Lusophone connection but as a way to work through her mother's death.

Luso-African capoeiristas such as Marianne and Dieudonné do not follow the trend of transmigration common to the generations of Manjaco before them (Gable 2006), likely due to the instability resulting from the civil war of 1998–99. Marianne took her first trip to Guinea-Bissau in 2016, despite her mother's misgivings. She met with family members she had never seen before in her parents' home village and fell in love with the country—its beaches and welcoming atmosphere. She admired the strong pride Bissauans had for their culture. "I feel so at ease when I'm there, without really knowing why," she wrote to me on Facebook, followed by two emojis: one smiling with tears and the other with googly heart eyes. She told me she hopes to move there someday. Before she took her heritage trip, Marianne connected to her origins through capoeira, seeking out fellow Lusophone communities and cultural knowledge that ended up contributing to the aesthetic of her capoeira community. In other words, once she familiarized herself with capoeira, she had a platform to connect with her Lusophone background in new and profound ways.

These kinds of trips and searches for heritage within West Africa— across different cultural and linguistic lines—are not always so visible under the monolithic rubrics of a singular "Africa(n)" as a trope of fixed, undistinguished traditions. Neither is place making in relation to origins so clearly traceable, especially due to the frequent overdetermination of ethnic and national subjectivity. My provocation serves to pivot focus toward other "practices of diaspora" (Edwards 2003) that double as practices of heritage through symbolic and material resources occurring simultaneously in West Africa, involving overlapping regional and Atlantic migrations. West African capoeiristas are creatively, resourcefully, and strategically looking to ritual and everyday objects in Dakar.

Conclusion: What Belts Do

> C'est quoi ces histoires de cordes-là?
> (What is the deal with these belts?)
> —ALEXANDRE

After receiving the second belt—yellow and white—at the *batizado*, Bigue explained her feelings about the achievement: "As a woman, I was shy, and then getting my yellow-white belt made me feel like I will no longer be afraid to be in combat with the men. Belts are important. They show that you work hard, and now I want to show I deserve the belt I have."[5] Feeling a similar pride but also concern about deserving her belt, Elena expressed that, although she felt she didn't deserve to advance to the level of *gradé* (advanced student), receiving it would encourage her to push herself to deserve it if she wanted to spend her life becoming a true capoeirista.

The belts as finished products embody a value system that speaks beyond degrees of skill in capoeira training and take on meaning in their use as people collect them, cherish them, and tie them ceremoniously around their waists to get into the mindset to play capoeira. Considering the "social relations of symbolic production, circulation and consumption" of artistic production, multiple logics and geographies are at play in the context of Dakar that create legitimacy and value (Bourdieu 1993, 140). Here, capoeiristas piece together a value system based on what they can access to replicate the original Brazilian objects but end up drawing on a range of social and cultural resources that result in an interwoven embodiment of heritage. Heritage becomes, for the group, both direct and indirect, at once foreign and familiar and, in the case of capoeiristas of Afro-Lusophone background, cultivating a familiarity with their heritage that was once distant.

Heritage is an everyday practice. Objects are bound up in the historical circulations that at times are exposed and at other times are hidden or disrupted by their different and multiple uses in a contemporary context. Black cultural production and heritage making in urban West Africa forces participants to rethink what is an everyday object, a symbolic or special object, a vehicle of self-discovery, or something that represents a

3.7 A *cabaça* painted red, green, yellow, and black, with cowrie shells and a Nimba mask, significant symbols in West Africa. Photograph by the author.

people (multiply conceived) or history. Contrary to the charge that race and diaspora *impose* external, irrelevant frameworks on Africa, West African diasporic practices and regionalism intersect in ways that show a local pursuit of global Black heritage interplays with empire, diaspora, and racial self-making emerging from their own historical and migratory contexts. Heritage is not only something that emerges from the past; it is also not necessarily aligned with a bounded constellation of people, places, and practices (Ferguson and Gupta 1997). Continental West Africans seek out a sense of belonging and connection to heritage by drawing on both the historical African diaspora and the contemporary migrations and diasporas of the region. Embodied in everyday objects is the possibility of constructing heritage (figure 3.7).

Young people in West Africa today are creating their own relationships with the concept of heritage and their backgrounds by putting West African political, cultural, and historical frameworks in dialogue with other Black Atlantic practices. Exposed to a world of seemingly endless cultural possibilities and avenues for self-expression, building a linear narrative of self by way of "tradition" requires a creative dynamism that joins cultural substitutes with pan-Lusophone, pan-Francophone, and Black Atlantic practices. This combination redefines the otherwise confining trajectory of postcolonial nation-states narrowly shaped by the colonial agenda that constructed self-serving and divisive political boundaries and social categories. Capoeiristas in Dakar in pursuit of everyday objects for their practice show interwoven sources that are as diverse, yet related, as their own community.

SPIRITUAL BAGGAGE
NEGOTIATING THE BODY AND RELIGIOUS POSSIBILITIES

Around noon, my phone buzzed with a text message from Lamine that simply read: "The sheep has arrived." It was Tabaski in 2015, the Senegalese celebration of Eid al-Adha, one of the most significant holidays on the Muslim calendar. The occasion warrants a lamb feast in just about every household. I arrived at Lamine's family home to find him in high spirits and dressed in an all-white *xaftan* (matching two-piece outfit worn by West African Muslims often on special occasions). We greeted his mother, who was busy preparing food in the backyard. An exceptional cook on an ordinary day, she had surrounded herself with several organized buckets of sheep parts that could only mean a tantalizing feast to come. Lamine gave me the tour of his room and with a humble laugh showed me his embarrassment of riches: a stack of event T-shirts he had collected from capoeira gatherings and a pile of smooth stones used to change tones when playing the berimbau, capoeira's central instrument. He even pointed out a thinned spot of hair, earned from learning how to spin upside down to add to the catalogue of physical traces of his life as a capoeirista.

Lamine was ready to become one of Afreecapoeira's leaders, the last *gradé* (advanced-level student) left in the association and one of the few Senegalese who had not yet moved away, quit the group, or become consumed by other responsibilities. He was one of the most committed capoeiristas, earning a fifth-year belt in only three years—but he was also one of the most hesitant. His attendance at training in 2015 had become increasingly spotty. He showed up late to practices and left early, displaying a waning commitment, but he continued to show up nonetheless. Once at the Blaise Senghor Cultural Center he announced that he would no longer sing or play berimbau. He watched longingly the others playing and couldn't help but give them tips and make corrections. As soon as the formal session ended, however, he picked up a berimbau to improvise a solo. Dieudonné commented, "It's like he is between 'yes' and 'no.' He'll play when he's forced to, but he doesn't put any heart into it anymore." In 2016, Lamine announced his departure from capoeira altogether, handing over all of his instruments, belts, and uniforms to a fellow instructor. He articulated his discomfort as a Muslim producing music that was associated with spiritual beings—a reference to the historical connection of capoeira with Candomblé religious practice in Brazil. Lamine's years of training to master the legacy of enslaved Africans in Brazil that he so admired was plagued by capoeira's spiritual baggage.

In this chapter, I examine how urban anxieties about feeling disconnected from heritage, from a sense of authenticity, and from an ethical self manifest in the search for answers through religious activity, spirit-based ritual, and ambiguously secular activities that, like the Afro-Brazilian combat game capoeira, center the body. As Xavier Livermon (2020, 52) has argued about the inherent heteropatriarchy of the nation, "The body remains an unexamined site for understanding and negotiating the disconnect between political control of the state and control of the economy." Furthermore, capoeiristas in Dakar both draw on and actively reject diasporic influences. I show how capoeira draws out anxieties and innovations that speak to religious practice and spiritual worlds imaginatively explored or actively kept apart in Dakar through a framework of "forgetting." This forgetting in postcolonial Senegal speaks to what Victoria Collis-Buthelezi (2016, 116) reminds us: that "anti-colonial nationalisms are . . . birthed by loss as much as they offered something new."

In the first part of the chapter, I draw on Lisa Lowe's theorization of liberalism as a strategic ordering of historical events. She sees liberalism and its historiography as a dominant narrative that illustrates racial capitalism as not only progressive but inevitable. She also sees it as a narrative whose violence is situated in misremembering, or actively forgetting. In the case of my research, forgetting looks like Muslim West African capoeiristas who fear a so-called animism they believe is embedded in capoeira but who cannot access the potential historical connections with Islam that Brazil has actively erased. In the second part, I move from forgetting to "remembering," by which I mean the bold and imaginative ways that other

West African capoeiristas are making spiritual and secular links to restore and reclaim lost kin and lost knowledge from coloniality and slavery. By looking at the imaginaries that urban and working- and middle-class Senegalese living in Dakar produce about capoeira's relationship to Islam (predominantly practiced in Senegal under particular Sufi brotherhoods) and to spirit and ancestor worship, I articulate how coloniality structures the affective conditions of both fear and promise, often disrupting the legibility of Black Atlantic forms of protection and healing. Stated differently, Black performance can foreclose as much as it inspires.

The growing body of literature on global Black Muslim communities recognizes Senegal as a key node in recent debates about racial empowerment, racism, coloniality, and spiritual and cultural citizenship through religious practice (Babou 2021; Carter 2021; G. Ndiaye 2020; Rahman 2021). The religious traditions at stake—both indigenous African spirit-based practices and Afro-Brazilian iterations—carry with them the burden of racist colonial and anthropological discourses that positioned African spiritual practices and institutions as "animist" and therefore outside Western modernity (Idowu 1973; Shaw 1990). These discourses have been countered by research centering Afro-Atlantic dialogues (Matory 2005) within Afro-diasporic religious networks. Scholars have analyzed Dahomeyan Óyò-Ife, Brazilian Candomblé, Haitian Vodun, and Cuban Santería to refute this racist legacy, demonstrating how they are sophisticated, modern, and transnational forms that have also solidified national sensibilities (Apter 2005, 2017; Daniel 2011; Matory 2005). The work of these pioneers has significantly shifted the analytic possibilities and allows us to think about the Black Atlantic world as a landscape of connectivity and innovation between continental and diasporic Africans throughout history.

Nonetheless, the continued stigmatization of indigenous spiritual practices and their uses in postcolonial West Africa reveals the global reach of coloniality. Lowe describes liberalism's strategic ordering of historical events as a "forgetting," or what Michel-Rolph Trouillot (1995) called "silencing." What is remembered and narrativized is only teleological progress rather than the exploitation that is the condition of possibility for liberal "freedom" that historically relies on the "unfreedom" of racial and gendered others. Like the silencing and forgetting of the connections shadowed by liberalism, I also see coloniality as the continuity from the colonial period of forgetting, obscuring, invisibilizing, marginalizing, and demonizing of practices deemed uncivilized, immoral, foreign, or even (perhaps ironically) sacrilegious that are discursively constructed as "African."[1] The demonization of indigenous African spirituality often targets its performative nature, how its expressions of religiosity are performed through dance and music (Covington-Ward 2021). In other words, the coloniality of Black performance extends to—or, perhaps, is rooted in—the realm of spirituality. The structural intimacies of the Atlantic world, often fraught and brutal, also demonstrate a politics that, Lowe argues, contained *past conditional* possibilities—in other words, alternative outcomes and solidarities than what seems plausible in our modern state of racial capitalism.

For some Muslim capoeiristas, capoeira's relationship to religion represented a barrier to their wholesale adoption of the martial art. Africanist historians have argued that "the study of leisure illuminates social practice and the process of its formation—and puts critical political and cultural issues into relief" (Akyeampong and Ambler 2002, 1). This chapter explores how capoeira draws out anxieties and innovations that speak to religious practice and spiritual worlds imaginatively explored or actively kept apart in Dakar. West African capoeiristas navigate concerns about the art form's relationship to spirit-based practices and religiosity, as well as the very practice of capoeira *as* a kind of spirituality—a physical and metaphysical practice of the deeply internal work of self-transformation linked to a historical understanding of the pursuit of freedom. Their preoccupations offer insight into how secular leisure, spirituality, religiosity, and creative approaches to "freedom" unpredictably coincide.

Black performativity through spiritual ways of being and engaging—including sartorial presentation and carrying spiritual objects—offers a deeper look into the coloniality of Black performance. When practitioners of Judaism fled the Portuguese Inquisition to Senegambia, some became *lançados* (exiled Jews who became settlers in West Africa) not only through intermarriage with Africans but also through adopting hybrid spiritual practices. They were derided by the colonial system, although Inquisition officials were "simultaneously dismayed and fascinated by the utilization of 'heathen' rites" (Rarey 2023, 52). Black performance and spiritual performativity are often particularly threatening to colonial logics, yet they also tend to be enticing to outsiders. The afterlife of these simultaneous logics of disgust and intrigue make Black performance a tricky space for Black people to fully inhabit.

By looking at the imaginaries that urban working- and middle-class Senegalese living in Dakar produce about capoeira's relationship to Islam and to spirit and ancestor worship, I articulate how coloniality structures the affective conditions of both fear and promise, often disrupting the legibility of Black Atlantic forms of protection and healing. This chapter posed the greatest challenge for me in writing this book. Every time I attempted to consolidate the ethnographic data, theoretical debates, and historical evidence to understand capoeiristas' religiosity alongside capoeira's spiritual and secular life, the foundation gave way, exposing a whole world of new questions. Every attempt to tease out one thread revealed that the subject is already a textile of woven elements that are impossible to examine without taking a microscope to the intricate lattice that initially appeared smooth. And there were knots, disguising where any of the tangle began and therefore with no clues about how to detangle it. Tugging on one thread also resulted in movement elsewhere, without a clear indicator of where the threads were strung together. I present the chapter, thus, as an intentional work in perpetual progress to highlight what is really of interest in this book: the tangle itself.

Part 1: On Forgetting

The first European explorers to Africa made contact in Senegambia in 1441 and enslaved a small group they took back to Portugal in 1444 (Bennett 2018). Hispanicized Senegambians—called *ladinos* in Iberia and *bozales* from Africa—were also the first enslaved Africans in the New World (Bennett 2018; S. Diouf 2013; Sweet 2004). As Sylviane Diouf (2013) demonstrates, Senegambians were some of the first to bring Islam to the Americas, and Muslim Senegambians were at the heart of major slave revolts, including the Malê Revolt of Bahia in 1835, marking their presence in the space of Brazil. Yet Senegal's significance at the outset of the making of the modern world and the historical circuits that unfolded are not common knowledge in either Senegal or Brazil.

Samba's Dilemma: Class Aspirations and Atlantic Expectations

What has long been known as *African traditional religions* is a massive umbrella term for ancestor veneration; ritualized healing from a range of individual ills; and other cultural practices that signify human relationships with spirits, the afterlife, and the "natural" world (Idowu 1973; Shaw 1990). The difficulty in defining these practices lies in the colonial perception of their reality (or lack thereof); the vast range of simultaneously overlapping and highly distinct "African traditional religions" across the continent;

and the inadequacies of Western concepts—specifically, Enlightenment dichotomies that separate the secular from the sacred through something called "religion." The French conceptualized indigenous spirituality in Africa as *fetishism* or *animism*, terms that live on in West Africa. A word such as *Vodun*, for example, as the historian Ibrahima Seck (47, 2014), director of the Whitney Plantation Museum, has explained, "means 'spirit' and is used to designate any kind of deity that human beings call on to solve their problems. The equivalent is 'tuur' among the Wolof, 'pangol' among the Sereer, and 'orisha' among the Yoruba." This range of terms suggests the importance of spirituality across West African cultures. Even during the colonial period in Senegal, when what the historian Mamadou Diouf (1998) has called a "threefold modernity" emerged—Christian, Islamic, and political—all of these developed with influence from autochthonous Senegalese traditions or ancestral cults, stemming from what today are considered ethnic groups. The Casamance region in southern Senegal is home to the Diola, "the largest group of adherents of a traditional religion within the Senegambian region" (Baum 1990, 370), but these animist traditions are less evident in present-day Dakar.

Lamine is an upwardly mobile, middle-class Senegalese capoeirista and a dedicated Muslim. During my research period, he was putting his master's degree in project management to work at a French organization that supports sustainable economic development in West Africa. His capoeira *apelido* is Faísca (Spark). Watching him play capoeira is to be in awe of the way he is able to bend and twist his relatively tall figure without interrupting his flow. From a crouched position he can flip backward on one hand and gently lower himself into a controlled headstand with minimal effort (figure 4.1). He can cartwheel into a solid handstand, playfully inverting his imposing height, before pulling his limbs into a defensive position low to the ground. He moves with just as much fluidity when he is dressed in white jeans and a collared shirt for a special New Year's Day *roda*. Lamine's favorite sequences became almost predictable to his capoeira peers, likely because of his approach to training: a mind-numbing repetition of movements or songs until they became part of his body's growing repertoire. He came to master both rote memorization and improvisational creativity.

As a capoeirista, Lamine worried me and others in the group for years. His hesitation to step into a leadership role and his conflicting aspirations to become a great capoeirista were illustrated in his consternation over capoeira music. He expressed anxiety about playing the berimbau because he knew the instrument carries spiritual energy and can make some capo-

4.1 Lamine in a defensive movement on the beach in Dakar for a capoeira photo shoot. Photograph by Bizenga Photography.

eiristas go into a trance. He feared that singing particular songs, such as "Sai Sai Catarina / Saia do Mar / Venha ver Idalina," which beckons a mermaid to come out of the sea, could potentially summon real spirits. "There are things you can see and things you can't see," he said. "How can I know that what I'm doing is not praising idols? One day, something terrible might happen to me and I won't know why." Lamine's concern echoed that of other West Africans I interviewed who were ambivalent around the spirituality they perceived to be embedded in capoeira. Aziz, a close friend of Lamine's from Burkina Faso, said, "The spiritual side of capoeira, Candomblé, made me react. I could have been inhabited or controlled by certain spirits without being fully aware of it." He decided to strengthen his religious practice of Islam to protect himself from the spirits that could be embedded in capoeira practice. When I asked him whether he had encountered these spirits, he responded, "Not really," but added that "often in the game you are super-excited and you don't know why, the music and all that. But I don't know if it's really tied to spirits." While naming Candomblé lends a concrete object to point to, the spiritual ambiguity many were concerned about is described as manifesting as music, energy, or other invisible potentialities.

To manage the spiritual potential, Lamine attempted to treat capoeira purely as a sport and a historically valuable artifact, shying away from its associations with metaphysical aspects. Diasporas are often embodied, and therefore gendered (Livermon 2020). Senegalese embodiments of diasporic culture clashed with the expectations around being a proper Muslim man, which requires keeping one's body protected from violation by idolatry and bad spirits.

Coloniality stems not only directly from former colonizing agents but also from a patterned structure of interaction that is performed and reenacted in the postcolonial period (Taylor 2003). Diana Taylor offers the example of a newspaper article from the 1990s describing the "discovery" of a previously uncontacted group in the Brazilian Amazon. The original, historical colonial encounter was reenacted through the journalistic narrative structure and performed for the national audience, reinforcing the imagined community of settlers now called Brazilian citizens. Similarly, when animism is quantified as statistically insignificant among the Senegalese population, we see the use of quantification to minimize indigenous spirit-based practices at the foundation of the country's social life. Representing the indigenous community of the nation's capital (but only a tiny percentage of the population), Lebu rituals hold significant symbolic power in Senegal, even though they are associated with little political or economic power (Kringelbach 2013). Lebu spirituality is also symbolically significant because it provides an indigenous authenticity specific to Senegal in an otherwise predominantly Islamic society structured by Sufi brotherhoods. However, the quantified rendering of their social impact would suggest otherwise.

Embodying capoeira practice, and embodying a capoeirista, also captures anxieties about what the body can and should be used for. Embodied performance in West Africa can be a site of social and political ideologies. For example, Adrienne Cohen (2021, 43) discusses "a broader understanding [in postsocialist Guinea-Conakry] of virtuosity as profoundly connected to virtue." Western epistemology produced a historically recent and false divide between secular morality and theological philosophy, which is not a preoccupation of thought traditions from African (and) Islamic contexts (Ogunnaike 2020). European colonialism later imposed racialized conceptualizations of the embodied ways Senegambians learned the Qur'an, framing African Islam as more feminine, more "cultural," and less cerebral and intellectual than Arab Islam (Ware 2014). Lamine's dilemma manifested most clearly in his compartmentalization of the use of his body: He would sing but not play the berimbau. He might show up to watch training but not train. He might instruct others but not join in himself. He might define capoeira as a sport and leave out the cultural or spiritual connotations, thus foregrounding the idealized capoeirista body to achieve becoming a more complete ideal of a masculine, productive, worldly citizen or cosmopolitan body.

Lamine also used his body to perform dignity for a gaze entangled in coloniality, otherwise known as bourgeois respectability in postcolonial Senegal. At times he emphasized that his is always a Muslim body, a human vessel for God's message and spiritual guidance. Achieving completeness in that respect required balancing a ratio of bodily practices: less time spent attempting a new capoeira acrobatic movement one hundred times to program it into his physical body, and more time spent enriching his religious self through the embodied practice of prayer. His commitment to learning anything he set his mind, body, or soul to revealed not only exceptional dedication but also that his moral ideals were in tension: Black freedom, Islam, and coloniality, whose frameworks can disrupt the first and be problematically entangled with the second.

The mystical and the "rational" or "modern" are not necessarily at odds in Senegal. As Ricardo Falcão (2014, 843) has documented, Senegalese reported an increase in mystical elements with respect to sports, as well as "increasing rationalization of the body . . . accompanying an increase in professionalization." What I call "compartmentalization" comes into play with what Falcão (2014, 843) sees as the "tensions between Cosaan and Dund Toubab"—that is, between Senegalese customs and white/Western lifestyles—particularly with activities that center the body. However, the presumed dichotomy between a "white lifestyle" and "local custom" does not fully encompass the Afro-diasporic space of capoeira (Livermon 2020). Societal pressures to conform to modernity, productivity, and maturity clash with diasporic criteria: carrying on a legacy; representing Senegal in the new moment in capoeira's history; being productive in carrying forward Moctar's groundwork; living up to the symbolic labor expected of Lamine by his teacher, his group, and himself. Discourses about what young bodies can and should do in Dakar are linked to expectations about the productivity of certain kinds of bodies. Lamine's class position gives him access to information that influences how he chooses to fashion his body. Furthermore, the mandate of capitalist productivity for masculine citizens, alongside the realities of a generation of working professionals struggling with unemployment—particularly after the devaluation of the CFA franc in 1994—are at odds with how young people see themselves, the use of their bodies, and their historical connection to the diaspora as Black people discovering a legacy of Black histories of struggle. The metaphysical bodies of ancestors in the diaspora are at odds with the desires and expectations of young professionals—of being good religious subjects and of operating in a world in which white supremacist standards of labor, dress, and comportment shape how the country sees itself. This is epitomized by the ubiquitous phrase "Senegal du demm" ("That is why Senegal/Africa doesn't advance" or, in Wolof, "Senegal doesn't go forward"). With the daily mantra of the country lagging behind, who can devote themselves to "leisure"?

Leisure is its own form of protection, not from extreme circumstances, but from the restrictive hold of postcolonial life for young people that so often demands conventional, conservative ways of being. On our way to the middle-class Point E neighborhood (part of the European residential areas in the colonial period) for capoeira training one day in June 2015, my taxi got caught in the congestion of an *embouteillage* (traffic jam) (Melly 2017) caused by a law students' strike at the Université Cheikh Anta Diop (UCAD). When I recounted the holdup at training, Lamine recalled his history with student strikes as a child: "They almost busted my head one time. I had to go into the residential neighborhood to protect myself." Lamine is of a generation of Dakarois born around the 1989 youth movement, sparked in part by the 1987–88 *année blanche* (blank year), an invalidated academic year (Diouf 1996). He was in his twenties when the second major youth-led movement emerged in 2012 to protest President Abdoulaye Wade continuing to rule beyond his term limit. Lamine's generation of young people in Dakar are considered more educated and yet much less employed than the older labor force, producing a particularly visible class of working-age, educated young men perceived as just sitting around (Bocquier 1992).

Capoeira represents a form of artistic expression, as well as another approach to "the political," that does not fit neatly into the realm of popular cultural production in Senegal. Modes of artistic expression such as hip hop have often been highlighted in scholarship because of their legible modes of civil engagement and their success in shaping electoral outcomes in the country.[2] However, expressive forms linked to racial empowerment, postcolonial fashioning, *and* leisure "should be valued beyond [their] resistant potential" (Livermon 2020, 109–10). West Africans pick and choose relevant elements of diasporic forms, as we have seen with both Rastafarianism and hip hop (see, e.g., Savishinsky 1994), and student strikes have

4.2 Two of Doffu Maam Bamba Yi's promotional T-shirts. Photograph by the author.

become common at UCAD, as they have at many institutions of higher education in West Africa. One of Dakar's crown jewels, UCAD plays a central role in the training of state functionaries, medical doctors, lawyers, and prominent intellectuals. However, structural adjustment policies of the 1980s led to decreased state investment in social infrastructure, with one consequence being a spike in violent crime and unemployment among young people in Dakar. This was precisely the moment when hip hop took root as a tool of political expression (Fredericks 2014).

Hip hop represented a different kind of diasporic return than capoeira, with different implications for race, religiosity, and cultural production. On the fifth day of not being able to recover my suitcase after landing in Dakar during one of my research trips, a dear friend and lifelong Baye Fall (Sufi) artist, Ahmadou (known as Doffu Maam Bamba), gave me T-shirts advertising his music. One featured a photo of him kneeling at the bedside of the spiritual leader Cheikh Modou Kara Mbacké Noreyni, a controversial figure whom Ahmadou and I met together in 2009. The other T-shirt featured a photo of a group of young Black American boys, most of them younger than ten, posing shirtless for the camera (figure 4.2). Their grimacing facial expressions implied they were trying to look older, using their stance to overcome their smallness and play tough guys. Bordering the photo, Doffu Maam Bamba superimposed one of his song titles, "Lo Gueume Doff Si Way" (What You Believe Is Crazy).

The line is a signature of his music and refers to how the saint Cheikh Amadou Bamba was not believed during his time; history has shown that he brought a powerful spiritual message. I commented that the shirt featured "Black American *taalibés*," referring to Qur'anic schoolchildren that undergo full-time study and are viewed as exemplars of the spiritual path, which infuriated Ahmadou's friends/fans. How dare I compare these "ghetto" boys to the honorable children in Dakar's streets who were learning the Qur'an and begging to learn the value of humility? This anecdote reveals the double-edged sword of the coloniality of Black performance, which in this instance relates with hip hop. It is appealing as a global trend, and even compelling as a form of global Black cultural pride, but it carries the potential for anti-Blackness—in this case, among Senegalese Murids who use hip hop to moralize and distance themselves from the criminality presumably embedded in Black American modes of expression.[3] Yet Doffu Maam Bamba oscillates between performance of what Livermon theorized as Afro-diasporic thug masculinity in African contexts and a kind of Baye Fall respectability. Sufi music videos are on the rise in Senegal (Ogunnaike 2013), and screenshots of Doffu Maam Bamba Yi from two music videos reveal two sides to the coin of being a Baye Fall performer in Dakar today (figures 4.3–4.4).

The fear that diasporic forms are inspiring but spiritually threatening also speaks to a fear of indigenous Senegalese spirituality. Marame Gueye (2013, 24) theorized: "In the beginning, rap music had negative connotations in Senegalese popular culture. Rap musicians were not taken seriously and were humorously likened to madmen because in Wolof, especially among the subgroup of the Lebou, the term *rap* means a spirit that inhabits someone's body and makes the person sick or mentally ill. Rap music was understood as an escapist form for idle youth who were overly fascinated with the West." The Wolof word for mad person is *doff*, which is precisely the name my friend chose for his stage persona: Doffu Maam Bamba means "Crazy for the Elder Bamba" (a reference to the Murid saint). His name and slogan respond to the accusations of madness made about visionary faith leaders. Gueye's observation about the initial hesitation Senegalese had about rap music provides a window into contemporary African interpretations of diasporic Black arts: They do not

4.3 A screenshot of Doffu Maam Bamba Yi embracing another Murid in the music video for his song "Lo Gueume Doff Si Way."

4.4 A screenshot from a joint music video of "But Bii," with Doffu Maam Bamba Yi and a local Dakar rapper, Dof Ndeye.

involve correcting through authenticity or origins claims but, rather, are created as new forms arise in the diaspora and come into dialogue with African sociopolitical realities. Gueye is likely referring to "rab"—the abrupt pronunciation of *b* can sound similar to *p* in Wolof and thus creates an association with the *rab* cult of the Lebu people indigenous to Dakar, who practice spirit possession. Associating rap with the *rab* cult shows that diasporic arts that are African-derived but created elsewhere and then circulated in Africa in the late twentieth century interact with a complex set of cultural, spiritual, and social contexts. In other words, the meanings Africans produce about these diasporic forms cannot be predetermined. The negative associations with spirit possession by the Senegalese, I argue, was attributed to both diasporic/foreign influence (a Black American/Western form) *and* local influences and African indigenous spirituality, with its spirits and the tools for addressing spiritual concerns in the ritual context of *ndëpp* (discussed later in the chapter).

Lamine set himself apart from political actors who took to the streets in protest, revealing that even something as ostensibly trivial as leisure can speak in the realm of the political in other ways. Instead of joining the movers and shakers within a burgeoning youth political movement in Dakar, he sought out the political in everyday ideas, practices, and affective structures (fear, longing, desire) of Senegalese youth, showing that his demographic does not neatly conform to the tropes of a working-class, politically active youth. Senegalese identity is porous, flexible, and incomplete. What it means to be Senegalese—and, more specifically Dakarois—is shaped by a global dialogue about Blackness through art and political expression. It is also shaped by how class aspirations, opportunity, and social status are inherently, but often invisibly, shot through with colonial logics.

Islam and spirit-based traditions or ancestor worship were both linked in the colonial period by a racial hierarchy that diminished the ways in which Africans engaged in spirituality and worship. French colonial administrators introduced the term *Islam noir* (Black Islam) to distinguish what they saw as a less threatening version of Islam that was a thinly veiled animism. Islam in West Africa is almost as old as Islam itself (Ware 2014). Islamicization—predominantly among Pulaar, Wolof, and Mandinka communities—was, in fact, one of the most significant foreign cultural influences in the region before the effects of French colonial rule (Ngom 2003). Islam is practiced in a fashion that incorporates existing indigenous practices while also maintaining early Islamic practices now lost even in important sites such as Saudi Arabia (Ware 2014). An understanding of indigenous spiritual practices is further complicated by the historical dynamics of Senegambia as a region shaped by *ceedo* (so-called animist empires) rulers and Islamic empires vying for political and spiritual dominance (Barry 1997). French colonial officials constructed the descriptor *Islam noir* as "a recently arrived, second-rate, poorly understood, syncretistic, and therefore nonthreatening brand of Islam" (Ware 2014, 20). This characterization was also an act of epistemological violence aimed at discrediting West African Muslim empires, which frequently defeated French military efforts in the region (Ware 2014). Therefore, the presumed binary between Islam and spirit worship is shaped by a colonial logic and is wholly incorrect. Is Islam a Black religion? It has a complex history in Senegal that is influenced by colonial logics of African inferiority while also intersecting with Black African anticolonial legacy and Black empowerment (continental and diasporic). Islam also has a similarly complex history in Brazil, past and present, that in some moments is synonymous with Black empowerment and has also operated to distinguish Muslims as a privileged group from other Black or African positionalities. Each context involving the racialization of Islam is relevant in understanding the anxieties and imaginaries of this moment.

At the heart of defining what is a political or principled practice is one's moral framework, especially for young people in Senegal for whom religiosity is so crucial. Religiosity is at the center of notions about the idealized or aspirational subject, of decisions around one's role in society, and, most concretely, of discourses centered on the social body and its relationship to metaphysical entities (spirit bodies or imbuing objects with spiritual potential). Lamine's concern with the *haram* (religiously prohibited) aspects of capoeira is impossible to understand without looking at how the art form is entangled with the coloniality of Black performance. Hegemonic ideas about a modern postcolonial society structure what is an appropriate use of the body and of one's productive hours and years. Many aspects of daily life in Senegal might be perceived as *haram* but are tolerated without issue. For example, the wildly popular sport of *lamb* (traditional Senegalese wrestling) involves music, dance, and autochthonous spiritual practices infused into Islam.

Why, then, might Lamine be particularly wary of capoeira? Lamine located spirit worship in Brazil—or, perhaps, *dislocated* it to Brazil. His approach to what he perceived to be Candomblé potentially embedded in capoeira music was influenced by how both "animism" and Islam in Senegal were rooted in French colonial discourse that condemned the former as uncivilized and undermined the latter as a false version of the "real" religion in the Arab world. Similar to Ayo Coly's argument that the figure of the African woman's body becomes a symbolic tool of dialogue between the postcolonial and colonial states, the performing or worshiping African body more generally carries a racial burden that urban young people inherit and therefore have to navigate.

One aspect of diaspora was compelling to Lamine: capoeira as an aesthetically beautiful and physically challenging martial art form that evokes an empowered Black history. Another aspect was problematic to the point of needing to be excised: its ambiguously defined Afro-diasporic spirituality. Race is inherent in both of these imaginaries of diaspora, yet only one is viewed in overtly racial terms (i.e., capoeira as the quintessential Black/African martial art). The African-derived spirituality entangled with capoeira also operates in racial terms: the structural anti-"animism" in Senegal that positions indigenous spiritual practices against modernity and middle-class respectability but is discussed in an Islamic framework only as *haram*.

Capoeira and Spirituality

The question of capoeira as possessing or interacting with spirituality requires a reflection on its ontology. Capoeira was never a stable object (Höfling 2019). Furthermore, its Africanness is constantly being constructed and contested. Ana Paula Höfling (2019) astutely demonstrates in her work on the history of staging, performing, and choreographing capoeira that it is impossible to separate "real" capoeira from performed capoeira, perceived to be inauthentic and untraditional. She posits that the two seemingly distinct genres—*capoeira regional*, characterized as a whitened and modernized version, and *capoeira angola*, characterized as the more traditional, African version—are manifestations of the discursive binaries characteristic of Brazil's twentieth-century national project ("tradition/modernity, Africa/Brazil, 'folk'/erudite, and retention/loss"). She argues that instead of constituting the invention of tradition, capoeira's history of moving from criminalization to legitimacy offers an example of the "tradition of invention," with teachers and performers constantly reinventing and taking creative license for what is then read, respectively, as folk (angola) and modern (regional) (Höfling 2019). One key example is the innovation of Mestre Canjiquinha, who incorporated elements from Candomblé into capoeira and thus added to the puzzle of trying to understand the shared elements and distinctions between the two. While this example relates to anxieties around capoeira's "staged" elements obscuring its traditional core, I also want to draw attention to coloniality's erasing impulse. The nonlinear trajectory of capoeira's historical life means that Candomblé and capoeira could have shared conceptual frameworks, music, and movements that were forgotten or actively erased, and then revived by mid-twentieth-century capoeiristas bringing together multiple African-derived legacies.

Part of the challenge of defining capoeira comes from its co-construction, the dialogue of practices emerging from the same conditions. While capoeira is not considered a religious practice in and of itself, it developed alongside Candomblé in the same environment of the slave markets of colonial Brazil. Historically, capoeiristas, if not also initiates of Candomblé themselves, have often participated in that religious tradition by drumming and singing for ritual ceremonies designed to bring out the spirit of an *orixá* divinity through possession of its human conduit (Matory 2005; Talmon-Chvaicer 2008). Many symbolic elements of Candomblé have made their way into capoeira songs, as well, lyrics that signal the close relationship between these two hybrid Afro-diasporic traditions (Lewis 1992). For instance, many songs offer praise to particular *orixás* (Brazilian Portuguese spelling of *orisha* in Spanish contexts), such as Ogum, the god of iron and war, and Iemanja, the goddess of the sea, as they also call for protection of the bodies and souls of the players who are about to enter the *roda*.

Afro-Brazilian cultural practices were denigrated and even criminalized by social elites for centuries (Hanchard 1999b). As Josivaldo Pires de Oliveira and Luiz Augusto Pinheiro Leal (2009, 21) state: "Both [capoeira and Candomblé] throughout their histories have received attention from Brazilian authorities, for various purposes. In capoeira, the trajectory varied between uses and abuses favorable or costly to its practitioners. In Candomblé, the violence against its practitioners characterized the societal dialogue with the ancestral knowledge of Africans in Brazil." Candomblé is often lauded as quintessentially "syncretic"; however, under the conditions of colonial power and slavery, practitioners most likely appropriated Catholic symbolism as a result of the repression of African cosmologies rather than voluntarily, as is suggested in the more sanitized framework of "blending" or "mixing" (Nogueira 2020). As Black consciousness in Brazil has gained social momentum in recent years, Candomblé and capoeira have been propped up as centerpieces for a larger political project to address issues of racial inequality (Collins 2015; Smith 2016a).

While the vast majority of Brazilians today identify as Roman Catholic, many monotheistic Brazilian capoeiristas engage in a kind of secularized appreciation of Candomblé as a way to honor the historical foundation of the tradition; however, they still do not see any real spiritual potential in the practice. There are three generalized camps with respect to the question of capoeira and spirituality. One espouses the idea that capoeira is purely secular and therefore "inclusive" of practitioners of any faith, a notion that serves as a veiled mechanism to erase Afro-diasporic spirituality. Second, there is a growing movement of "Capoeira Gospel" that seeks to remove musical elements perceived to be associated with African-derived spirituality and replace them with Evangelical Christian concepts (de Brito 2017). Then there is the third camp, which highlights capoeira's Bantu and Yoruba cosmologies as foundational to the practice and its historical intimacy with Candomblé. For instance, the Bantu cosmological influence is manifest in the physical arrangement (a circle) and the movement style (upside-down movements such as cartwheels), corresponding to the *kalunga* hypothesis, in which the universe of the living and the dead exist in two halves of a circle (Desch-Obi 2008; Talmon-Chvaicer 2008). In this last camp, capoeira is seen as the contact point between the world of the living and the inverted world of the dead.

It is common for capoeiristas to cross their bodies or kiss a necklace of a Christian cross before they enter the *roda* to play. These protective or preparatory habits are not required; they are, rather, a widespread convention that corresponds to players' individual styles. Nevertheless, small acts such as these speak to the ambiguity of capoeira's relationship to religiosity: It contains elements of Catholicism, evidenced in the graduation ceremony being called *batizado* (baptism), and an aspect that signals a kind of syncretism. However, there is also the possibility that these aspects were meant to be satirical. A direct kick aimed at the chest is called a *benção* (blessing), which the anthropologist J. Lowell Lewis (1992) believes is social commentary on the brutality of colonial missionaries who sought to root out Afro-diasporic spirituality but represented their violence as a blessing. Furthermore, although largely unacknowledged, capoeira also contains elements that can potentially be read as having Islamic origins.

Bolsas de Mandinga: Vessels of Black Atlantic History and Colonial Angst

The ambiguity of capoeira's relationship to spirituality is embodied in the sacred bags known as *bolsas de mandinga* or *patuá* in Brazil and as gris-gris in Francophone West Africa. The Portuguese and Spanish Inquisitions punished people who produced and used these objects, and the French issued a decree in Saint-Domingue (Haiti) in 1758 prohibiting their use (Dayan 1995; Rarey 2023). In the Atlantic context, the word *Mandinga* refers not only to the European ethnonym for Manding-speakers in West Africa but also to the objects (pouches carrying sacred texts, usually worn on the body) and the practice of "magic," or manipulating spiritual forces for the purposes of protection, usually against intimate violence (Rarey 2023). A person wielding these forces is called a *mandingueiro*. The Mandinka people were highly skilled traders in the West African Sahel who have an array of regionally specific denominations and dialects grouped under the Manding language family. They were also skilled in the production of protective amulets against violence or harm. In the hands of Africans, *bolsas de mandinga* were feared by the Portuguese as objects of sorcery or devil worship, despite their wide use in Portugal (Mudimbe 1988; Rarey 2023). Mandingas were brought to the Americas and reproduced by enslaved Muslims from Senegambia (S. Diouf 2013; Rarey 2023). The use of amulets, however, was widespread across the Spanish and Portuguese Atlantic in early modern history and began to be prosecuted under the Inquisitions because of their perceived non-Christian, "African" connotations (Rarey 2023). In fact, most amulets began to be referred to as *mandingas*—divorcing them from the ethnonym of the same name—once non-Africans began seeking them out in significant numbers (Rarey 2023).

In capoeira, *mandinga* is a core concept that has a range of meanings. Most concretely, it refers to an individual's mastery of trickery to dupe and outmaneuver their partner through movement, expression, or pace. The personal noun *mandingueiro/a* refers to someone engaged in this corporeal cleverness, but it goes beyond the game to refer to a person's character and how they strategically move through life. What is still referred to as *mandinga* or *mandingueiro/a* in Brazil today (referring to the power to manipulate forces through physical objects for the purposes of healing or resolving social issues) is akin to what is known in Senegal as maraboutage or Marabouts. Many Senegalese wear gris-gris concealed under their clothes and protect their babies by putting gris-gris sourced from and blessed by Marabouts around their waists. In addition, the Baye Falls disciples of a subgroup within the Murid Sufi order often adorn themselves with large necklaces composed of amulets, and neotraditional wrestlers display gris-gris during combat (Chevé and Wane 2018; Repinecz 2020). It would likely offend Senegalese Sufi respectability to compare the parallel practices of *mandingas* and maraboutage. However, maraboutage, while at times controversial as a popular form of resolving social issues in Senegal, is understood to be within Islamic structures, as a Marabout is a Muslim spiritual figure. To compare maraboutage to the mystical forces associated with an African-derived spiritual practice in Brazil is thus to link it to an untethered, unruly indigenous or "pagan" ritual from which Muslims should distance themselves. Distancing of oneself from an ambiguous African spirituality echoes the colonial logic of subordinating indigenous Black practices to modernity and proper institutionalized faith.

White settler Catholic society in Brazil feared Islam, as well as African ancestral and spirit worship, in part because they were, in some ways, one and the same. Islam in West Africa, as everywhere, was superimposed on the preexisting indigenous spiritual modalities (Ware 2014). Amulets are used across West Africa, including for Vodun on the southern coast, but when employed by Muslims they are paired with Qur'anic verses produced by a Marabout or spiritual guide. As discussed in the previous chapter, objects that make up the mundane in West Africa have the potential for reinscribing and localizing diasporic objects and practices.[4] However, this category of everyday objects also holds knowledge about what is buried in Senegambian history in Brazil, that which is glossed over. In the everyday of Wolof and Fulani in Senegal, jewelry is used, along with leather pouches, as amulets: "The *corval* [an intricate gold bead] is hollow and may have once served as a receptacle for charms or for a sachet of perfume. However, in my experience Senegalese jewelry is often hollow but seldom contains anything. On the other hand, men's *gris-gris*, or talisman cases (flat packets, usually made in leather or silver), commonly hold small items and function as amulets" (Johnson 1994, 42). Ruben Andersson (2014, 63) notes that clandestine Senegalese migrants headed for Spain often stripped themselves of their amulets, which were used for invisibility en route when they were in danger or required rescuing, as those migrating in similarly daunting circumstances across the US-Mexico border enlist the protection of spiritual and other charms (see also De León 2015). An everyday object in West Africa thus takes on a new migratory context for protection.

When we lift the blinders of compartmentalization, we can play with the possibility of recovering Senegambian histories in Brazil and, therefore, Afro-Brazilian inspirations for postcolonial Senegal. A compartmentalization approach might find proof that capoeira and Islam were unrelated in colonial Brazil. For example, James Wetherell's 1860 travel musings included a section titled "Blacks," with one of the subsections titled "—In fighting," in which he describes capoeira. Another subsection, titled "Ornaments of Blacks," makes reference to Islamic bracelets and charms (without naming any connection to Islamic West African regions where people often adorn themselves with silver and bronze jewelry). He writes, "Many of the black men are accustomed to wear iron bracelets, some of them of twisted wire, like the old Irish Torques, some of iron chain, and some simply a ring of iron, the ends scarcely touching, so as to allow it to be pulled a little open to introduce the hand. Brass and iron rings are much worn, and several frequently on the thumb; *these are said to be charms* against the bites of snakes"

(Wetherell 1860, 114, emphasis added). Whereas "Fighting" implies hostility and "Ornaments" implies aesthetics or frivolity, both descriptions unintentionally demonstrate shared epistemologies and protective practices. What Wetherell calls "charms" used to protect against snake bites suggest the same use of *mandinga* amulets that took many forms and were worn on the body. West African Muslims today often wear silver rings, some with protective scrolls encased inside them. Along with "Ornaments of Blacks," the "Writings of Blacks" section also mentions "Mahommedans," a term for Muslims in that period. Yet Wetherell's descriptions of capoeira, titled "Blacks in Fighting," are unrelated to these sections.

One way to read these two presences is to think of their distinction. Islam was perhaps associated more with West Africans and their descendants, while capoeira emerged initially as a practice among West Central Africans. However, the racial descriptor "Blacks" used by Wetherell demonstrates the emergence of a racial category in the colonial era that was not only imposed by enslavers and colonial administrators but was also a reality of the shared experience of captive Africans and Afro-Brazilians. Blackness was a construct of the intentional innovation to reconstruct and piece together a range of African musical, spiritual, and other embodied practices that were distant and unrelated on the African continent. Furthermore, if we dwell on the archival intimacy forced by colonization and slavery, we cannot ignore the proximity of observations that landed Black "Mahommedans" and "Fighting Blacks" under the same observational umbrella. Perhaps least obvious of all—or what Matthew Rarey (2023, 14) would provokingly call an "insignificant thing"—is jewelry Wetherell remarked as "said to be charms" that is the capoeiristas' bodily skill of *mandinga*, or Black technologies of protecting and preserving the body under the most dehumanizing circumstances.

The relationship between Senegambian and Brazilian Black histories invites scholars, capoeiristas, and religious practitioners to develop more context-specific lenses regarding race and racialization. In Brazil, Candomblé is increasingly a symbol of contemporary Black Power movements, and more people are drawn to becoming practitioners. Islam, however, is not known to have been brought by African practitioners to Brazil and has gained visibility there only in relation to recent African and other migrant groups.[5] In other words, Islam is not widely understood to be a "Black" or "African" religion. It therefore is not valued in the same aspirational, Afro-futurist ways as Candomblé, which is seen as a religious refuge and model for Black liberation in everyday life in Brazil. That said, *within* the world of Candomblé, practitioners are beginning to investigate historical connections between the two religious practices. Scholarship on African Atlantic spiritual practices, especially within the brutal context of the transatlantic slave trade, demonstrates that the differences between specific traditions are sometimes less important than the larger approach to spirituality as a moral guiding force. In writing about the Mâle Revolt for instance, Olúfẹ́mi Táíwò (2022) brings our attention to the Vodun-inspired Haitian Revolution that, in turn, influenced an Islamic-inspired Bahian revolt. He also points out that warring empires on the African continent (Muslim Hausa and Yoruba) came together in the Brazilian context of racialized slavery. While capoeira and the Malê Revolt are not directly linked, Táíwò sees the shock waves of the Bahian revolt as having led to an increase in *quilombos* (maroon communities) and inspiring more capoeira activity that "humiliated police in the streets of Rio de Janeiro" (Graden 1996; Táíwò 2022, 213).

Looking at the two most significant instances of slave rebellion in Brazil, one was linked to Islam (the Malê Revolt of Bahia), and the other is linked to capoeira. Many capoeiristas believe the practice was used as a form of military combat in Quilombo do Palmares, a maroon society formed in the seventeenth century that lasted nearly a century. While there is no documented evidence of capoeira's presence in Palmares, there is an abundance of nineteenth-century literature describing capoeira as a practice of everyday resistance by enslaved people (Soares 2001; Talmon-Chvaicer 2008). Describing the painstaking preparation of protective talismans by Afro-Brazilian Marabouts, Diouf (1998, 187) offers, "In the Americas as in Africa, Islamic talismans were an integral part of the warriors' panoply. . . . Each fighter received a protection that would consist in the repetition of a special formula, dozens, hundreds, and even thousands of times. The preparation of a rebellion by the Muslims was thus a long process." Rarey (2023, 215) goes a step further, referring to the secrecy of spiritual power encased in the Mandinga pouches as itself a revolutionary act, a "retreat from aesthetic conditions of slavery" in conditions in which "public visibility of the body was implicitly tied to violence." In capoeira, a player's *mandinga* is described as cleverness through physical prowess but is often synonymized with "magic," hinting at *bolsas de mandinga* as magic, sorcery, or other types of spiritual power. Instead of the object imbued with divine energy, the capoeirista's body, and how they wield it, is the source of metaphysical power. In other words, *mandinga* in capoeira is an embodied and performed iteration of the same divine warrior magic as Muslim amulets.

Muslim Africans in Brazil and Afro-Brazilian capoeiras are often co-present in blogs and academic scholarship, but without a direct link. Each appears as a symbol of resistance—two expressions of Brazil's iconic freedom movements—with one (the Malê Revolt) contained in an event, and the other (capoeira as everyday resistance) crystalized in the form itself. Extended analysis that draws direct connections between the rebellious associations of capoeira and the Muslim revolt remain to be investigated by scholars or practitioners. The space that connects them is the imaginary of resistance. If it turns out that no concrete connection existed historically, that would not negate the shared space, because it had generative potential for modalities of freedom embodied in what became the future: Senegambian Muslim capoeiristas in Dakar and Banjul navigating spirituality, Blackness, and the moving and music-making body.

Islamic elements of Afro-Brazilian capoeira might also be contained within capoeira's core concepts. The *corpo fechado* (closed body), for example, speaks to the ambiguity of "African origins," as well as the ambiguity of spiritual connections. The closed body is central to Candomblé philosophy, referring to spiritual protection from harm. Here again we see an overlapping concept with capoeira in which capoeiristas describe needing a closed body in certain moments of the game as a shield from strikes, while also needing to open up to make themselves receptive to dialogue with the other player or to create a false vulnerability, inviting the opponent into a trap. *Corpo fechado* in capoeira is mostly secularized. Especially in the teaching context, where most of capoeira arguably occurs now, the concept of a closed body is both a physical manifestation and figurative lesson about being aware of your surroundings in the *roda*. T. J. Desch-Obi writes about the Central African cosmologies of protecting the body from external and spiritual disruption through *kalunga*, but the gris-gris amulets are also conceived of as closing off or shielding the body from harm in an African Islamic epistemology. Sufi traditions in particular invest in amulets that carry *baraka* (the blessings of God). These physical manifestations of God's blessings are often worn as necklaces to protect the body. Furthermore, some capoeiristas have speculated that the chorus of one of the most popular capoeira songs, "O La Ê La Ê La" bears a strong resemblance to the Islamic "La Ilaha illAllah" (There Is No God but God).

The epistemological foundations for Dakarois anxieties around ancestor worship are an iteration of the relationship between Islam and coloniality in Senegal. On the one hand, Islam is the state religion and structures political and social life; as such, its official institutions carry out the continuities of the colonial state (Villalón 1995). Its hegemonic power creates tension around the bounds of a religious life and polices the false barrier between the secular and the religious, a barrier into which indigenous ritual and cultural practices do not slot neatly. On the other hand, Muslim sociore-ligious movements in colonial Senegal and among enslaved Senegambi-ans have been vanguards of anticolonial, antislavery initiatives. Europeans saw religious conversion to Catholicism as a benchmark for civilization and progress, a racial schema designed to order humanity in relation to the standard of white supremacy (Diouf 1998). However, both Islamic and Catholic institutions sought to suppress indigenous spirituality: "Both Muslim and Catholic forms of worship asserted themselves over genies and ancestral spirits, which from then on retreated into private space, ob-scure regions of the memory, of the seaside (Gorée, Dakar, Rufisque), and of the river (Saint-Louis)" (Diouf 1998, 678). Indigenous spiritual geogra-phies were literally pushed to the margins of the country. Diouf describes "colonial urban logic" as a compartmentalizing force "that delineates the spaces of life, leisure, work, and religious practices" and, in particular, "a spatial translation of religious practices." Coloniality is not difficult to trace with respect to the overtly racial discourse of the French categorization of colonial subjects in West Africa (Diouf 1998; Wilder 2005). However, in re-lation to Islamic modernity in Senegal, the question of the racial structure of religious discourse is more complicated. This is evident in the demarca-tion of some objects as sacred, secular, or superstitious, a fundamentally racialized practice of delineating space, material, and cultural production and assigning them to a hierarchy of civilization.

The Portuguese Inquisition went after healers, prosecuting what were seen as not only religious violations but also the strong efficacy and protec-tive powers of "African fetishism" (Rarey 2023). Black religious pluralism and cosmopolitan performativities in Senegambia and the Upper Guinea Coast were threatening in their cultural fluidity and refusal to compart-mentalize in a context of violent compartmentalization by the Inquisition. That "flexibility" is no longer valued in postcolonial Senegal, and the ex-teriority and inferiority of the body are spaces of caution, concern, and careful compartmentalization. Performativity of so-called cosmopolitan-ism today is more of an adherence to the rigid standards of gender and modernity, which was not the case in colonial Senegal even in the 1950s, where Muslim men who were sexually non-normative were embraced as Afropolitan dandies (M'Baye 2019).

Mandinga Madness in West Africa

What does the capoeira concept of *mandinga* do for West African capoeiristas? The etymology of the word tells us it is a simple ethnic category. However, we can also examine its use in capoeira, as it leads many to believe the practice is aligned with animism or disruptive of social order. Christopher, like many West African capoeiristas, expressed dissatisfaction with Eastern martial arts, which he saw as too direct and confrontational and rendering one's intent too visible:

> If that situation, this case occurs, I think that capoeira already will greatly help me. Why? Because we learn the ruse, the *mandinga*. . . . And that's what I was saying is the shortcoming of [other] martial arts. It's so, uh! They expect just a, the direct blow, bam! bam! You know? The frontal, the linear. Yet capoeira, it's circular. And a person who is in the linear, they will be a bit lost. You *mandinga* them a little bit, and voup! A *compaso* [a type of inverted circular kick] that comes out; they never saw a *compaso*.

For Christopher and many others, trickery is one of the most useful aspects of capoeira. They value the circular, the unexpected, and the ambiguous character of capoeira over the "linear" and more "direct" style of other martial arts. The circular or "free" aesthetic that West Africans perceive in capoeira is also the characteristic many of them saw as the indication of capoeira's Africanness.

At the same time, the fluidity and unpredictability of capoeira's aesthetic is often the target of criticism by audiences unfamiliar with it. Some West Africans describe strangers—and even their loved ones—approaching them to accuse them of madness. Their bodily comportment falls outside the realm of recognizable and socially sanctioned movement, and they are sometimes deemed outcasts. Adama Badji, the founder of the Capoeira Association of the Gambia, shared with me that he almost lost his wife because she did not understand why he did capoeira and feared she needed to distance herself from it. Others also talked about family members who were unable to find the sense in what seemed to be idle activity—or, worse, they felt they were engaging in something potentially dangerous due to the ambiguity of movement that could not be socially located.

In a funny twist of events, Aziz, an advanced student in Afreecapoeira, described his introduction to capoeira as a confusing moment in which he was carefully trying to avoid a madman who seemed to be harassing him during his first training session. He was hooked after seeing Sylvèr, a Congolese instructor who was known for his strength, speed, and acrobatics, carrying out one of his signature moves. "He did it once in the Gambia," Aziz said. "He pushed against the wall and swung his legs over. When I saw that, I said, 'Wow! Seriously, I have to learn how to do that.' In the beginning, I had difficulty with *ginga*. It was a pretty uncomfortable position." He was impressed at the display of masculine virtuosity to which he aspired while encountering the discomfort of the first stages of disciplining the capoeirista's body. Then Aziz encountered another form of discomfort:

> As soon as I got there I understood that it was Sylvèr and Gery that ran the class. And then I see someone that takes me from the side, and he says, "Go ahead. *Cadeira* [chair position]. Loosen up. Loosen up." At some point I said to myself, "Guys, you see there is a crazy man who took me aside, come save me!" [He said,] "Go ahead relax. Move." And I told myself, "But this is not what the others are doing." The crazy man in question turned out to be Moctar. I didn't realize that this crazy man was actually the master, and I saw him do his *mandinga*.

Cool acrobatics were an initial appeal, but Aziz was confronted with the gendered ambiguity of a capoeira energy flow, likely the same aesthetic other unfamiliar audiences in the region experienced. What he saw as "madness" was in fact Moctar's use of *mandinga*, the desirable quality of capoeira that can take years of experience to embody.

This fear of idle or excessive movement is particularly looked down on because of how it speaks to an unconventional expression of masculinity, especially in wasting time on unproductive pursuits. Yet Black African masculinities are not constructed in a vacuum; rather, they are forged in relation to the transnational system of oppression brought about by racial capitalism and the inspiration Africans have always found in global Black gendered performativity (Appert 2018; Livermon 2020; Matlon 2022; M'Baye 2019; Quayson 2014). While most studies emphasize the adoption of Black masculine performances—even if they are not widely received by urban African publics—capoeira's spiritual connotations in Senegal show how the desire to draw on diasporic Black masculinities can be internally fraught for some men. For others, it is precisely in this new type of masculine embodiment that they find freedom not just from normative corporeality, but as a way to use the body and the shared energy of the *roda* to create a daily practice that transcends restrictive economic, social, and political possibilities. While not necessarily adopting gender or sexual non-normativity, they find freedom through the pleasure of leisure, indulging in the space between free time and wasted time.

As I reached the end of my fieldwork, I heard rumblings from other Senegalese Muslim capoeiristas who were beginning to think through the possibilities of Islamicizing capoeira by adding Muslim prayers to the music. Considering their creative solutions alongside Lamine's dilemma, I pose the question: Why can't capoeira—a container of, at least, Catholicism, Bantu cosmology, Yoruba Ifá, and other spirit-based practices—be perceived as simultaneously Senegambian, Islamic, and Black? Can capoeira's African origins be Muslim, too, coexisting with the truth of its overwhelmingly Angolan roots? Coloniality disrupted these Atlantic connections at every step. Can Senegalese Muslim capoeiristas today comfortably attach themselves to origins, claiming the continental, the diasporic, and the imagined of what might have been? All of this spiritual baggage contains more hidden gems than we can imagine.

Part 2: On Remembering

> If the goal of racialized modernity was to create a homogeneous self and a singular normativity and set them in opposition to pathologized others, responses to race in Africa have undermined that singularity by affirming the validity of other norms, other ways of being in, experiencing, and narrating the world.
> —HARRY GARUBA, "Race in Africa"

While steadfast monotheistic beliefs and practices weakened capoeira's appeal to some Senegalese capoeiristas, others were inspired and enriched by it. They saw the practice's spiritual ambiguity as a strength.

Ndëpp Repair: Sacred Movement and Sacred Place

Although Apollo grew up in a Muslim family, ancestor worship, as it is in much of Senegal's overwhelmingly Muslim society, was at the foundation of his monotheism. Diouf (1998, 677) notes, "Expressions of religion (beliefs, imagined worlds, knowledge and practices) participate in a discontinuous space where local practices are entangled with the Islamic and Christian professions of faith." Apollo attended an international capoeira event in Cotonou, Benin, in April 2011 and recalled that "we did Candomblé," using the Brazilian terminology as his reference point for describing the Beninese Vodun initiation (which he considered but ultimately did not undertake). He said, "My family here in Senegal also does Candomblé. They call it *ndëpp* or *tuur*.[6] We've practiced it for a long time. I had a grandfather [who lived] abroad, and when he came back, he broke all the things and said they were fetishes. Now my family doesn't practice it anymore."

In one respect, Apollo's grandfather's destruction of the "fetishes" speaks to a monotheistic Abrahamic framework that diminishes animist or polytheistic beliefs. However, in the specific context of coloniality, we cannot discount how autochthonous spiritual practices and cosmologies were racialized in the colonial period, deemed uncivilized, and used to justify mass reeducation through missionizing state infrastructure, legal structures, and a symbolic reordering of socially acceptable public practices.[7] The Brazilian context that Apollo is familiar with as a capoeirista (Candomblé) operated as the baseline for his description of African spiritual practices (Vodun in Benin). He privileged his identity as a capoeirista to provide a language for regional and local spiritual practices (such as *tuur* in Senegal that are, in fact, at the foundation of his upbringing). Similar to how *Candomblé* operates as a catchall term for Black Atlantic spirituality among Senegalese capoeiristas, *ndëpp* is used as a stand-in for indigenous spiritual deinstitutionalized practices in Senegal. In other words, centering indigenous practices of any kind is more important than elaborating their specificity.

Looking at just the indigenous Senegalese terms, *ndëpp* and *tuur* are not synonymous. While *tuur* involves an engagement of ancestral shrines across ethnic groups in Senegal, *ndëpp* refers to a specific practice associated with the Lebu, considered the main national indigenous group and historically intermingled with Wolof; Lebu people hold symbolic power, even though their political and economic power eroded after independence (Kringelbach 2013). The ritual ceremony of *ndëpp* is mostly led by priestesses (called *ndëppkat*), often before a participant audience composed predominantly of women, and involves drumming, dancing, and animal sacrifice, which people use to appease ancestral spirits in the service of healing a person from a bad spirit possession (Ndiaye 1986). The belt of gris-gris is central to the priestesses' power, as "the priestesses direct all the operations, ensuring in particular . . . the protection of the public against the 'bad' *rab[s]*, thanks to the amulets with which she is heavily loaded" (Ndiaye 1986, 67, my translation). Scholarship from early French anthropology to psychology has analyzed *ndëpp* in detail, primarily describing it as a treatment for mental illness that practitioners understand to manifest in the form of possession (Balandier 1948; Collomb and Ayats 1962; Monteiro and Wall 2011; Sylla 1994).

"We have *tuur* in my family," Apollo shared and described each member as possessing strange behavior that other family members could not explain; this led the family to seek out someone who "reads shells." The diviner revealed that they were neglecting their *tuur* (a spirit linked to their family or lineage), which was to blame for the strange behavior and negative occurrences in the family. Apollo said, "I was manipulated into thinking this was the root of the problem." He continued to be in a process of challenging inherited assumptions about what was acceptable and unacceptable spirituality. Apollo used the terms *Candomblé* and *Vodun* interchangeably. "I think in capoeira with Candomblé, Vodun, the slaves that were deported to Brazil, they didn't have a religion at that time," he explained. "They lived with that. So I think it's logical that they refer to themselves using that." His assessment that these religious traditions were akin to having "no religion" speaks to coloniality, as well as to the problematic definition of *religion* common to Western delineations and how African spirit-based practices are often defined in opposition to it.

Scaling out to the Atlantic connections, Apollo's comparison of Candomblé to *ndëpp* was not a particularly apparent one to make. Candomblé is a direct outgrowth of a range of Bantu spiritual practices, as well as Vodun and Ifá practices, depending on the spiritual "nations," as Candomblé has many variants that claim lineage in different African origins. It was developed by practitioners in a dialectic of maintaining spiritual traditions while adapting them to new contexts. *Ndëpp* as a ritual practice—or the *rab* cult in which it is practiced—is not a spiritual tradition shown to have been reconstructed in the Americas; nor does it have a specific connection to Brazilian Candomblé. It is practiced by the Lebu ethnic group, indigenous to Dakar's coast and not largely represented among the ranks of enslaved Senegambians taken to the Americas (Seck 2014).

Apollo defines his pursuit of a deeper engagement with an embodied knowledge of his Africanness as a Senegalese Muslim Peul and Sereer who nearly underwent initiation into a Yoruba religious practice in Benin that was routed through Afro-Brazil. Apollo expressed that, although he was already both a Muslim and a knowledgeable capoeirista, it was in Benin that he first learned about aspects of capoeira that "very much enriched [him] spiritually." Beyond the overt religious activities, the practice led to internal shifts within him. In his words, "I was no longer myself." It was through the embodiment and performative enactment of diaspora that a transformation took place, without displacement to Brazil. Apollo became more familiar with his background, his country, and his region through the transformation that diaspora inspired to pursue a deeper knowledge of West Africa and Black Atlantic spiritualities.

If we focus attention on the messiness of categorization, synonymizing, and making associations, we see a productive ambiguity, a useful confusion and conflation that speaks to the flexibility required to work through and beyond the logics of coloniality. Performers playing around with remapping, or resisting the mapping of African-based religions and cultural practices, are also critical of the Senegalese state and are therefore thinking radically about what it means to be Senegalese. A key dynamic in that radical thinking is the "delight" of not being able to be clearly defined that accompanies many African-derived religious practices (Khabeer et al. 2014, 133). For example, Apollo chose the name Sangomar for his capoeira group because of the pride of place common in Brazilian capoeira. In ecological terms, Sangomar is a sandbar at the mouth of Senegal's scenic Sine Saloum Delta, but it is also a sacred pilgrimage site for Sereer ancestor and spirit worship in a ceremony called Pangool. President Macky Sall wielded the symbolism of this sacred site to rename the ostensibly first Senegalese offshore oil-drilling operation; his symbolic indigenization of state and multinational capital enterprise leveraged indigenous Sereer practices that keep the memory of the great Sereer kingdom alive.

Diouf (1998) provides a clue into the historical shift caused by Catholicism and colonialism that pushed ancestor worship to the margins and shadows of Senegalese life. In describing the genies associated with regions of Senegal and urban sites in Dakar, he explains that the imposition of monotheism and colonial urbanism transformed into "processions and libations." Thus, the sacred takes a new geographic form: "It is presumptuous of buildings to try to contain them." Combating coloniality at the state level looks like the performative renaming of capital enterprise to an indigenous concept/name/place. From the capoeira community, combating coloniality looks like diaspora—claiming an imagined origin of the sacred place of Sangomar or *ndëpp* out of Black longing—without displacement, drawing from the region that is already home. Sangomar is a site of pilgrimage for Sereer spirituality; Apollo said, "Sangomar is my identity"; yet he himself does not identify simply as Sereer. He does not reproduce the colonial logics of ethnic purity, instead seeing Sereer and Wolof as not having a "big difference between them. . . . They have a similitude."

Apollo offered his identification with ethnicity, heritage, and rural nostalgia for origins by saying, "It was the connection with Sangomar and Candomblé; it wasn't about ethnicity. *I don't see that as relevant.* It represents the sacred, a sacred place. Capoeira in Brazil, they valorize their identity, and they sing Bahia. I can't sing Gorée because then I steal it from Moctar. I could, said Ouidah, but I'm not Beninese. When I looked for something that's what came to mind" (emphasis added). His thought process was imaginative beyond direct ethnic heritage, and practical. The sites of the slave trade in West Africa constituted obvious symbols to mirror how Brazilian capoeira symbolizes Black pride in place of the troubled history that produced Black subjectivities. Yet the question of nationality, and the need to respect the work of the regional founders of African capoeira schools (such as Moctar on Gorée Island and Mestre Fassassi in Benin), led Apollo to think about what it means to have African spirituality specific to Senegal and available to Senegalese beyond a narrow rubric of ethnic membership.

In colonial Senegal, religion, ethnicity, and political subjectivity were inextricably linked in ways that affected the relationship between class and place (Diouf 1998). Senegal's spiritual geographies tell a story that diverges from the dominant narrative of what constitutes the nation. Each region of Senegal, and each neighborhood of Dakar, has a spirit that dwells there (Diouf 1998). Sites and practices of ancestor worship such as *tuur*, common across many ethnic groups and religious affiliations in Senegal, represent, for many young Dakarois, an idea, rather than their own quotidian practice or childhood memory; nostalgia for village life is a common trope for generations born in the city. For Senegalese capoeiristas looking to make the art form speak to their political, personal, and ideological goals, autochthonous spirituality (relationships to different categories of spirits) brings to mind practices such as *ndëpp* and places such as Sangomar.

Like Apollo, Jacqueline, a capoeirista in her early thirties of Sereer ethnic background, found *ndëpp* useful for its diasporic potential. Capoeira as the "African" martial art was what drew her to train. "I really like the movements. It's pretty," she said. "It also interested me that it's something that comes from Africa. So as an African, why do martial arts that come from Japan?" Turning to the relationship between Brazil and Senegal, Jacqueline evoked *ndëpp*, a Lebu-Wolof trance ritual used to cure bad spirit possession and other psychological ailments:

> Brazil and Africa have relations because if you leave African land, you are part of a family when they bring you to Brazil. Each African family

has a totem and even great-great-grand parents. If, for example, you are in Brazil and one day you come to Senegal and there's a *ndëpp* ceremony, if they sing your totem, you will fall into a trance. If you go to Gorée and they sing your totem, [even] after one hundred years, if you are part of that family, you will fall into a trance. Even from Africa they can sing and touch you over there.

In other words, the source of diasporic repair is in the singing female healers, *ndëppkat*, whose voices free the body of harm and evil or even "return" diasporic kin to their roots through inducing trance. Why—in the wide range of West African indigenous spiritual practices—does *ndëpp* arise as connected to the kind of bodily, racial, historical, and imaginative work some Senegalese capoeiristas are trying to think and move through? At first glance, *ndëpp* has become the point of reference because of its visibility in popular culture (Deliss 2014; Mueller 2013). However, *ndëpp* also speaks to the symbolic weight of an indigenous Senegalese practice that cannot be traced to outside influence. While televised as a national spectacle, *ndëpp* is simultaneously a target of scorn, as seen in Apollo's grandfather's shattering of the totem. Neo-Pentecostal movements, such as the Universal Church of the Kingdom of God, have also deterred their members from both the Muslim use of gris-gris and indigenous *ndëpp* healing ceremonies in their contemporary missionary campaigns (Samson 2016). Jacqueline said excitedly, "Even white people come to get healed!" as if to prove *ndëpp*'s potential and redeem its value beyond the colonial gaze. Apparently from her perspective, white people coming to *ndëpp* to address mental health problems makes it compelling for moving beyond racial distinction of performance spaces. In colonial Senegal, Marabouts' most popular clientele for gris-gris were elite mixed-race *signares* (derived from the Portuguese *senhoras*, or ladies) and other mulatto women (Diouf 1998), much like the Black traditional healers in the Americas who drew significant numbers of white clients even during slavery (Sweet 2011).

Seck (2014) discusses the impact of enslaved Senegambians on North Carolina. While he discusses a Lebu presence among the Senegalese ranks, and writes about *ndëpp* as compared with other spirit-based practices on Whitney Plantation Museum's website, he does not elaborate on any possible evidence of diasporic versions of the practice in the Americas. However, one can infer that these enslaved communities perpetuated versions of the ritual on American plantations, and I hold some space that evidence may one day be found. But diaspora without displacement redirects our attention to what is already present in the imaginative agility and lived experience of West Africans on the continent. *Ndëpp*, Jacqueline's inspiration for her racial self-making and spatial "reasoning" for linking Black geographies, is a healing practice she knows to have the power to strike in the bodies of living Black kin anywhere and return the souls of those already passed (and past). In her conception of *ndëpp*'s capacity, diasporic healing and connection is already ongoing in embodied spirit worlds in Senegal.

In the same way that Candomblé has become a catchall for Black Atlantic spiritualities, *ndëpp* seems to have served a similar purpose for Jacqueline. A distinct ritual practice, some Senegalese capoeiristas used it to refer to anything that would otherwise be categorized as animism in Senegal. What's remarkable is that Jacqueline referenced *ndëpp*—practiced predominantly by the Lebu ethnic group—rather than the specific spiritual practices of her own Sereer background, such as Pangool. While Jacqueline identifies as Christian, she conceptualized *ndëpp* as a spiritual technology capable of reconnecting African captives who perished in the Americas with their descendants on the African continent without ever returning home. In other words, she was playing imaginatively with what are believed to be strict ethnic and religious delineations. She saw capoeira in a similar vein, not just as a way to memorialize a painful history, but as a material method of correcting the separation between enslaved and continental Africans and returning diasporic souls home, embodied in their African kin. Jacqueline conceptually wove together history, religion, and the body in a global, expansive understanding of Blackness and Africanness. Senegalese capoeiristas such as Jacqueline and Apollo look to forms of bodily expression that express pride in "African" ways of moving and expressing that are otherwise stigmatized or underexplored. By highlighting a particular function of the *ndëpp* ceremony, Jacqueline wondered aloud about the possibility for Brazilian kinship to which she felt connected through her practice of capoeira. Her unique contribution was not simply in recognizing a parallel in a diasporic community. It was also in seeing the ability of *ndëpp* to return the spirits of ancestors who died in captivity through inducing trance in their descendants.

Colonial logics related to how spirituality is gendered impact the meanings of *heritage* and *Africanness* for those trying to develop cohesive spiritual imaginaries. The *rab* cult was "feminized" after Islamicization, meaning that it became more closely associated with women's spheres, while Islam reinforced religious and political institutions controlled by men (Mueller 2013; Zempleni 1969).[8] This historical shift works in tandem with the idea that women are representative of tradition and folklore as a result of the masculinization of the political and public sphere following the founding of the nation-state. The imaginary of heritage, authenticity, and Africanness (as opposed to Westernness) is bound up in women's "traditional" ritualized spaces, bodies, and practices (Coly 2019).

Neoliberal restructuring in the 1990s expanded the NGO infrastructure in Senegal, as it did across Africa (Ferguson 1990; Piot 2010; Thioub et al. 1998). Women gained more economic opportunity through these organizations, especially in urban centers such as Dakar, even though they did not gain more influence on public policy (Morales-Libove 2005). Jessica Morales-Libove's dissertation on Wolof *tours* demonstrates that Senegalese women use dance spaces in Dakar to grapple with increasingly restrictive gendered expectations under increasing economic precarity. While Jacqueline did not describe *ndëpp* in explicitly gendered terms, evoking a ritual dance space in which women are healers (*ndëppkat*), and therefore one of the few spaces where the gender hierarchy is reversed, does similar symbolic work. The antidote to coloniality can sometimes be found in spaces where female leaders wield powerful spiritual skills.

How do West Africans connect not only with the history of the slave trade as an abstraction but also with the souls, entities, or bodies of kin lost across the Atlantic? Both Lamine's dilemma and Jacqueline's proposal are indicative of how religion, racial empowerment, discourses about the body, and coloniality operate in the postcolonial space of Dakar. Similar to Lamine, Jacqueline's perspective is one that butts up against the colonial distinction of irreconcilable categories—that is, monotheism versus spirit-based or ancestor worship. Rather than approach the diaspora with compartmentalization the way Lamine does, she demonstrates an alternative approach. She sees potential in putting Afro-Brazilian and Lebu practices in dialogue for her own construction of Black expression and decolonization.

Conclusion

Capoeiristas who evoke practices such as *ndëpp* add them to the repertoire of African resistance to erasure and oppression and draw on them to imagine futurity. What persists that "Islamization and colonization have been unable to obliterate" is not just a romanticized precolonial society particular to certain ethnic groups such as Wolof or Sereer (Ngom 2012,

102). Indigenous, regional, continental, and diasporic events, cosmologies, and embodied practices inspire Dakaroise young people's political imaginaries. Felwine Sarr (2020, 116) makes a similar case for a range of African cosmologies as fruitful models for the future when he writes, "[They] relativize the omnipotence of the subject. . . . A vitalist ontology is shared by several systems of thought of societies from different African cultural areas; among the Bantu peoples, the Dogon, the Sereers." Coly (2019, 6) reads the controversial Senegalese film *Karmen Geï* as a model for how the main character "draws from indigenous African expressions of the sexual female body to model some future directions of a fully emancipated and emancipatory African feminist criticism." Capoeira has joined the repertoire of indigenous African resources as a tool for imagining an emancipatory, anticolonial future, despite its being "foreign" and the fact that its characterization as a tool of resistance is questioned by scholars.

Diaspora without displacement allows for attunement to the myriad outlets for personal discovery, heritage connections, and historical rectification pursued by young Dakarois. In this framework, I understand their imaginary of these potential relationships or possibilities not just in terms of an external diasporic influence of a Black cultural practice from elsewhere (Livermon 2020), but also as arising from the constraints of modernity, respectability, and liberal notions of progress at home. The process of forgetting is layered. It involves the decentering in historiography of Central Africa's cultural contribution in Brazil, which, as noted earlier, occurs through Nagôcentrism (Heywood and Thornton 2007); the erasure of Islamic practices brought by enslaved Africans (Senegambians and others) to Brazil; and the forgetting of the diverse African origins of symbolism, ritual, and spirituality in capoeira. This is particularly the case as the practice moves into a commodified, sanitized, and deracialized context in the contemporary moment. Coloniality in the form of forgetting or historical silencing means concepts such as *corpo fechado* and *mandinga* are no longer remembered as Islamic in Brazil. Subsequently, forgetting also obscures the potential Islamic origins of the practice for twenty-first-century Senegalese Muslim capoeiristas. Once capoeira made its way to Senegal, West African capoeiristas read it as predominantly tied to African diasporic spiritual imports, legible only as a troubling (and perhaps idolatrous) spirit-based practice for Muslims.

Senegalese young people are learning about what is Senegalese, what is Wolof, and what is Afro-diasporic at the same time. Perhaps more important, they are coming to this knowledge through an embodied practice that is itself a mysterious Atlantic amalgam; capoeira's connected global histories are unfolding at the same time that capoeira circulates, obscuring what it was and what it is. The gaps and baggage capoeira carries also expose the instability of what is considered spiritual or religious and, therefore, what were the influential elements in the construction of this diasporic performance project. Ultimately, these kinds of transatlantic mysteries force us to rethink national historical frameworks. If "mixture" and "syncretism" are at the heart of Brazilian identity and culture, then the racial triad of indigenous, African, and European—and the religious blends of African spirit worship with Catholicism—are not all-encompassing. Monotheistic legacies in Brazil are not only Catholic; they are also Islamic. They are not only "syncretized" with African spirit-based practices after the fact but are *already* defined by them in the case of Islam—not to mention that West and Central African cosmologies have also already been merged.

This entangled legacy requires that we rethink what we know to be Senegal. Essentializing is problematic not only because it reduces identity to a fixed, knowable, and often a-historical essence but also because it presumes to know which cultural origins define a group of people. By listening to the imaginaries, the "what ifs," and examining which forms of embodied knowledge are compelling for people trying to make sense of themselves, we can piece together their potential (ancestral) pasts, as well as what historical and spiritual forces they draw on and cite as aspirations for their future. What is forgotten through coloniality's strategy of erasure is remembered by those who are curious and courageous enough to try to fill in Atlantic gaps.

CHAPTER FIVE

AFTER TOURISM
DIASPORIC CHAUVINISM AND THE RENEWED REGIONALISM OF WEST AFRICAN HOST PILGRIMS

Dakar buzzed with energy in December 2015 as a high point of the year approached. It would soon be Maggal, the annual pilgrimage to Senegal's holy city of Touba to commemorate the life of Cheikh Amadu Bamba, commonly known as Serñ Tuba, a saint and the founder of the Murid-diya Sufi brotherhood (Babou 2007). Three million Muslim disciples of the brotherhood prepared to descend on the sacred site, while countless others in the diaspora gathered—from living rooms in Philadelphia to mosques in Paris. They, too, sang sacred poetry that collapsed their geographical distance from the pilgrims in Senegal (Dang 2013).

The timing of that year's Maggal set in motion a pilgrimage of another kind: While millions of Senegalese headed east to Touba, a group of university students and young professionals took advantage of the national holiday to travel south. Leaving one capital for another—Banjul, in the Gambia—they journeyed six hours by van, overnight, to participate in a weeklong event celebrating the ten-year anniversary of the Capoeira Association of the Gambia. West African capoeiristas often travel to one another's events, and a yearly trip to Gambia was becoming a tradition for Africa

5.1 Stage at the Alliance Française in Banjul decorated for the International Day for the Abolition of Slavery. Photograph by the author.

Capoeira–Ilha de Gorée (Afreecapoeira). Members hoped to support their Gambian peers in developing the newest capoeira association in the region. Along with regional guests, the event featured Brazilian instructors living in France, accompanied by ten of their European students, many traveling to the African continent for the first time, on a pilgrimage to a place they framed as an origins site for capoeira.

The encounter culminated in a performance marking the International Day for the Abolition of Slavery in Banjul. The show would be held at the Alliance Française, a legacy from France's first colonial act of establishing French-language institutions after the Berlin Conference, at which major European empires met to divide and conquer the African continent through military intervention and formal colonial rule (Calvet 2010) (figure 5.1). In preparation for the show, the visitors from France doled out marching orders to the performers to carry out the vision of their Brazilian instructors. Sereia, a top student of the *mestre* (master), made sure that not a single detail was out of place or out of time.[1] She instructed Solomon, one of the Gambian capoeiristas, to take off a necklace that displayed the iconic revolutionary Che Guevara because, she explained, "Che

Guevara was not born in the slave time." Despite the week of collaboration by European, Brazilian, and West African martial artists in the name of commemorating abolition, Brazilian *mestres* and their French students led the workshops, choreographed the performances, and chose among themselves who would be featured. It is standard for a visiting group to run workshops within international capoeira networks, but under the premise of a "return to Africa" trip, the behavior of these visitors exemplified what I have defined in this book as *diasporic chauvinism*, an assertion of ownership and expertise that, ironically, excludes African participation in what is an inherently amalgamated Black Atlantic tradition. Given their level of experience in capoeira, that might not seem strange to some. Many of the European (mostly French) students had trained under Brazilian *mestres* for years, and several made regular apprentice pilgrimages (Griffith 2016) to Brazil to hone their skills. West Africans, including the Gambians who were on their home turf, were not chosen to narrate scenes for the performances and were left out of the evening's lineup of solo performances, only to be hastily patched in at the last minute. Throughout much of the performance that night, the blocking pinned them to the sides of the stage as the story of Black liberation unfolded in the French cultural center.

After the formal show, the Brazilians and Europeans and the energized audience cleared out of the Alliance Française amphitheater to continue the festivities, dancing in the courtyard and enjoying pizza, fruit juice, and a secret bottle of cachaça they shared among themselves. In the same moment, a few of the African capoeiristas lingered on the stage, some expressing a sense of disappointed hopes. Siaka and Ebrima from the Gambia had trained for months in anticipation of the opportunity to showcase their new acrobatics. In the midst of this post-show lull, Kassoum, a member of the Senegalese capoeira association, picked up a berimbau that had been left on the floor of the now vacant stage and casually began to play. I joined him by picking up a pandeiro, timing my accompaniment with his relaxed rhythm. Siaka, from the Gambian school, silently kneeled in front to propose a capoeira game. Organically, a spontaneous *roda* evolved, with only the members of West African schools. This collective effort moved against the compounding disappointments of diasporic expectation. The informal scene became tacitly instructive, with Afreecapoeira students from Senegal teaching the Gambian students how to enter the *roda* and how to play the instruments, all with silent motions so as not to break the delicate energy of the moment. When two French capoeiristas happened upon the scene, they stood respectfully to the side. Despite being at the center of all of the week's events, they chose this time not to participate right away. Instead, they simply witnessed this impromptu West African collaboration in a diasporic practice.

Like the informal *roda* that took place after the Senegalese TV cameras stopped recording the twentieth-anniversary event (see chapter 2), this collective effort to play with no audience but one another marked an organic event that resulted from the mundane and compounding disappointments of diasporic expectation. The choreography and creative preparations for a staged performance of capoeira are important, if frequently undervalued, sources of knowledge (Höfling 2019). So, too, are the accidental, failed, audience-less *rodas* that happen not in the formal organic way that is standard for capoeira (capoeiristas mostly play with themselves and with an audience of themselves) but, rather, because of who was centered during the performance (whiteness and expertise in Black performance) and who was excluded (the marginal capoeiristas picking up where exclusion left off to improvise a regional promise of something new).

West Africans—typically understood as hosts and tour guides for capoeira events with international visitors, as well as the embodiment of Africa as origins—routinely embark on pilgrimage, from Dakar to the Gambian slave fort or from Lomé, Togo, to the Door of No Return in Ouidah, Benin. Their routes and practices seek to engage with diaspora—imagined and real, historical and contemporary; through relationships, networking, and interactions; and in places both geographically based and imagined. Victor Turner (1988) wrote about the sequential structure of pilgrimage, from the pilgrims' preparations to every step of the journey through the return home. What distinguishes pilgrimage from other types of travel is the break from the structure of daily social life to undertake a journey to a special event, a sacred site, or a place with deep foundational significance to a community. Many West African capoeiristas described Brazil as the "Mecca of capoeira" and, therefore, a place they needed to visit in their lifetimes (see, e.g., Griffith 2016). Without Brazil as a viable option for pilgrimage, events where capoeiristas from Brazil and other places "return" capoeira to Africa create something akin to pilgrimage to Brazil for West Africans. The traveling of West African university students for half a day to a neighboring country is unlikely to be viewed in the extraordinary light of pilgrimage in the way that diasporic "tourist pilgrims" and global capoeiristas embodying diasporic return by taking a sacred journey to the continent of capoeira's imagined and real origins are considered the true pilgrims

(Ebron 1999). With global capoeiristas visiting, those who already live there (in this case, Gambian capoeiristas) are positioned as hosts. They do not travel and are even less likely to be regarded as undertaking pilgrimage. This chapter explores what happens when African young people who have immersed their lives in a diasporic art form travel to encounter the embodied diaspora. In some ways, Brazilian *mestres* represented their practice and embodied the diaspora. Rather than analyzing how Brazilians are impacted by a journey of "return" to the homeland of their practice and national history, I examine how the lens of diaspora is an ever evolving inspiration for self-discovery and community building and, simultaneously, an obscuring framework that emphasizes historical racial formation while color-blinding the present. Diaspora is an explicit and embodied exploration of what Blackness can mean, what its relationship is to whiteness, what its heritage is, and how regional and international collaborations are unfolding. From the "failures" of diasporic return due to the disruptive force of coloniality, the unanticipated renewal of West African regionalism emerges.

I aim to complicate the notion of diasporic embodiment with respect to place and temporality. Anthropological constructions of diaspora have focused on those who left or were taken against their will, with less emphasis on those left behind. If we are to take seriously diaspora as a condition (Campt 2005; Edwards 2003) rather than a place or predetermined set of demographics, then we have to keep open the possibility of all contemporary Black subjects experiencing the longing for sovereignty and continuing historical trauma of the slave trade. Diaspora is also an act performed and embodied through practices that Africans take part in and perpetuate. They form communities partly in the shadow of a diasporic elsewhere. The question then becomes: What is diaspora in the context of martial artists from various class backgrounds, who come from countries across West and Central Africa in search of work and education and who circulate among regional urban sites for cultural activities? West Africa contains rich histories of migration, adventurous travel, departures to refuse European rule, and sacred pilgrimage (Rahman 2021; Yamba 1990). Small-scale networks of West African capoeiristas working to develop the practice in the region exist not in contrast, but as an added layer, to the porous, expansive West African regionalism rooted in Senegambia (Barry 1997). Diaspora as an analytic in contemporary West African networks within and between Africans and international visitors enhances our understanding of the kinds of practices, relationships, and ideologies that are compelling to young people seeking history, belonging, leisure, and discovery of what their bodies and voices can bring to their understanding of themselves.

These types of interactions are not predetermined. I have seen instances elsewhere in West Africa in which pilgrimage-like relationships between Brazilians and Africans did not play out in ways indicative of diasporic chauvinism that marginalizes contemporary African participation. However, the similarity of the stories emerging from these types of events in Benin, Togo, and the Gambia by European groups suggests that this is a growing trend. White apprentice pilgrims who train capoeira in Brazil and France develop an intimacy with Black diasporic pilgrims' experiences. In pilgrimage events, this leaves little room for the experiences of African host pilgrims, who are positioned to embody the static past, the "unskilled" present, or the invisible host. Whiteness plays out not only as a display of privilege but also as a cooptation of the Black histories and artistic forms that are at the center of what is "returning" and what "remained." The confluence of white privilege and diasporic chauvinism obscures other generative phenomena. For instance, the mundane, ongoing pilgrimages of West Africans enact diaspora as bodily practice and social schema of global connection with Black people. The common framework of diaspora masks the significance of these activities.

An island slave fort and its holding cells were just some of the sites on the agenda of the pilgrimage group that arrived in Banjul in December 2015. Perhaps *pilgrimage* is an insufficient word to capture the dialogic nature of these events. Brazilians came to discover the Africa of their heritage. European travelers came to discover the Africa that was partly responsible for the Afro-diasporic combat game they have embraced under the tutelage of Brazilian *mestres*—but they also came to speak to Africa. They arrived with the confidence of their years of bodily conditioning, their Portuguese-language skills acquired to keep up with the commands in capoeira class, and the blessing of their instructors, who, back in Europe, the United States, or Canada, operate as the embodiment of capoeira's African qualities (Robitaille 2014). They arrived to tell Africa about the artistic traditions of self-expression and liberation enslaved Africans spawned in Brazil, as if to report back to the Motherland from the colonies. Over the course of about a week, they moved from site to site, spreading the gospel of capoeira in a series of private and public performances, trainings, and gatherings that strung together a statement of origins and return, the beginnings and the now of capoeira, and the ways the embodied practice unlocked a window into the Atlantic world.

Practitioners play out the politics of racial positioning and the narrativization of the history of the slave trade during international cultural events. I argue that these types of events, in this case framed as a "cross-cultural exchange," produce diasporic chauvinism. The term *diasporic chauvinism* refers to a hierarchy of ownership of narrative and knowledge and a monopoly on expertise undergirded by various forms of privilege. The privilege Brazilians and their white students possess is facilitated by a hegemonic narrative of the African diaspora in which Africans are perpetually and strictly the embodiment of origins, foreclosing the possibility of their being pilgrims. In this narrative, Africans function as both historical relics and passive hosts to the experiences of capoeira "pilgrims" from elsewhere, whether they are Brazilians of African descent or white European practitioners. These Brazilian experts privilege the intimacy of long-term relationships with their students in Europe in ways that often reduce their African capoeira peers to symbolic props. Having trained under Brazilians both inside and outside Brazil, Europeans, Americans, and other (primarily white) students of capoeira in the Global North also engage as "experts," thus appropriating diasporic chauvinism. Theirs is an assertion of expertise and authority through their proximity to Brazilian teachers. Thus, the dynamics that unfold during capoeira roots tours reveal the fraught dynamics and problematic tropes of pilgrimage and return in the African diaspora.

If the focus shifts from the issue of return for diasporic exiles to the construction of West African participants as "hosts," we can raise questions concerning how contemporary African subjects are situated and situate themselves in this narrative of historical reckoning. What can their *disappointment*—which assumes expectations and a failure to meet them—tell us about the affective structure of African aspirations for connection through diaspora? What happens to our definition of *diaspora*—as a practice of process; a mode of being and becoming; a search for homeland, belonging, and repair from the ongoing damage of the past—when we see continental Africans as another kind of pilgrim? What is diaspora when defined by practices of continental Africans as a mode of creating community and union among Senegalese, Ivorian, Guinean, Central African, Bissauan, and Gambian pilgrims who are seeking out and struggling with the discovery of familiar places? What is diaspora without significant displacement? Can the term expand to include the postcolonial predicaments of marginalization—seeking belonging, healing, connection with wounded kin—or must we use a different term due to the positionality and innovative work of continental African peers?

The Problem of Pilgrimage

Increasing attention has been paid to Global South alliances and histories as a critique of the centering of the Global North, or "the West," as a self-proclaimed project of modernity (Trouillot 2003). If the Global South emerged as a celebratory category implying a new world order that would challenge Euro-American imperial hegemony, scholars have begun to critique the ways in which new hegemonies, hierarchies, and other inequalities are being reproduced (Cesarino 2017; Dávila 2010; Thomas and Campt 2008). Performative events of both the commemoration of abolition and pilgrimage help to further understanding about diasporic circulations and racial formation from the sites of contemporary urban West Africa (Clarke 2004; Pierre 2012). These types of events illustrate that the temporary displacement of participants in pilgrimage reveals hierarchical arrangements of intimacies and expertise discourse with more clarity.

Pilgrimage is a practice intimately tied to the idea of place and directionality. It also tends to carry a spiritual connotation. Sites and relics of the slave trade hold an emotional weight akin to the spiritual journey of religious pilgrimage (Brand 2011; Davis 1997). "Roots tours," as such trips have come to be called since the 1970s, are a kind of pilgrimage, a return of Black diasporic people to different sites in Africa associated with the transatlantic slave trade. Afro-descendants in the diaspora and white foreigners are increasingly engaging in roots tours to the African continent, curious about both the atrocities and the instances of Black resistance that emerged from it. Roots tours have also increasingly become one of the major ways that practitioners pay tribute to the deep historical significance of capoeira. They serve as a reminder that while capoeira has become popular in gyms and dance studios around the world as a form of fitness and exercise, the tradition is painfully and inextricably tied to the global forces of imperial expansion and enslavement out of which it emerged.

Typically, these trips include roughly a dozen students from capoeira schools in Europe that are headed by European or Brazilian *mestres* and other advanced instructors. They are organized collectively by the visiting group and the African capoeira school in the host country, which also invites practitioners from the surrounding region. In 2015, the Capoeira Association of the Gambia formally hosted the event, in partnership with Josselin, a French expatriate working in the Gambia who had become central to the organization. Josselin had played a major role by teaching classes, finding financial sponsorships, and organizing public events. That year he offered his family's home in Banjul as the central residence and rehearsal space for all participants. Before moving to the Gambia, Josselin had trained *capoeira angola* in eastern France, with a group led by brothers from southeastern Brazil, who were the experts leading the week's events.

International capoeira events held across West Africa that cater to international visitors follow a standard agenda, whether they occur in Benin, Ivory Coast, or the Gambia. Often the practitioners play capoeira in public spaces, almost always in at least one bustling outdoor marketplace. There is typically also a formal tour or a capoeira event planned at a site linked to the transatlantic slave trade. Those considered the highest-ranking experts conduct workshops on capoeira sequences and techniques, culminating in a choreographed performance for the general public. While the impetus for these gatherings and performances is framed as a pilgrimage, indicating a symbolic return for descendants of enslaved people, the trips are not, of course, limited to Afro-Brazilians and typically include few students or instructors of African heritage.

There is clear tension between the framing of the event and the embodiment of its discourse. Those who attend these trips to West Africa are mostly white Europeans, as are the experts who lead them, serving as the agents of capoeira's return to Africa. As a result, the meaning of the pilgrimage or return becomes more universalized: the return of capoeira to its origins by all capoeiristas, regardless of their racial positionality. While the majority of capoeiristas visiting West Africa continue to be white Europeans, Brazilian experts are visiting the region more regularly, so these international gatherings take on more of the feeling of a traditional diasporic pilgrimage to an African homeland. Brazilian pilgrims are typically migrants who settled in Europe or the United States to set up capoeira schools, who then take their students on a journey to the African continent—often a first for all of the travelers. Less frequently, Brazilians visit directly from Brazil.

Building on Victor Turner's (1988) assessment of the social and material dynamics of sacred pilgrimage, we can think more explicitly about the relationship between hierarchy and political economy that shapes the social phenomenon. Race is a central feature of the historical narrative of diasporic pilgrimage. It acts as an explicit organizing principle in part through the use of the tropes of exile of the enslaved, racism enduring in settler colonial society from the past and ongoing in the present, and the idea of Black belonging through the act of return. In the context of a diasporic pilgrimage intertwined with the commodification of culture, the boundary between tourism and pilgrimage becomes slippery. Race implicitly structures the interpersonal and structural relationships among the various pilgrim positionalities. During the week of Maggal, the simultaneous and overlapping pilgrimages occurring in Senegambia (and the expanse of its concomitant digital diaspora) reveal the different frameworks of diaspora circulating in the region that speak in various ways to the aftermath of slavery, colonial rule, racial formation, and the unfolding postcolonial state.

Many people who cultivate themselves as capoeiristas in countries around the world have become invested in the artistic legacies produced in the context of the slave trade. Some have even become politicized about racial inequality in their host country more generally as a result of their involvement with Black expressive forms (Griffith 2016). However, the Black Brazilian body is also an object of consumption for white Western practitioners (Robitaille 2014). Black Brazilian instructors embody a differently racialized self through the physical movements of capoeira and the racially marked semantic value that accompanies those movements (Robitaille 2014). The fact that the capoeira pilgrimages to West Africa are primarily attended by white, European foreigners demonstrates a step further in this phenomenon. The desire of white practitioners to trace the return speaks to a much larger investment in inhabiting not only the physicality (Robitaille 2014) but also the affective and spiritual positionality of Afro-descendants and African diasporic relationships.

Lauren Griffith's work on American capoeiristas who travel to Brazil "in search of legitimacy" through intensive training sessions brings to light a phenomenon she calls "apprenticeship pilgrimages." Griffith delves into the parameters of authenticity on all sides of the equation, not only looking at the validation that foreigners (mostly Westerners) seek on pilgrimages but also examining the debates regarding who has the right to represent Brazilian capoeira abroad. Scholars have documented parallel phenomena with Western tourist pilgrims seeking healing and spiritual well-being through yoga or Buddhism in India and elsewhere (Baumann 2001; Hoyez 2007; Maddox 2015). In these instances, those who undertake the journeys often attribute specific meaning to geographical places that require forms of pilgrimage for internal and social transformation (Hoyez 2007). As Griffith (2016, 50) remarks about Americans attending capoeira workshops in Salvador, Bahia: "Travel . . . is an important way for *capoeiristas* to augment their cultural capital."

The same idea can be applied to the French capoeiristas who travel to West Africa ostensibly as capoeira pilgrims. Upon setting foot on the African continent for the first time, they enter the social landscape as experts from afar. Some of them have already made multiple apprenticeship pilgrimages to Brazil. Now, on their return-to-the-source trip to Africa, they arrive not simply as knowledge-seeking pilgrims but as already baptized, advanced students. Trips to Africa represent the next stage after pilgrimage, where they engage as experts by way of their proximity to diasporic legitimacy. They assert superior knowledge concerning Brazilian national culture and thus exercise a kind of appropriation of diasporic expertise and of the explanatory power of diasporic chauvinism.

Capoeira tourism in West Africa has become the next stage in the global intimacy of the coloniality of Black performance. Lisa Lowe (2015) argues that a "colonial division of intimacy" forced four continents into a system of labor and social relations that are intimately (and violently) intertwined under liberal colonial logics that attempt to erase the history of those entanglements. Twenty-first-century frameworks of diaspora similarly compose and produce their own regime of intimacies that might look different from colonial arrangements at first glance but ultimately reproduce hierarchical logics of race and gender. Practitioners from Brazil, Europe, and West Africa circulate to discover, collaborate, and build cultural institutions. The intimacy of cross-cultural exchanges occurs in the name of bodily practices that celebrate Black cultural production across the Atlantic. Figures, sites, and creative outputs of enslaved people unite the diversity of these martial artists. It is precisely through practitioners' dedication and curiosity that the coloniality of Black performance emerges, when global capoeiristas with greater access to diasporic expertise end up marginalizing African participation. Euro-American capoeiristas engage in cultural tourism and apprenticeship pilgrimage to Brazil (Griffith 2016) after being exposed to Brazilian migrants selling their cultural labor in Europe. Many travel to Bahia, the "Mecca" of capoeira tourism, which is a space that Christen Smith (2016a) calls "Afro-paradise"—imagined geographies where Blackness is violently managed by the state in part to offer up the spectacle of Black cultural production for the consumption of international tourists. This spectacle of Black violence and Black culture is in service to a white settler colonial society profiting from tourist dollars and the global fascination with the Black exotic and the Black erotic, as well as Brazil's reputation as a fantasy playground (Williams 2013).

In this era characterized by a new wave of temporary diasporic returns, Brazilian repatriates to Africa are also deeply implicated in Europe's ongoing coloniality with West Africa (Ndlovu-Gatsheni 2013; Quijano 2007). We therefore cannot understand diaspora without looking at multilayered circulations: migration, tourism, pilgrimage, return. I argue that diaspora in its current framework has obscured the ongoing coloniality of cultural production and political economy. Furthermore, I propose a new way of looking through the lens of diaspora to see how everyday collaborations among West African urban networks offer emergent models of cultural institutions that celebrate Black cultural production.

For Turner (1988), the process of pilgrimage strips away prior social categories, and pilgrims are unified in *communitas*, however momentarily. Some scholars of capoeira have described the art itself as an inclusive and unifying practice that suspends social divisions to a point (Lewis 1992; Wesolowski 2020), while others demonstrate how race, gender, and other axes of identity are integral to how capoeira communities are formed (Griffith 2016; Humphrey 2020; Robitaille 2014). I argue that in diasporic pilgrimage with Africa as the sacred destination, global racial hierarchies are heightened. Through capoeira pilgrimages to Africa, racial divisions and their consequences are more clearly revealed, and through the failure of the "cultural exchange" and global connection anticipated by all, other connections grow stronger—in this case, with respect to West African regionalism. West African regionalisms are not new social frameworks, by any means (Barry 1997). However, in the context of secular pilgrimage in the twenty-first century, young people can forge regional ties in a new way through diasporic aspiration.

Scholars have examined how culture becomes a commodified object in the context of these kinds of trips, even if commerce does not encompass all of their motivations and ways in which individuals can be affected by the experience (Ebron 1999; Holsey 2008). I want to acknowledge the commodification of heritage, of diasporic return, and how neoliberalism has opened up these experiences to anyone, even the descendants of former colonial rulers and slave traders. The scholarship should move past the assumptions about commodification that produce a dichotomy of tropes: diasporic consumers of return experiences, on the one hand, and opportunistic African hosts who seek to profit from them, on the other. The literature on roots tours points to a desensitization to these sites on the part of Africans who live in proximity to them, an indifference accompanied by economic opportunism. Studies of African opportunists and diasporic pilgrims show how the commodification of culture, heritage, and history is always in play for both parties. However, moving past this dichotomy reveals how host pilgrims offer new understandings of the contemporary dynamics of return, heritage, and diaspora.

Pilgrimage and Place Making in the Gambia

The organizers from the Capoeira Association of the Gambia and their French partner intended the cultural crossroads event to be a collaborative narrativization of the return of capoeira to the African continent, and through it a geographical construction of the slave trade that centered the Gambia. With its relative political stability and vast beachfront, the area in and around Banjul has become a tourist hotspot.[2] The resorts, restaurants, and other industries catering to tourists drive significant revenue to the country, alongside peanut exports and remittances from the Gambian diaspora abroad. One of the central activities of the event included a visit to Kunta Kinteh Island.

The history of the Capoeira Association of the Gambia is somewhat unusual, but it reflects a trend common to other groups in the region: multidirectional diasporic influence. As the association's founder, Adama Badji, explained to me, a Black American friend of his from Pennsylvania who provided a great deal of support for the association was teaching him boxing on the beach in 2005 when Mestre Valú, an Afro-Brazilian capoeirista on vacation, spotted them. Valú was on a mission to "bring capoeira to Africa." According to Adama, when Valú saw the men boxing on the beach, "the spirits told him that I was the person he should give capoeira to in Africa." From that day forward, Adama has taken capoeira on as his only profession. He made it his mission to learn as much as he could during his limited two weeks with Valú and then to spread the art form across the Gambia. Adama taught as many children as he could, recruited adults, and established the association.

The Capoeira Association of the Gambia promoted the event on its Facebook page as an international gathering of capoeiristas to participate in a "cultural crossroads" and an "international cultural exchange," to coincide with the International Day for the Abolition of Slavery. The participants were a group of French capoeiristas, many of whom had never been to Africa before. Afreecapoeira from Senegal was also invited, as were a few members of another group, Ginga Nagô, from Guinea-Conakry. Those from the capoeira school in Dakar were referred to as "the Senegalese"; those from Europe as "the French"; and the two leaders of that French school as "the Brazilians." The event demonstrated dynamics that illuminate the relationships among various actors in the market of symbolic and material exchange of Black cultural expression in urban West Africa. With West African, South American, and European capoeiristas coming together for cultural exchange and to memorialize the history of slavery in the Gambia, the expectations were high for diasporic "return." In practice, however, several agendas came into conflict over issues of geographical symbolism.

The Gambia was not necessarily a predetermined place to discursively construct the origins of capoeira; nor was it the most representative site of the transatlantic slave trade. Yet it is through this event (and others like it) that the symbolic locations of the slave trade and the origins of capoeira are being constructed. Historical relics such as the dungeon on Kunta Kinteh Island provided material justification/evidence for the locating of slavery in this specific place, along with the spaces of everyday life in urban Banjul and the fishing village of Tanji (all destinations of the event). These places were transformed into sites foregrounding the history of slavery, marked by the performance of a capoeira *roda* by international and regional guests. This temporary troupe performed in a village square in Tanji, played instruments while promenading through outdoor markets, and entertained beachgoers with acrobatics while training along the sandy shoreline. Throughout the week, they presented capoeira *rodas*, workshops, and impromptu musical performances across Banjul, Tanji, and Kunta Kinteh Island.

West African Host Pilgrims: Refusal, Silence, and Expectation

> To create a *de-colonialized* archive, Africans need to first excavate historical silence and the forms of violence that it entails.
> —FRIEDA EKOTTO, "A Reflection on Gender and Sexuality as Transnational Archive of African Modernity"

The French capoeira instructor, Josselin, planned the day trip to Kunta Kinteh Island, one of the featured activities (figure 5.2). In the fifteenth century, European imperial powers settled the site, naming it James Island. The British used the island as a slave-trade port from 1588 to 1807, during which time captured Africans were incarcerated for several weeks, then sent to Gorée Island in Senegal before they were shipped to the Americas. In 2003, the island became a United Nations Educational, Scientific, and Cultural Organization (UNESCO) World Heritage site, and in 2011 visual artist Chaz Guest successfully petitioned President Yahya Jammeh to rename it Kunta Kinteh Island. Scholars have written about the sociopolitical dynamics of African American pilgrimage to the Senegambian slave trade

5.2 Capoeiristas aboard a pirogue singing and playing music on the Gambia River headed toward Kunta Kinteh Island. Photograph by the author.

sites of Kunta Kinteh Island and Gorée Island, exploring the symbolic power Africa holds for diasporic Blacks and the reparative work of the return journey (Bellagamba 2009; Clarke 2004; Davis 1997; Ebron 1999; Hartman 2006; Holsey 2008; Pierre 2012; Tillet 2009). In many of the re- tellings of these journeys, local Africans are described as either opportu- nistic and apathetic with respect to the sites' history or resigned to silence due to the shame of being associated with the slave trade—through either enslaved relatives or relatives who owned and profited from the enslaved.[3]

Positioned at the crossroads of pilgrim and host, Siaka, an instructor with the Capoeira Association of the Gambia, spent much of the day mak- ing the journey smooth for the visitors, negotiating prices for boat tickets and settling minor disputes. When Cebola, the Brazilian *mestre*, flew into a rage over the cost of being carried on a Gambian man's shoulders from the castle shore to the boat back to the mainland, Siaka acted as mediator, tamping down the conflict as a police officer was brought in to settle the dispute. Musa, the boat guide responsible for our transportation by canoe to and from the island, laid out the affective guidelines for our encounter with this site of the slave trade: We should not feel happy in this place, even though it is beautiful, but we should also not cry, which is why we would hear Mandinka freedom songs. Black and white are coming together now, he explained. We are to forgive but never forget on this solemn journey of reflection and remembrance.

Siaka was a skilled capoeirista who expressed excitement at the opportunity to expand his knowledge by participating in the event. However, during this day trip his role as one of the main Gambian hosts, rather than as a pilgrim, created the presumption that his participation in the state-run tour of the slave trade fort was routine. Instead, the darkness of the place, coinciding with his discomfort around whiteness (both everyday whiteness built into the infrastructure of his daily life and the heightened whiteness of the interactions with these foreigners), kept him bound to the boat. Siaka reached his limit as a capoeirista host at the slave dungeon nestled in the Gambia River, off the coast of the capital, that flows into the Atlantic Ocean. Instead of participating in the tour, he remained on the periphery while the others circulated with Lamin, their state-sponsored guide.

While Siaka stayed behind, one of the French capoeiristas, Jean-Paul, responded to a request from Lamin for a volunteer to reenact being chained standing up inside the tiny prison cave that once held as many as fifteen people. Lamin explained that those who survived after two weeks were shipped to Gorée Island, then loaded onto ships headed for the Americas. While they waited, the captured men and women were made to defecate in the cave while food was flung at them through a small window. Assuming his role in this reenactment, Jean-Paul responded with a joke, laughing and saying to the group: "Bye. We're not coming back!" The Brazilian capoeiristas, having opted out of the official tour, meandered around the island on their own. We discovered them at the end of our route, taking selfies with broad smiles and flashing the surfer "hang loose" hand symbol. Several of the French capoeiristas disobeyed Lamin's instructions and the historic landmark's guidelines as a place of mourning, which strictly prohibited swimming. They snuck behind nearby shrubs, disrobed, and reemerged on the dock in bathing suits before diving and cannonballing gleefully into the Gambia River's depths. None of the African participants swam. The waves the French created by their splashing disturbed the fishing boat still holding Siaka and the boat guide, Musa, causing it to rock and bob.

Later in the evening, Siaka ambivalently gave me his account of the day. The crickets were bellowing and BBC radio was blaring on the recording I made at the house where we were staying, almost drowning out the soft-spoken Siaka. Several times throughout the day I had asked him to share his experience with me. Each time, he began to speak, but then declined to elaborate:

SIAKA: Do you remember where we stopped last time?

CELINA: Well, I had an idea of what I think you were going to say . . . , but I don't want to put ideas in your head, you know?

SIAKA: OK. Can you tell me?

CELINA: What I think?

SIAKA: Yeah.

CELINA: There's something I think has been weird here. I don't know if it's the same thing you feel, but, like, there's a weird separation. [*Nervous laugh.*] And, um . . . I find it troubling, a little bit.

SIAKA: OK. It's, like, if . . . I know that most of the people also . . . see that, too. You know. This is something I am . . . They are like that. You understand what I mean.

CELINA: French people?

SIAKA: Yeah. They are like that.

CELINA: They're like what?

SIAKA: They're like this.

CELINA: What is "this"? I mean, what do you mean?

SIAKA: Can we proceed and then we stop and we talk about this later? What do you want to ask me?

Siaka would share weeks later that he had assumed I understood his thoughts about whiteness and was uncomfortable with an open, and now recorded, discussion centering his thought process with respect to the trip to Kunta Kinteh Island. I then awkwardly stumbled into a question about how he saw the future of capoeira in the Gambia. In response, he described the usefulness of the event in furthering his group's mission. "You go in the Gambia," he said, "there will be capoeira." After a bit more conversation about the event—and frequent commentary on my state of physical distress because, as he put it, "mosquitoes are always after you"—he abruptly returned to the original topic: "So you asked me something about the beach today and James Island yesterday." When Siaka chose to describe thoughts he had previously withheld, his insights came tumbling out in a clearly defined narrative:

> Today at James Island, it is my second time. . . . I didn't want to [leave] the boat. I don't want to hear the story . . . of what happened some years ago, hundreds of years ago. I don't want to hear it. I once [was] there with some friends, and when I heard the story, my day get ruined, you know? With my friends, you know? We weren't able to have any good conversation and stuff like that, so . . . that's why I don't like [to go]. . . . But at the end they told me we'll being going straight to Banjul without stopping, so that's why I got on the boat. If not, that's why I'm not joining the boat to the island, you know? . . . I didn't listen to the history. I stayed here on the bridge with the fisherman [Musa, the boat guide]. I was helping him to do some catches. I have experiences of fishing since I was ten. My brother was a fisherman [and] I'm named after a very famous fisherman. He's the most famous fisherman in my district. He still lives there but now, [he's] old! [*Laughs*.]

When the capoeira group concluded its tour with a grand performance at the end of the week, some of the same European men who had been making jokes about being trapped in a slave dungeon and then swam on the swimming-prohibited historical island performed in the *puxada de rede* (fisherman performance) scene. The centrality of diasporic return in pilgrimage obscures the complicated structures of feeling for the Africans playing host pilgrims. Each person in the brightly decorated West African canoes (pirogues) that day had a different embodied relationship to the space of the island. Siaka's position as a Black Gambian capoeirista, in light of his own pilgrimage to a slave-trade site through the exchange of knowledge and capoeira interactions with these expert visitors, would not allow him to set foot on the shore. Lisa Stevenson (2014, 2) has thought through affective states of hesitation and uncertainty, urging ethnographers to dwell on the unknown and listen to "the thing unsaid" that "disrupts the security of what is known for sure." Similarly, Saidiya Hartman (2008, 2–3) offers a methodology of recognizing the gaps and silences that are integral to the study of the enslaved and the racialized, which she describes as "achieving an impossible goal" by "listening for the unsaid, translating misconstrued words, and refashioning disfigured lives." Siaka demonstrated a level of trust in me, a fellow capoeira pilgrim of the African diaspora, to understand the meaning buried in his silence. He also demonstrated the weight of the thing unsaid, an unwillingness to put into words the impact of this history on him and to put his body in the space of the island. Perhaps the weight of the thing unsaid could be expressed only through the act of not expressing it, for words would serve only to trivialize it.

Siaka refused the experience of historical traumatization as he was steeped in a capoeira *encontro* with Afro-Brazilian, European, and other West African peers for an event commemorating the abolition of the transatlantic slave trade. He did so not with grandiose statements but with silence. Silence can be a practice of creating space for harm or oppression as passive resistance to the state of normativity. It produces an archive of unconfronted marginality in African contexts (Ekotto 2020). Siaka did not utter what he was refusing when he chose to stay on the boat and not step foot on the slave fort, and he refused to name the social dynamics unfolding in the capoeira event. Audra Simpson's (2014) "ethnography of refusal" comes as she confronts the disjuncture between being an ethnographer and Native American: She takes on the refusal of her interlocutors to offer themselves and their knowledge up for anthropological capture that historically has extracted so much from them. Digging through the lives of African (global and continental) subjects to find the remarkable nature of their politics, their social relationships, and their imaginaries would be to reproduce the characterization of African lifeways as outside of so-called modernity. So how do we escape reproducing coloniality while also calling out racial harms occurring in capoeira events that rely on racial hierarchies but often go unnamed?

After "failure," we find the most productive iterations of what diaspora and diasporic return were meant to achieve. For many West Africans, although travel is significant, cultivating relationships and interactions with people rather than places is what gives them meaning. Even with familiarity, places can invoke pain—apparent in Siaka's refusal to set foot on Kunta Kinteh Island. No one but Musa, the Gambian boat guide and fellow fisherman, was attending to him during his subtle but significant reaction. Siaka acted as expected in his position as local host, but when he refused to leave the boat, almost no one recognized the reason for his reluctance to continue his duties. Few noticed that Siaka—already unsettled and silenced by his interactions with the French capoeiristas—refused to step onto the former slave dungeon island. Unlike the international pilgrims, he did not go to the island to provoke feelings of pain and sadness in himself or to satisfy curiosity. He already carried with him what motivates his daily practice and devotion to capoeira.

Contrary to the common trope of African opportunism in roots tourism pilgrimage, the Gambian capoeiristas were the most economically disadvantaged martial artists, yet they sacrificed the most to carry out the event for their regional and international guests. Josselin urged me to take particular notice of their position: "You should write that Gambians are the poorest capoeiristas in Africa. These guys have nothing. Absolutely nothing. They sleep on the ground. In the village they all call them crazy. . . . But they are so brave, they come and train so hard, and they just want to play." While Josselin described Gambian capoeiristas in terms of a deficit framework, Anna, a Gambian capoeirista, maintained that while "having nothing" is a reality, it is rooted in a colonial legacy that exposes many African nation-states to exploitation. She framed frustrations with the white takeover of their capoeira group as indicative of a larger issue of economic inequality in her country: Foreigners appropriate most of the capital, while "Gambians own nothing." Again, in the deficit framework, Josselin's admiration of the fortitude of the Gambians he works with further situates them in a radical alterity. Their love of capoeira is so extreme as to be marveled at, because the dire nature of their economic circumstances would usually be a deterrent. This reading is a misrecognition of how many Gambian practitioners frame their practice as a form of liberation, a historical obligation as Black Africans. For example, Siaka framed capoeira as a duty of reclamation:

> [French people] know that capoeira is something very good, something you can use to fight and something you can use to express yourself. So they don't want it to be only a sport of Black [people]. . . . In general, the white don't want the Blacks doing it then. Yeah, so, and now me—what I wanna. . . . A friend of mine is a master online, too, and he told me [that] now at the moment, there are more whites capoeiristas than Blacks . . . , which means that we have to develop. Really, it's ours.

For many West African practitioners, they are enacting what should be the ordinary state of affairs for free Black people to learn and pass on their cultural heritage.

A Gambian capoeirista's refusal to step off a fishing boat onto the shore of a former slave port is not the focus of studies on diasporic pilgrimage. The complexity of Africans' relationship to the history of slavery, and to a late capitalist present, situates them at a radical economic disadvantage in relation to African American pilgrims (Holsey 2008). Scholarship in this field has begun to develop more complex models to problematize notions of return for Black people in the diaspora who are seeking a resolution to a lost history, as well as a temporary escape from racism at home (Williams 2018). There remains, still, a perspective on West Africans' positionality that is overlooked: Africans as pilgrims. Their pilgrimage is not defined by the distance of their journey or by the loss of an African homeland. They are pilgrims because of their desire for diasporic connections thwarted by the uneven development and social misrecognitions bred by late capitalism. Their pilgrimage lies in the pursuit of a Black future through a Black past, broadly and creatively defined.

Their pilgrimage to the spaces of capoeira conviviality during these kinds of cultural exchange events also reveals the limitations of what pilgrimage means for them, like the painful inability to set foot ashore a slave dungeon in one's own country or the silent resentment at seeing privileged white foreigners laugh and play in that space. West African capoeiristas have not been historically displaced from the continent the way enslaved people were at the height of the transatlantic slave trade, but they view Afro-diasporic people as formerly enslaved kin or counterparts. The lived experiences of West African capoeiristas shaped how they approach capoeira as practice and space of joy and community. They live with economic and social plunder in the wake of colonization and slavery every day in the form of neoliberal reforms (Chalfin 2010) that dispossess local economies to privilege international exploitation.

Diasporic Chauvinism: Interrogating Expertise

Many of the West African capoeiristas felt that the weeklong encounter was shrouded in tension and discomfort from start to finish. Ostensibly, the Gambian and European organizers structured the gathering. To that end, all of the visitors stayed at Josselin's home for the week, although lack of space forced a few of the men from various countries to sleep under tents in the yard. The few women in attendance shared a private bedroom, while most of the men slept on mats in the living room. As the days went by, divisions appeared that reflected a descending hierarchy with the Brazilian guests and their European students at the top; visiting Senegalese and Guinea-Conakry contingents in the middle; and, finally, the Gambian capoeiristas who hosted the event at the bottom. It is not easy to untangle the politics of Black expressive cultural knowledge—its production, reproduction, embodiment, and identified experts, disciples, and novices. At times,

African participants criticized themselves and their own knowledge of the practice. As one Gambian noted: "Some of our people, they know nothing about the rules. Sometimes when I break the rules I feel really embarrassed." He felt shame, despite being part of one the newest capoeira groups in the region and thus understandably less knowledgeable. The discourse and perceived hierarchies around expertise are raced, classed, gendered, shaped by uneven accessibility, and mediated by capitalist commodification (Ebron 1999; Griffith 2016; Hartman 2006; Holsey 2008; Pierre 2012). In the case of capoeira roots tours, high-ranking Brazilian practitioners are the experts, with good reason. They are often directly embedded in the lineages of capoeira from the Brazilian source. In the context of pilgrimage and cross-cultural exchange, diasporic chauvinism traffics in, and is disguised by, the discourse surrounding merit, expertise, and hierarchy.

Cebola, the Brazilian *mestre*, viewed the economic precarity of the Gambian capoeiristas, and what he observed of Banjul more generally, as a point of solidarity with his own working-class upbringing in Minas Gerais. In the evenings, he shared stories of race and class discrimination that he experienced in Brazil, admitting that since he had moved to France about a decade earlier, these dynamics have remained much the same back in Brazil. Describing Josselin's residence, he noted: "You see this big house we're staying in, and then you see how poor the rest of the people are living in the city." While Cebola's thoughts did not appear insincere, there was a troubling gap between his statements and his interactions with the Gambians and Gambian history. What is novel here is not the circulation of stereotypes or generalizations about Africans held by whites and foreigners. Instead, it is that those who have dedicated their lives to a form of cultural expression that valorizes African roots fail to recognize the agency, contribution, and partnership of contemporary Africans. There is what Africa represents for diasporic Blacks, and then there is the reality of an uncomfortable gap in their narrative of diasporic belonging.

This exclusion became explicit as the Gambian event went on, often taking the form of a reluctance to communicate in a language Gambians could understand. When the Brazilians taught workshops, they spoke in primarily French or Portuguese, which many of the French practitioners could understand after years of training and traveling to Brazil. Only a fraction of the time did anyone translate into English, the shared language of local hosts and several of the Senegalese guests. The Brazilians did not spend much time interacting with the West Africans, despite the fact that the event was billed as a workshop for the Gambian hosts to learn from more experienced instructors. In many instances during the workshops, the Brazilian brothers Cebola and Maré expressed frustration with the Gambians for not properly executing movements. The Brazilian experts ran workshops, directed *rodas* (in which they disciplined West Africans' behavior), and choreographed the final performance. The activities, movement sequences, and cultural dances were already familiar to the French students, so they performed with greater ease and confidence while the West African hosts and guests were treated with either indifference or a sense of annoyance for their lack of knowledge.

While diasporic chauvinism sometimes manifests in the explicit exclusion of African participation, re-Africanization, or innovation (described in chapter 2 in relation to the twentieth annual celebration of Afreecapoeira), here it was displayed as a form of privilege by diasporic experts. The Brazilian instructors and their groups discussed their visit as a journey of return, the discovery of African origins, and a cultural crossroads or exchange. Yet they rolled out what seemed to be a prepackaged set of activities, directed entirely by their group, without consideration of the new context or attention to the desires, input, or leadership of the West African groups present.

As the literature has extensively shown, the process of return is a complex one for diasporic pilgrims. Like the African Americans on roots tours, Brazilian capoeira practitioners of African descent are similarly navigating their position as pilgrims, yet in their case, they have privilege in relation to West Africans because of their proximity to white support and the financial opportunities of living in Europe. For diasporic Blacks, this is a journey of rediscovering the self through *place*. In doing so, they construct the very place they seek by projecting their African imaginary onto it.

The Disguising Act of Expertise: White Appropriation by Proxy and Proximity of Diasporic Chauvinism

Embodiment and historical representation were frequently at odds in this "cultural exchange." European participants often invisibilized the link among race, embodiment, and history (particularly when it came to whiteness). Although West Africans have had access to information about capoeira only since the advent of the internet and the global circulation of the Hollywood film *Only the Strong*, released in 1993, white Europeans often accuse Africans of not being "aware of their own history" regarding the martial art form (see chapters 1 and 3). As a Dutch capoeirista shared with me on our way to Kunta Kinteh Island: "It's a brave history for the African people that a lot of them don't know anything about. But they need to know. We can't just stop the conversation at all the tragedies of slavery. There were incredible and inspiring things that came out of it, too, and people need to know about them." His project with Adama, the Door of Return, aimed to bring seven Brazilian capoeira *mestres* to the Gambia to play capoeira and be given "African names." The good intentions and personal investment of the Dutch capoeirista speaks to the level of intimacy many capoeiristas around the world feel for the historical foundations and contemporary implications of their practice. It also highlights the role through which many white capoeiristas feel entitled, as practitioners and expert initiates, to assert their place as mediators of diasporic relationships. As such, they become the unlikely brokers for Africans in search of new possibilities for repair and return.

Instances of diasporic chauvinism appropriated by white European capoeira practitioners take on an entirely different valence because of their historical and present-day white privilege. White expertise over Black cultural forms in the context of the Gambia was most visible in the collaborations for the final performance during the International Day of the Abolition of Slavery, revealing that with the international visitors in charge, historically representational embodiment would be explicitly addressed in certain ways—and invisibilized in others.

The French group visiting the Gambia designed the show to pay homage to the history of capoeira spreading from Africa to Brazil, with the development of the *capoeira angola* genre being a key moment. Two white Europeans were initially selected to play the game of capoeira. Their role was to embody the legacy of the Black Brazilian artistic pioneer Vicente Ferreira Pastinha (Mestre Pastinha). What is important to note here is that the Brazilian instructors who were in charge of the artistic direction of the show centered their French students, leaving the African participants to the mercy of a foreigner's vision. The automatic authority of Brazilians and the privileged position of skilled European capoeiristas made both parties experts on the narrative of capoeira—of its historical significance and, therefore, which elements to emphasize in the storytelling. Souvenir, the main instructor for the Senegalese group, spent years studying the movements, music, and historical context of capoeira. He has maintained relationships with a wide range of contemporary groups and *mestres* around the world. Yet the perspective of capoeiristas such as Souvenir held little weight in this environment, in which Brazilian and European practitioners were experts by default and African practitioners were perpetually perceived as novices.

Souvenir brought me in to play pandeiro (tambourine) for a portion of the show that aimed to depict the beginnings of *capoeira angola*, a style that developed from a racially defined cultural movement led by Mestre Pastinha. In the 1940s, Mestre Pastinha sought to re-Africanize capoeira in Brazil amid critiques that it had been "whitened" since Mestre Bimba had standardized elements of the practice for national public acceptance and broader participation. When Sereia, a French woman of Arab descent who was a key organizer during rehearsals and events, saw me, a Black woman, with the other musicians, she grew angry. The depiction must be historically accurate, she explained, and no women were participating in *capoeira angola* at its inception the 1940s. Souvenir reacted quickly, whispering to me, "There were definitely no white people, either." The rest of the African practitioners were responsible for serving as the background orchestra. By Sereia's logic, the gendered bodies of the performers were a barrier to an "authentic" historical representation; gender diversity was categorically inappropriate for the reenactment, while there was no concern over the color-blind casting of white players to occupy the center in the representation of capoeira's historical "re-Africanization" in Brazil.

Creating spaces of leisure and play for tourists, in turn, renders those same spaces sites of segregation and symbolic or literal violence for locals who are marginalized. The hypervisibility of white foreigners in the African diaspora has been examined in the context of short-term visits such as tourism and longer-term engagements such as the Peace Corps and white expatriates (Pierre 2012; Roland 2011; Smith 2016a; E. Williams 2013). In the 2015 capoeira encounter, white practitioners displayed their Black cultural expertise for various audiences over the span of a week: performing for tourists on the beach and locals at the Alliance Française event; acting out stylized renditions of Brazilian fishermen and fisherwomen in *puxada de rede* dances; and representing *capoeira angola*, the embodiment of the mid-twentieth-century re-Africanization movement. While these styles are staples of any capoeira school around the world, in the context of "cultural exchange" and the "return to African origins," these specific performances revealed how race, gender, geography, and coloniality challenge the notion of an "inclusive diaspora."

This inclusivity stems from the commodification of capoeira and other Black cultural forms. Some scholars of capoeira have framed it as a "non-hegemonic" or inclusive space in which social divisions fall by the wayside when one enters a capoeira community, and anyone can advance in its ranks (Lewis 1992; Wesolowski 2020). This view reflects a merit-based framework and the assumption that expertise in a bodily practice is enough to claim ownership of its historical framing and embodiment representations. Like many "merit" systems, extant privilege gets reproduced. On the ground in capoeira pilgrimage we see the reproduction of white women's aspirational power and the continued absence of Black African womanhood. No African women were central to any part of the show beyond the opening scene depicting the African origins of capoeira, in which Anna from the Gambian group and two others performed the Mandinka *jambadon* dance linked to the ritual of circumcision. As mentioned earlier, Bigue, the only West African woman visitor to the Gambia, left the event early because she was uncomfortable with white European women being put in charge of so many of the performances, *rodas*, and workshops, as well as their behavior toward her that made her feel unwelcome. The centrality of white women specifically exposed Black women's absence and marginalization in these events.

To engage Sara Ahmed's (2006) provocation that race and racism shape—or, more precisely, *discipline*—how bodies are oriented in space, we must think about how race and gender work in the realm of embodied performance practices. Whiteness temporarily and performatively inhabits Black bodies, histories, and spaces through the practice of Black cultural forms. Ironically, racially defined culture is leveraged in a process that highlights the injustice of the past while simultaneously invisibilizing contemporary contexts of racial inequality and the uneven access produced by white privilege. This dynamic, in turn, justifies or allows white people to comfortably inhabit the role of "expert" in cultural traditions, histories, and legacies of Blackness. Their dedication to training and privilege of possessing the time and resources to engage in apprenticeship tourism afford them the chance to become highly skilled in technique and develop accompanying knowledge. Meanwhile, white practitioners assert narrative control over events of the African diaspora under their jurisdiction. Through their proximity to Brazilian instructors, they center themselves within Black Atlantic traditions and embodiments as privileged practitioners with cultural and historical narrative authority.

Many from the Dakar group leveled critiques at the French participation in the capoeira gathering. Most striking, the French group separated itself from the Africans during the cultural exchange and, coupled with its management of most of the capoeira activities, assumed an air of superiority. Solomon noted that the French capoeiristas ate apart from the larger group during communal meals, while others pointed to their behavior inside the capoeira *roda*. According to several West African participants, the exclusionary nature of the white Europeans' interaction with them was paralleled by their aggressive behavior and control of every *roda*. Solomon described to me his experience with the white French co-organizer, Josselin: "He normally shows some racism. I know this is a problem between our own internal association [in] the Gambia, but actually it's going beyond. I mean, he develops strategies that will bring barriers. There are specific places where the French are supposed to go for having lunch. There are places for Gambians; Gambian will be this area."

As Solomon shared his perspective, I sat with my discomfort that while the capoeiristas visiting from Senegal and France were given accommodations inside Josselin's house, the Gambian capoeiristas staying on-site slept in the courtyard. In the morning, an abundance of fresh baguettes and a breakfast spread was made available for the European guests, with plenty left over each day; the food was only offered to the Afreecapoeira for an added fee. One of the white European guests, seemingly also uncomfortable with the separation, chose to sleep in a tent outside with the Gambian capoeiristas. Solomon's comments speak to the relative frequency of foreign visitors and the fact that racism is not an exceptional occurrence but an ordinary element of the social infrastructure of the association and, possibly, of the Gambia more broadly. Despite his attempt to establish the issue as mundane, after expressing his thoughts he disclosed the personal hurt he felt as a result of racial isolation. Typically, those who host tourists have more awareness of the inherent divisions between visitors and hosts than tourists do of their hosts' contexts, particularly regarding racial differences between the groups (Roland 2011). Solomon described physical segregation between Gambians and French visitors as a pattern, as "barriers" created partly through a precedent Josselin set over the years with other events he had organized. Since Josselin's arrival in the Gambia, and due to his connections to resources and sponsors, he seems to have taken over the operations and the vision of an association originally founded by Gambians. Other Gambians from the group also described a long-standing hierarchy of resource distribution, food sharing, and lead instruments playing that privileged Europeans and that Africans felt was indicative of underlying racist attitudes.

Souvenir and other West Africans remarked that the capoeiristas visiting from Europe did not take seriously the premise of the event as a historic occasion of exchange and return. He asserted that they "really came for vacation" rather than the reciprocally pedagogical relationship he imagined would motivate one to participate in this kind of trip. This perception attributes questionable morality to the visitors, accusing the latter of being self-interested vacationers disguised as pilgrims of a cherished art form. Hiding behind a façade of cultural exchange and a discovery of imagined diasporic origins not only discredited the Europeans' stated intentions of being peers in pilgrimage. It also collapsed the aspirations of African host pilgrims to connect to diaspora through embodied, collaborative engagement. The Gambian, Guinean, and Senegalese participants said they gained valuable knowledge from the Brazilians' expertise, but many expressed overall disappointment with the event.

Renewed Regionalism Through Disappointment

There are many affective states that structure these kinds of encounters: moments of unbridled joy, wonder of discovery, fierce competitiveness, and creative excitement. Disappointment, one of the least anticipated outcomes, is perhaps the most telling: It speaks to the collision of anticipatory desire with the reality of misrecognition. This manifestation of expectation speaks to something prior: The unexpected yearning for diaspora from Africa that is not fully explained by African opportunism (i.e., migration, cosmopolitanism, or economic gain). This expectation of and from diaspora is not self-evident, just as racial self-identification is not self-evident in postcolonial West Africa because of the ways that Blackness is seen as existing elsewhere and as an apolitical default for Africans. Yet the commitment to capoeira, as previous chapters show, demonstrates a complex practice of racial self-making paired with blind spots about the racialization histories and processes autochthonous to the region. Examining disappointment reveals an anticipation of something a priori while also being produced at the same moment that it fails.

Hope, as an affective phenomenon, can be a modality through which entitlement, aspiration, and racialized subjectivity operate (Parla 2019). Disappointment here emerges as the outcome of a failed hope for diasporic connection in the Gambia. But the story continues, as disappointment carries the potential for unanticipated alternative arrangements to satisfy the original aspiration of building communal ties through embodied practice and a diasporic imaginary. Different from the unconscious way that race influences hope in that context, disappointment gives way to a continuation of regional intimacy that was *initially* motivated by a diasporic framework. This explicit commitment to the pursuit of Black ties through Black performance serves to keep the framework of diaspora compelling long after its concrete and legible manifestation has, in a sense, failed.

Nonverbal forms of expression, communication, being, and performing reveal not only the tensions but also the forms of connection that emerge from these kinds of events. Divisions along racial and national lines were apparent in where people sat on the bus during Gambian day trips; where they ate; and even how people interacted in the capoeira *roda*. Socio-spatial configurations and the orientation of bodies to surroundings revealed the problems of pilgrimage in practice rather than just the imagination of the differently positioned pilgrims. To explore the meanings embedded in West Africans' practice of pilgrimage, return, and belonging, cultural expertise is central to the embodied practice of return, place making, and network building. Expertise and knowledge production are contested terrain, rife with aspirations, disappointments, and erasure, while the quiet work of doing diaspora and unrecognized diaspora in practice are simultaneously in effect among the West African practitioners.

The spontaneous *roda* of West Africans arose after a weeklong cultural exchange that centered them symbolically but did not include them structurally. West African capoeiristas reopened a space after the formal events closed, re-centering their bonds with one another. What goes unrecognized are the creative innovations of those responding to the inherently disjointed nature of diaspora, a concept that, Stuart Hall (1990) and Brent Hayes Edwards (2003) argue, is also built from the articulation of difference rather than simply from sameness. By routing their aspirations and activities through diasporic narratives and art forms, they wound up building stronger regional ties among local capoeira institutions. Through the "failure" of equal inclusion in the formal activities, they were able to connect with their national neighbors in a subtle but significant turn of events. The Senegalese contingent sought friendly competition to improve their skills individually, improve the status of their group, and share knowledge with their Gambian neighbors to elevate the reputation of capoeira in the region. The Gambians sought mentorship and to create memories with the visiting West African capoeiristas and repeatedly lamented that there was little interaction either inside or outside the *roda* among the groups of varying nationalities.

This is especially intriguing, considering that many of the West African youth inclined toward capoeira are often seeking international, rather than regional African, Black connections, partly to escape the limitations of postcolonial African national projects, imagined to exist at the bottom of the global hierarchy. When the first cohort of Senegalese capoeiristas traveled to Brazil, some did not return. Years later, the same thing occurred in France. West Africans in general, and Senegalese since independence in particular, are often looking for a way "out," yet scholarship on Senegalese migration demonstrates that it can be a means of staying rooted back home (Babou 2021; Hannaford 2017).

For the many non-Senegalese practitioners who train in the Senegalese group—a majority, in fact (see chapter 3)—the relationships from these capoeira networks give them a sense of belonging in the face of social isolation they experience as migrants in Dakar. Their secular pilgrimage is not determined by the specificity of the place to which they travel. They journey for the pleasure of people, simultaneously opponents and friends who challenge and impress them and sing with them about the tribulations and oppressions of slavery. In preparation for the 2015 event, the diverse group of Dakar-based martial artists gathered in their main instructor's living room, waiting for a 3 a.m. van to take them to the Gambia. One member, Christopher, set the tone for their departure, delivering a motivational speech inspired by Al Pacino in the film *Scarface*, which he had been studying for weeks on YouTube to improve his English-language skills. Around 1 a.m., he stood before his drooping comrades and delivered a passionate monologue about the necessity to operate in the Gambia as a unified team, sticking together and supporting one another even in the face of enemies or opposition. Christopher's military metaphors added to the drama of a martial arts convention, encompassing both collaboration and competition. Most important, he concluded, the group should keep in mind their aim: to learn something new to bring back. With that, he opened up the floor to anyone expressing themselves in any language. The speeches unfolded one by one, untranslated. The capoeiristas spoke in Sango, English, and Wolof, even though French was the only language that was fully intelligible to all present.

The road to the Gambia is best taken at night, so the energy they poured into the seven-seat van from their initial launch faded into quiet chatting and snacking, then sleep, despite the bumpy Sine Saloum Delta road. As the sun rose on their approach to the first Senegal-Gambia border, they filled the van with music. Like the Maggal pilgrims, these martial artists journeyed south in song. A single pandeiro circulated among them from one musical number to the next as they shared the responsibility and privilege of carrying the rhythm. One of the more skilled members took over the pandeiro, slapping his palm against it in a 6/8 beat and began improvising in French: "We're taking a trip for capoeira, from Dakar to the Gambia." He passed the tambourine to his fellow Central African and close college friend, who launched into a capoeira musical classic but embedded the names of everyone in the van in the lyrics. This was the soundtrack to their pilgrimage to Banjul, one of the most exciting moments of the year. For some, this would be their first opportunity to meet and train with Brazilian capoeira *mestres*. For others, it would be the first time leaving the borders of their home country, Senegal. All told, it was a rare opportunity to display the fruits of their assiduous training—three, four, even seven days a week for some—and sharing that dedication with an international group of peers traveling from as far away as France and as nearby as neighboring Guinea-Conakry.

On the surface, this van of African pilgrims was no more than a group of university students making the most of a weeklong holiday trip with members of their extracurricular club. In the mundane, we find the extraordinary, a display of the being and doing of an unrecognized iteration of diaspora. This manifestation of the African diaspora's central paradox that it is the articulation of difference that makes diaspora shows the simultaneous presence of difference and unity, movement stemming from a diversity of experience and positionality (Edwards 2003). Constant singing in the interstices of an event is characteristic of capoeiristas everywhere. The group engages in classic capoeira exercises, such as taking turns singing or improvising from the classic repertoire of songs in Brazilian Portuguese. But in this van, the participants asked one another to sing and improvise in whatever language they chose. It is typical to improvise in capoeira music, and with the majority of schools outside of Brazil, the levels of comprehension of Portuguese vary widely. The understanding is that capoeiristas will eventually learn cues, phrases, and possibly full sentences through familiarizing themselves with the music.

In this case, there was a similar opacity of understanding; no one translated their words into French or another common language in these informal outbursts of song. As was the case during the ride to the Gambia, and in various other moments during my fieldwork, some encouraged improvisation involving commentary about the diversity of West African languages, regardless of the fact that the rest could not understand. For instance, one member sang in Sango, with only a few French words sprinkled in that indicated he was commenting on the trip to the Gambia. Only one other member, also from the Central African Republic, could understand. In this way, West Africans took the standard practice of singing in a language most do not understand (Portuguese) and inserted their own linguistic background. This does not just serve to "vernacularize" or "indigenize" a "foreign" art form but, instead, creates space for the diversity of West African linguistic expressions that represent the complex reality of capoeira in this region.

Through the disappointment of what they expected from the embodiment of the diaspora coming to visit and share, many West Africans found expertise among one another. Souvenir, from the Dakar group, echoed Solomon's concern about the social segregation of the international visitors during the event, saying: "They're not integrated at all." His disappointment was not simply for himself, an advanced teacher, but also for the loss of opportunity for his Gambian neighbors. He observed that Cebola showed his European apprentice a rhythm, then instructed the apprentice to pass the technique to the Gambian capoeiristas: "He should stay and make sure they learn it and understand it, engaging with them directly by himself." He further lamented that the Gambians who organized and hosted the event had a real need and rare opportunity to learn from the expertise of the Brazilian visitors, but that the activities, music drills, and movement sequences all catered to the French students. Souvenir felt the Brazilian experts were not teaching the basics, which were key for the stage at which Gambians found themselves as capoeiristas. Instead, they focused on more advanced movements, such as *sequêcias de Bimba* (traditional paired movement sequences for the genre *capoeira regional*), which Souvenir felt was not useful for the Gambians at this stage.

At the end of week, a few of the Gambian capoeiristas untied the Brazilian flag–colored ribbons used to decorate the performance space that Aissatou made and braided them into bracelets that they distributed primarily to the members of the African schools (figure 5.3). This gesture signified the regional unity that had emerged and blossomed alongside the exclusionary practices of the French and Brazilians. The spontaneous, mentoring *roda* reminded me how, throughout the week, members of the Senegalese group spent every day of the event teaching their Gambian peers various movements and musical techniques. For example, Kassoum from Dakar spent about an hour on the boat ride back from Kunta Kinteh Island teaching the less experienced Gambian capoeirista, Aissatou, how to play the berimbau. When Adama, the president of the Capoeira Association of the Gambia, noticed this, he praised Kassoum, saying, "I would be extremely happy if you succeeded in teaching her before you leave [back

5.3 The Gambian capoeirista Solomon, wearing his Che Guevara necklace, decorating the Alliance Française performance space with Brazilian flag–colored ribbons. Photograph by the author.

to Senegal]." Kassoum's attention to Aissatou's learning counteracted the effects of diasporic chauvinism.

As a follow-up to the 2015 event, the Gambian group was invited to Dakar on a kind of mentorship trip, to learn from and build stronger relationships with the Senegalese school. That event was a far more inclusive and interactive week of events. In a Facebook post about their visit to Dakar, featuring the T-shirts distributed only weeks prior in the event that took place in the Gambia, Jungle (an advanced student in the Capoeira Association of the Gambia) wrote, "Capoeira Association the Gambia, Afree Capoeira and Capoeira Sanke promoting peace love and unity. Thanks to Afree Capoeira for taking good care of us all." The photos featured in the post were of capoeiristas from across West Africa smiling in groups, posing in silly and playful ways at a supermarket, and laboring to carve berimbaus by hand or pull metal wires from old car tires for their *arames*. In another Facebook post, the Gambian capoeirista and skilled singer Cantador posted photos from the trip with the caption, "Hoping to see you soon Afree capoeira peace and love Senegal and Gambia." These visits continue to the present day, although they are not always formalized or well publicized. Months after the Gambian encounter, capoeiristas from

5.4 Moctar Ndiaye, founder of Afreecapoeira (*left*), and Adama Badji, founder of the Capoeira Association of the Gambia (*right*), playing berimbau at the Afreecapoeira training grounds during the Gambians' visit to Dakar. Photograph by the author.

that country set out for Senegal, some visiting for the first time. During the visit, the Senegalese group took them on a tour to Gorée Island and the House of Slaves, at the request of the Gambian visitors. Siaka, who had refused to be present on Kunta Kinteh Island, gingerly explored the slave chambers, lingering at the opening of the Door of No Return, guided and surrounded by the West African peers he had once hosted. They, too, held a public *roda* in a bustling marketplace, along with workshops and informal social gatherings. Unlike the international encounter in the Gambia, no documentary was published on Vimeo to commemorate the gathering. Instead, it was just one in a series of visits, events, and mutual exchanges predicated on mentorship, sharing knowledge, and the local institution building of capoeira in West African urban sites.

Unremarkable Stakes of African Pilgrimage

Capoeira pilgrimage events in West Africa are often framed as Brazilians bringing capoeira back to Africa. What exactly is returning? While African capoeiristas who help organize these events also participate in this narrative, it reinforces the notion that Africans are solely the embodiment of history and origins for the diaspora and, therefore, passive receptors "waiting" for the resolution of a diasporic return. The reality of the history of West African capoeira schools disrupts this hegemonic discourse. For the most part, the African founders of the region's first capoeira groups came to the art form on their own. They prioritized investing in their local communities and future generations of African capoeiristas before and long after any Brazilian or other foreign visitors arrived. They are also the ones who often initiate and consistently reach out to Brazilians and the global capoeira community for knowledge and to build up their networks and institutions.

The explicit and implicit concern with expertise created a hierarchy of the three main groups present at the event in the Gambia. Those who took center stage for the majority of the show during every section of the performance (music, dancing, and the three main commonly recognized varieties of capoeira today) were primarily the French capoeiristas. They had the most *proximity* (Ahmed 2006) to what is considered the true capoeira tradition—that is, training legitimized by Brazilian *mestres* and *contra mestres*. Occupying the middle slot in this hierarchy of expertise was the Afreecapoeira contingent from Senegal, one of the oldest capoeira groups in the region (since 1997), which boasts some of the most "developed" players in relation to the standard set by the French group. The newest group, with the most recent recruits, was considered the least experienced on the whole.

This hierarchy of experience and expertise, while seemingly objective and therefore innocuous, was determined by a set of standards that sidelined the rich, albeit recent, history of capoeira developed by West African practitioners over the past twenty-five years. More significant, this hierarchy of experience manifested in an ostensibly race-blind inversion of roles, in which skilled white practitioners centered themselves and their bodies as the primary carriers of this Black radical movement tradition. Meanwhile, teachers and students who so often explicitly invoke the figures of slavery and Africa in narrativizing capoeira and its history, somehow evacuated the art form's deeply racial implications and foreclosed any possibility that this history could inform present understandings of race or the ways in which they themselves are implicated in racial structures.

Moving through events premised on cross-cultural exchange, pilgrimage, and diasporic return, we see layers of misrecognition. The outcome reveals the pervasiveness of a dominant narrative of diaspora that informs community building in the contemporary period—or, rather, the limitations it contains. These events occur as a way to make place that speaks to the overlapping desires and agendas of the various participants. The presence of Brazilian and European visitors on pilgrimage to the origins of capoeira's cultural elements (as imagined by global practitioners) transforms the sites of mundane exploration (such as the outdoor markets of Banjul) and historical sites (Kunta Kinteh Island) into a particular kind of place: Africa. For the Gambian hosts, who are already home, this place is both mundane and historical.

West African practitioners are not performing Africa to make place for those international and regional guests. Their own capoeira practice, with or without visitors, demonstrates how Gambian capoeiristas are making the place of history, making the place of the Black Atlantic, and making the place of the slave trade as they *already* understand themselves to be situated in time and space. In this way, Africans are doing, being, and enacting the work of diaspora as they engage in regional pilgrimage and network building.

PROTECTING THE MAGICAL POSSIBILITIES OF BLACK MOVEMENT

Aziz, a Burkinabé member of Africa Capoeira–Ilha de Gorée (Afreecapoeira) who first discovered capoeira when he came to Dakar to pursue his doctorate in physics, with a focus on solar energy, shared his thoughts on the significance of West African capoeira, saying: "I find that it's our duty who know about capoeira to make it known to others. At the very least, we have this duty to popularize capoeira, make it so that people are conscious that it is there; it is a heritage that they have and that they have to appropriate. It's not normal that it was created by African slaves and that it is more widespread in Europe, for example, than here. I find that very contradictory."

The coloniality and promise of capoeira means the story is still unfolding in both respects. When I went back to Dakar in 2022 to see the changes since the twentieth anniversary event in 2018, I learned that Ashael had moved into an instructor role, and Elena had stepped into running the organization, along with several of her European capoeirista friends. Thinking of Arnaud's disappointment that Afreecapoeira was "all [African] foreigners," I couldn't help but sit with my own discomfort to learn that white foreigners were calling many of the organizational shots, causing fractures that even led some to leave the group. Several people shared with me an incident in which a white Spanish female capoeirista living temporarily in Dakar became a main instructor at Afreecapoeira. Perhaps unfamiliar with the religious norms of the city, she grew frustrated with students she thought were coming and going during training. She shouted at them, not realizing they were going to pray when the mosque down the street signaled the call to prayer. In this same moment, Apollo, who started his own group, Berimbau Sagrado, and now runs a capoeira school in France, shared that he and several other Muslim members back in Dakar were collaborating on fusing capoeira songs and Islamic prayers. The space of Afreecapoeira and its transnational reverberations continue to move through the delicate balancing act of remaining "free" of creative limitations and open to everyone while sorting out the never-ending question of what constitutes "Afreeca."

The model of regionalism shows the inspiration at home, influenced by and in dialogue with diaspora and not reinforcing nation-state lines. If diaspora in this case has served a purpose, it is to offer alternatives to thinking about heritage and geography and ways to think about and move the racialized and gendered body that open up new relationships with the past elsewhere, as well as the past in one's own family or one's ethnic or regional history. Simon Gikandi (2010, xvi) makes the case for a critical Afro-optimism, writing: "Social science has given us powerful and compelling studies of postcolonial failure, but it has not adequately recognized the poetics of survival that animates African being in hard times." As its central intellectual challenge, this book takes on complex layerings of here and elsewhere in postcolonial imaginaries of race and diaspora. It dwells on recognizing what history has tried to bury and on the misrecognizing that leads to unexpected solidarities and new connections. Diaspora without displacement does not mean without migration or movement. Rather, the framework serves to look at what other circulations emerge when we peel our focus away from the spotlight of diasporic return and look backstage, in the wings, or at those waiting outside who wanted to see the return play out but were never admitted inside. Positioned strictly as the embodiment of origins, the forms of displacement West Africans do undergo fly under the radar. Their displacement comes not in the form of contemporary migration out of the African continent or historical forced enslavement. Instead, West African capoeiristas are displaced from the center of what are intended to be moments of diasporic return, when people from Europe, the Americas, and across West Africa congregate in a symbolic and literal return to African origins. Pushed to the sides of the stage; overlooked for solos; and displaced as leaders, teachers, and creative authors, they play out the diaspora they sought in those spaces that fall outside of the gaze.

Race and diaspora are embodied practices, ideological frameworks, and political objectives in urban West Africa. Capoeira, an Afro-Brazilian martial art created during the slave trade, is emblematic of the African roots of Brazil's cultural traditions, yet West Africa's capoeira institutions can be understood as the form's "return" to the homeland. To many practitioners and scholars, capoeira in Africa represents a celebration of global Black survival and artistic expression in the twenty-first century. However, the recent history of West Africa's first capoeira schools, founded in the mid-1990s, represents more than the triumph of a repatriated diasporic practice. This is not the story of Brazilians bringing capoeira and liberation to West Africa; nor is it the story of a New World imaginary of Africa. It is the story of how West Africans have leveraged diasporic art forms, historical narratives, and political orientations to articulate themselves as Black, as kin to Black people across the diaspora. It is also the story of how they see West Africa as both a weathered site and a new frontier to ignite new engagements with history, slavery, colonialism, regionalism, and subjectivity. In the face of the "burden of modernity" that requires Africans to privilege "the foreign" over the indigenous, Afro-Brazilian cultural forms hold possibilities that can result in a return to what is local and African and, ultimately, to what Africans discover to be theirs to innovate (Bahi 2010). Diaspora does not always do the expected work of unifying the continent and diasporic communities as racial kin. It unexpectedly facilitates a new kind of postcolonial regionalism within grassroots artistic networks. While diaspora is the explicit premise, regionalism is an implicit mechanism and a barrier, as well as a goal for politically motivated Black artistic development.

Unremarkable Stakes: Decolonizing the Remarkable

> My commitment to Black life means I refuse to spectacularize Black abjection.
> —SAVANNAH SHANGE, *Progressive Dystopia*

The afternoon that Moctar sent a text message to his capoeira group saying that his mother had passed, several members rushed to catch the ferry to Gorée Island to pay their respects at Moctar's family compound. He was busy with memorial preparations when they arrived, moving around his courtyard barefoot in a bright blue boubou, making his way from guest to guest to shake hands, exchange greetings, and grieve. The martial artists decided to stay outside and wait for the right moment to speak to their *mestre*. After a brief period, he made his way to the narrow dirt road outside his home and, spotting the group, relaxed his tired countenance into a soft smile. The capoeiristas offered their condolences and said they would be on their way back to Dakar on the 4:30 p.m. ferry to give him space to mourn with his family. Surprised, he responded, "But what about the . . ." and raised his hands to strike an imaginary berimbau to the melody of a classic capoeira tune, "Tim Tim Tim la Vai Viola." A couple of us joined in singing while Moctar mouthed the melody. He then dropped his hands and said, "My mother appreciated these kinds of things. She would have liked for us to play music and be happy." We said a final goodbye, each of us shaking his hand or gripping fists. I asked him what his mother's first name was; he told me, Anna, reminding me of my grandmother Ann, who has also since passed. He shared that when he gives traditional capoeira nicknames (*apelidos*), he names many of the girls Anna, after his mother.

Anthropologists looking beyond the grim circumstances of our present have attuned their ethnographic sense to how people, often marginalized in various ways, have and always will imagine otherwise. I caution against coopting these inspiring potentialities into another mechanism that reproduces the "other" as otherwise from the norm or as exceptional. To look to the other for ways to imagine, do, think, and be otherwise dances a fine line of re-exoticizing "them." So how can we avoid repeating our past (and present) intellectual demons? Before initiating any search in this direction, we need to be grounded in the assumption that our interlocutors are unremarkable. It is only from this point of departure that we can productively— and, most important, ethically—conceive of how our interlocutors are imagining, thinking, acting, being, and doing together otherwise.

Turning to African diasporic subjects and the expressive forms that emerge from these communities to look for ways to imagine otherwise has been a productive starting place for moving beyond the inevitability of oppressive structural forces (Redmond 2014). A brief genealogy of African diaspora–oriented ethnographers highlights a decolonial tradition that can serve as a model for work rooted in the assumption of agency and humanity, as well as the unremarkability of their marginalized interlocutors (Allen and Jobson 2016; Hurston 2018). This lineage has shown how subjugated groups are situated within rather than outside modernity's structures, even when they are deemed to exist in a position of radical alterity (Thomas 2016). In my work, I see working- and middle-class West African martial artists as a force that is decolonizing the remarkable by engaging in leisure and play with boundless political possibilities.

During a routine administrative meeting after training at the École Franco-Sénégalaise in Dakar, Ibra (*apelido* Propheta), a Burkinabé who has spent much of his adult life in Dakar and a senior member of Afree-capoeira, decided to empty the contents of his worried mind by posing a question to the tired trainees: "My country is not well. What can capoeira do?" Ibra was referring to the recent coup that had ended the twenty-seven-year reign of President Blaise Compaoré through military intervention and democratic protest. The capacious imagination embedded in quotidian practices by African subjects all too often are overlooked when African experiences are read in relation to violence, economic precarity, ethnic or religious strife, and other overdetermined tropes of life on the African continent. Every other evening these young people show up to train for friendship, *ambiance*, and exercise. When political strife arises, many have seen the potential of their practice, something they frame as the quintessential tool of Black freedom. It continues to carry with it an inherent possibility for liberation in their own contexts, whether literal or otherwise.

When I spoke with Ibra later about his inquiry at the meeting, he laughed about my having taken the question literally rather than as the rhetorical provocation he meant it to be. Those who imagine otherwise, such as the anthropologist, are also playing with the reality of this potential, recognizing that the immateriality of the otherwise is a necessary component of its actualization, whether it is playful, metaphorical, or provocative. The method of physical and metaphysical liberation in which Brazilian capoeiristas engaged for centuries has become an activity of leisure for diverse groups in urban Senegal that, in one creative gesture, carries the potential for large-scale political implications. Participants draw from what was successful in fighting some of the most oppressive structures in human history—slavocracy and global white supremacy—and imaginatively apply it to their postcolonial challenges. They turn to a Black grassroots fighting form in which the trained body and mind are the only weapons necessary to achieve freedom. And they use it as a modality to imagine ordinary people such as themselves taking on this tradition to challenge political elites that disrupt the democratic process through the potential of a capoeira spirit.

In Dakar, young, urban West African professionals are in dialogue with Brazil—its cultural forms, networks, and state. Yet through expressive arts such as capoeira, postcolonial predicaments come to light, including the continuous process of constructing a nation entangled with multiple migratory trajectories and contested representation and grappling with its place in the global scheme. West Africans leverage capoeira as a mechanism to re-center West Africa as a Black space, drawing on diaspora (as earlier social and artistic movements in Dakar have) to frame Senegal as a crucial site in historical and contemporary global schemas that continually marginalize Black histories.

Coloniality is a phenomenon rooted in the colonial past. But, as Ayo Coly (2019) theorizes, it is also an extension of the present postcolonial discourses in dialogue with colonial discourses; diaspora thus can reproduce social hierarchy. The *coloniality of Black performance* is the idea that through the embodied expressive practices, Black performance can be troublingly blurred with Black performativity, which has consequences for the participation of Black, Black African, and non-Black practitioners. Despite the inescapable potential of coloniality, many see their artistic presence as reversing the monumental processes of history. Others, such as the Guinean instructor and comedic capoeirista Cheikh (*apelido* Memoria), playfully reimagine the possibilities beyond precarity in the present, like Ibra's provocation, which toyed with the idea of capoeira's "energy," "magic," and "atmosphere" as having the potential to contaminate political strife with a spirit of collaboration.

Those who allow me to write about them are cosmopolitan, transnationally oriented young people who have posed a conceptual problem—or, rather, nightmare—for much of the intellectual history of anthropological engagement in the region.[1] In the context of writing about these urbanites, their radical "otherwise" lies in the recognition of the unremarkable nature of their contributions before we can find what is remarkable about them. We have first to make room for narratives of Africans centered on the political promises of playfulness, joy, and friendship rooted in an everyday practice of pursuing Black heritage.

ACKNOWLEDGMENTS

As much as possible, anthropologists should speak to invisible systems to bring the workings of power to light. We should not speak for people, especially those who can, and do, speak for themselves. The people featured in this book are my peers in capoeira, and many are my friends. They have their own versions of their stories to tell and their own ideas about which stories they would or wouldn't choose to highlight. The shape and argumentative style are grounded in our shared experiences, but the result is ultimately my responsibility. I thank them first and foremost for allowing me to work with them to produce this book.

The theoretical work for this research began at the University of Pennsylvania. Deb Thomas, my loving mentor, saw me for what I would become and fiercely devoted herself to making sure I never gave up on my potential. On the note of love, Tim Rommen treated me like a whole person and trusted my ideas all the way through. John L. Jackson showed me that rigor and the levity of curiosity could coexist. Cheikh Babou opened my mind to a critical and anchored commitment to the work. Kamari Clarke also served as an encouraging mentor to me at the right moment. I also have my peers to thank from what we jokingly claimed as the "Penn School of Africana," along with my other home in Anthropology and other departments at Penn who muscled through ideas with me: Osei Alleyne, Diego Arispe-Bazán, Layla Ben-Ali, Lyndsey Beutin, Tiffany Cain, Jeremy Dell, Coleman Donaldson, Josslyn Luckett, Rasul Miller, Khwezi Mkhize, Zach Mondesire, Samiha Rahman, Keren Weitzberg, and Alden Young. Serigne Ndiaye guided me through my first trip to Dakar, and Courtney Keene presciently revealed to me that the city had a capoeira group. Thank you to folks I met through our mutual love of thinking expansively in and about Dakar: Youssef Carter, Wendell Marsh, Matthew Tinari. Bator was my first teacher of thinking critically and with care about Senegal: *Wala biggen boggen*! Kassoum Diakite Diop served as my de facto research assistant, with his sheer curiosity and support of my research aspirations.

I received support and productive feedback at Dartmouth College as a Provost's Fellowship Program Fellow (PROF), specifically as a Thurgood Marshall pre- and postdoctoral fellow in African and African American studies. My connections there have also supported the work and inspired me to be more imaginative: Robert Baum, Laura Edmondson, Trica Keaton, Chelsey Kivland, Summer Kim Lee, Laura McTighe, Emily Raymundo, Israel Reyes, Yana Stainova, and Michelle Warren. I had several Wolof instructors who gave me a precious gift. Thank you to Moutarou Diallo, Mbacke Thioune, and Cheikh Thomas Faye, and special thanks to Ibrahima (may he rest in power). Rebecca Bodenheimer took on the task of editing with grace and respect for the work. Elizabeth Ault understood early on what the book eventually became. I thank her, the two gracious anonymous reviewers, and the production team at Duke University Press for manifesting my vision.

I had the good fortune of finding mentors along my way. As a postdoctoral fellow in anthropology at the University of Pittsburgh, I found the support of colleagues such as Nicole Constable, Tomas Matza, and Gabby Yearwood, who mentored me while always treating me as an intellectual equal. Kaniqua Robinson was my writing partner when the world collapsed into the pandemic. Heath Cabot, Yolanda Covington-Ward, Ayşe Parla, and Jemima Pierre workshopped early versions of this manuscript, giving me invaluable feedback and, most important, encouraging me to be courageous in my writing.

At the University of Texas at Austin, I found brilliant and generous people who ushered me through the end of this work. I am so grateful to Kamran Ali, Khytie Brown, Iokepa Casumbal-Salazar, Maria Franklin, Oviya Govindan, Liz Ibarrola, Sofian Merabet, and Aaron Sandel, in particular. At the helm of the Center for Women's and Gender Studies, Christen Smith connected me to a community of incredible scholars. I am also deeply grateful to Shauna Carlisle, my coach in the Faculty Success Program of the National Council for Faculty Development and Diversity, and to our group, Katie Cruz, Ximena Sevilla, and Paris Whalon, for being my solid accountability crew.

I could not have crossed the finish line and survived the waves of self-doubt without my mental health guides. I am deeply grateful to Batsirai Bvunzawabaya, Ashleigh Gore, and Rose Zingrone for keeping me on a healing path so I could accomplish my goals.

The journey started in earnest after my dissertation defense, which my family celebrated with me by kicking off an unprecedented *pagode* music session in the Africana conference room at Penn. Jeff, Katie, and Simone have housed me, played music with me, and fed me through years of the writing grind. Gramma Ann has done everything from copyedits to deadline reminders, while believing so deeply in my abilities. You will always be with us. Tio Beto has always reminded me of the power of whose namesake I carry while being one of my biggest cheerleaders. Antar, Rasa, and Julian have been alongside me on this, hearing complaints, playing with ideas, and, most importantly, keeping our family legacy at the forefront of my motivations. My father, Ronaldo, has graciously allowed me the freedom to find my voice in relation to our heritage. No one has put in more emotional labor and professional guidance than my mother, Karen, who is unconditionally devoted to my success. Thank you both for falling in love with Senegal along with me and for always reminding me to just do my own thing.

GLOSSARY

The terms defined as Brazilian Portuguese may also have etymological links to West Central African languages such as Kimbundu or Indigenous Brazilian languages such as Tupí-Guaraní. Also, the names of capoeira movements vary slightly from one group to another; therefore the same word can signal different movements depending on the school.

AGOGÔ (Brazilian Portuguese): a two-tone bell used in capoeira music

AMBIANCE (French): positive or vibrant social atmosphere

APELIDO (Brazilian Portuguese): nicknames given in capoeira

ARAME (Brazilian Portuguese): the metal wire (often sourced from a car tire) used to string a berimbau

BATERIA (Brazilian Portuguese): the orchestra of instruments that drives a capoeira *roda*

BATIZADO (Brazilian Portuguese): literally "baptism," the ceremony where students earn a belt that advances them to the next level in the school's system

BENÇÃO (Brazilian Portuguese): literally (and likely sarcastically) "blessing," a standard kick that shoots directly forward, often aimed at the chest of one's opponent

BERIMBAU (Brazilian Portuguese): a central instrument in capoeira that resembles an arched bow

CABAÇA (Brazilian Portuguese): a gourd-based part of the berimbau that projects the sound

CAPOEIRA(S) (Brazilian Portuguese): the original term for practitioners of capoeira as they showed up in nineteenth-century archives

CAPOEIRA ANGOLA: a main genre of capoeira that emerged in the 1940s as a "re-Africanized" version (founder Mestre Pastinha)

CAPOEIRA CONTEMPORÂNEA: a modern genre of capoeira that does not strictly conform to the two traditional styles

CAPOEIRA REGIONAL: a main genre of capoeira that emerged in the 1930s and is considered one of the most traditional and standard forms (founder Mestre Bimba)

CAPOEIRISTA (Brazilian Portuguese): a practitioner of capoeira

CARNAVAL (Brazilian Portuguese): an annual parade throughout Brazil of colonial origins that occurs prior to the Catholic period of Lent and features samba schools that compete through costuming, dance, and music

CHAMADA (Brazilian Portuguese): the "call" when one player holds a pose calling their opponent to reset the game, often after a dramatic moment

CHAPA (Brazilian Portuguese): a direct kick similar to a *benção* but delivered from a side angle rather than facing forward

CORDAS (Brazilian Portuguese): the belts used to delineate skill level in capoeira, awarded at *batizados*

CORPO FECHADO (Brazilian Portuguese): literally "closed body," referring to a concept found across spiritual (Candomblé) and expressive forms (capoeira) in Brazil where the body is protected, either from spiritual methods or, in capoeira, from shielding oneself from harm by moving with the body gathered inward and arms at the ready to block attacks. The two areas overlap, when in some capoeira music the lyrics feature the concept of a spiritually protected body.

FRANÇAIS MBËR (Dakar Wolof): a linguistic register often associated with Wolof wrestlers speaking "broken" French

GINGA (Brazilian Portuguese): a fluid base step in capoeira

GRADÉ (French) / GRADUADO (Brazilian Portuguese): the first stage of an advanced-level student in capoeira

GRIS-GRIS (Francophone) / PATUÁ or BOLSAS DE MANDINGA (Brazilian Portuguese): protective amulets, often with spiritual connotations

JOGO (Brazilian Portuguese): a "game" or a bout between two opponents in capoeira

KINKELIBA (Wolof): a plant/shrub whose leaves are used as a common tea in Senegal

LADAINHA (Brazilian Portuguese): a category of songs called "litany" that opens a capoeira *roda*

MBALAX (Wolof): a popular music and dance genre based in neo-traditional Senegalese dance and percussion (specifically *sabar*) with singing in Wolof and Afro-Latin musical influences

MBOKK (Wolof): family or relatives (noun)

MESTRE/MESTRA (Brazilian Portuguese): master in capoeira hierarchy

MVET (Fang): a West Central African continental counterpart to the berimbau instrument

ÑAK (Wolof): non-Senegalese African

NDËPP (Lebu-Wolof): a spiritual ritual originating from and practiced among Lebu people in Senegal that is used to cure people of spiritual and psychological ailments

PARANAUÊ or PARANÁ Ê (Brazilian Portuguese): a refrain of the most well-known capoeira song first improvised by Mestre Genário making reference to the Brazilian state of Paraná

PUXADA DE REDE (Brazilian Portuguese): a neotraditional dance mimicking fisherman casting nets that is often performed by capoeira schools. It also has its own repertoire of songs with themes about the precarity of fishing, bodies of water, and praise music to Iemanja, goddess of the sea.

QUEDA DE RINS (Brazilian Portuguese): literally "kidney fall," a capoeira pose when you prop your side on top of your elbow and splay your legs forward or up in the air

QUEIXADA (Brazilian Portuguese): a circular capoeira kick that swings outward

RAB (Lebu-Wolof): the cult of the Lebu people indigenous to Dakar that involves the practice of spirit possession

RENCONTRE (French) / ENCONTRO (Brazilian Portuguese): a capoeira summit event often involving visiting instructors who offer workshops and long *rodas*

RODA (Brazilian Portuguese): the circle of peers where two capoeiristas "play" each other

SALTO (Brazilian Portuguese): literally "jump," referring to a backflip in a capoeira context

sër-u-njaago (Wolof): a Manjaco textile

set (Wolof): to clean or to be clean; also means neat or properly executed

teranga (Wolof): a Senegalese concept of core social value of hospitality or welcoming

tiges (French): thin tree trunks or stalks; used to make berimbaus from kinkeliba trees in Afreecapoeira

tubaab (Wolof): a white person or Westerner

tuur (Lebu-Wolof): a ritual practice of ancestor worship and drawing on ancestral protection common in Senegal

ucad: Université Cheikh Anta Diop in Dakar

volta do mundo (Brazilian Portuguese): literally "a turn around the world," when a capoeirista chooses to reset the game (often after an intense attack or when they are tired and need to take a breath) by extending their arm out and inviting their opponent to do the same so the two can walk slowly inside the circle before restarting

NOTES

Preface

1   The main mode of bodily communication in capoeira involves a variety
of kicks, spinning and circular or straight and direct, as well as creative
"escapes" and offensive or defensive responses. The goal is less to take
down one's opponent (although capoeira does involve takedowns and can
sometimes be quite violent) than for opponents to engage in an improvisational "conversation" in which they communicate through creative one-
upmanship, trickery, strength, technique, and even humor, all while the
audience of a circle of clapping and singing peers (*roda*) await their turn.

2   Siaka, a Gambian capoeirista, once generously framed my early resistance
to capoeira as "A fisherman's child will lose a taste for fish."

Introduction. Moving Origins

1   Because capoeira is understood to be a combat game, in which two opponents aim to interact both collaboratively and competitively to one-up
each other in attacks and showmanship, the action verb used to describe
capoeira is the Portuguese word *jogar* (to play), and a single match is
called a *jogo* (game).

2   Cheikh Amadou Bamba was the founder of the Sufi brotherhood Muridiyya and the symbol of a successfully nonviolent anticolonial campaign
against the French in Senegal. The French exiled him to Gabon in an
attempt to disrupt his rising popularity, but this had the opposite effect.
His exile is well known, and he is often depicted artistically for the miracle
he performed by laying his prayer mat on the ocean. Known by few is that
the vessel of his exile was the Brazilian ship *Pernambuc*.

3   Senegal is often referred to as a foil in relation to Guinea-Conakry for
resisting a postindependence relationship with France.

4   Also featured in my analysis is the group Owlavé Capoeira in Abidjan;
however, it falls outside the schema of African-founded schools. It was
started by a Brazilian woman, Mestra Marcia Kablan. She is married to the
Ivorian visual artist Cyprien Kablan, with whom she runs an artistic cultural and community center for Ivorian young people and diverse groups of
Ivorian and international adults. Kablan's capoeira school is integrated into
the regional capoeira network through mutual collaboration and support
for events. Several of the main groups listed also have members who broke

off to create their own groups, such as Berimbau Sagrado in Dakar, a *capoeira angola* group in Lomé, and, most recently, Capoeira Oriazambi Gambia in Banjul. This book, while it engages somewhat with these outgrowth groups, focuses on the original capoeira schools and associations in the region that have developed since the 1990s and early 2000s. One of these foundational associations, Ogun Eru in Cotonou, which is also the only African-run capoeira school in the region to have its own institutional space (a cultural center), has also recently expanded to open a branch in neighboring Togo. Similarly, Afreecapoeira in Dakar has several students from other African countries who have migrated elsewhere or returned home to teach as semiformal branches of the original Senegal-based school in Ecuador, the Democratic Republic of the Congo, Gabon, and France.

5 Regionalism based on geographical proximity and contemporary African migration within Africa contributes to other artistic worlds, such as Kwaito. Livermon (2020, 64, 69, 71) points to multiple forms of "black migration" in South Africa that contribute to diverse Black mixtures that coalesce in shared musical and aesthetic "affinities."

6 For most of the book, I treat *Brazil* and *diaspora* as synonymous. In specific chapters that deal with capoeira events with Brazilian visitors (chapters 2 and 5), I approach the two distinctly to theorize separately the racial dynamics of diasporic return to West Africa and Brazilian social hierarchy.

7 There is little documented evidence of women's participation in early capoeira in Brazil. However, criminal records from the late nineteenth and early twentieth centuries show cases of women who were likely part of the capoeira street scene and were said to have "violently attacked men," although the men's names were often kept off the record to "protect the masculinity of the victims" (Oliveira and Leal 2009, 123).

8 That is not to say it is not an African invention. It simply is not likely to have existed as we know it today in West or West Central Africa.

9 Historians and social scientists have aimed to debunk the romanticization of "African resistance" that often accompanies historiography and contemporary ethnography of capoeira (Assunção 2005; Downey et al. 2015; Talmon-Chvaicer 2008). In so doing, they often position themselves against an "Afrocentric bias" linked to the works of another group of scholars writing about capoeira in the past and the present (see, e.g., Desch-Obi 2008; Kambon 2018). In the words of Assunção (2005, 206): "The idea of capoeira as an ancestral cult of 'crossing the *kalunga*,' is based on present-day knowledge of Central African religious traditions, and was re-invented by Afrocentric militants in the United States during the 1990s." The charge of Afrocentric intellectual militancy is rooted in assumptions of poor empiricism, despite the reality that any and all scholars studying as ambiguous a form as capoeira must confront dubious colonial sources and a paucity of alternative forms of documentation. The label also creates suspicion around some projects that intentionally seek out African origins. With attention on the easy target of "Afrocentrism," the creole hypotheses

flourish without being as readily challenged. Desch-Obi (2008) directly addressed what he called the "creolization paradigm" and what James Sweet (2011) calls "creole essentialism" that minimizes African influences through the charge of essentialism, while effectively producing a kind of Brazilian essentialism (see also Desch-Obi 2012; Wade 2004).

10 Brazil, for example, has shifted from an overwhelming focus on Nigerian/ Yoruba influences (known as Nagôcentrismo) to recognizing the impact of an earlier and longer-standing migration of enslaved people from West Central Africa (Angola/Bantu).

11 Paul Zeleza defines diaspora as "simultaneously a state of being and a process of becoming, a kind of voyage that encompasses the possibility of never arriving or returning, a navigation of multiple belongings" (Zeleza 2005, 41). Working with scholarship that defines diaspora as a "process" and a "condition" defined as much by difference as by sharedness (Brown 2005; Campt 2002; Edwards 2003; Gilroy 1993; Zeleza 2005) shows that origins can be similarly processual, not as a final point in defining the self but, rather, as an active mechanism of political, social, and historical meaning making. The anthropologist J. Lorand Matory (2005, 3) troubled the narrative of a binary between African origins and diasporic constructions, offering, "The irony at the core of this story is that diasporas create their homelands."

12 By introducing the possibility of contemporary continental West African capoeiristas as diasporic, I write in the vein of critically engaging racial, gendered, and affective formations that come to define emerging diasporic political projects (Thomas and Campt 2008; Thomas and Clarke 2006).

13 Annie Gibson (2014) distinguishes between diasporic capoeira, referring to initiatives linked to the structure of Brazilian schools, and transnational capoeira, in which media and capoeiristas merely passing through create a grassroots practice that often uses locally produced instruments. Cuba, like Senegal, is the latter case; Gibson (2014, 1) describes capoeira in Havana as "Brazilian in practice yet Cuban in essence." There is an important distinction between diasporic capoeira and transnational capoeira; however, the bifurcation of the literature does not mirror this distinction. Tatjana Lipiäinen's study, for example, looks at an example of transnational capoeira, but the analysis falls under the category of inclusive capoeira paradigms that usually accompanies diasporic capoeira studies.

14 The inclusivity framework is encapsulated in Lipiäinen's origins argument based on a study of capoeira in Russia: "The very roots of capoeira are culturally mixed. Furthermore, capoeira's underlying aim has been the pursuit of freedom from a variety of hegemonic constraints, by African slaves, Brazilian poor and now also by transnational young-old, females-males, poor-rich, black-Asian-white-etc. Therefore, to portray capoeira angola today as purely black, Afro-Brazilian, or Baian [sic], cultural practice does not appear to reflect empirical reality nor Lugones' attitude of openness towards new constructions of self" (2015, 682).

15 Although African-founded schools such as Afreecapoeira fight to maintain their autonomy, they have social ties to major capoeira schools in Europe and the United States that are more directly rooted in Brazilian capoeira structures.

16 Interrogating postcolonial African subjectivity nonetheless requires interacting with Africa as a category, despite its constructedness. The concept continues to be salient both inside and outside of the continent (Ferguson 2006), and tracking the contested meanings of Africanness sheds light on a host of postcolonial social categories and lived experiences. It is out of this vein of reconstruction following the problematics (Apter 2017) or "problem-spaces" (Scott 2004) that this book emerges as a way to redefine how we see "Africa's" role in the African diaspora and the making of the modern world. I follow the work of Deborah Thomas (2011) and Andrew Apter (2017), who see their respective research sites in Jamaica and Nigeria as places *from which* to theorize race, modernity, and the making of history rather than simply as places that require these perspectives to elucidate their singular historical experiences. In that light, I encourage thinking with and from Africa to shed light on how we have come to understand that world and the grammars, categories, and structures in place that shape our everyday interactions within it.

17 As Keren Weitzberg (2017) argues in her historical study of Somaliness, asserting chauvinistic superiority (internally over women and externally over other groups) can be a key strategy in positioning oneself in relation to colonial and postcolonial legacies of power where racial and ethnic hierarchical formations become normative. Somali chauvinism is not built on a clear material reality of who is or is not "Somali"; rather, it shifts with the changing power landscape from European colonial rule to postcolonial Gikuyu nationalist rule. Diasporic chauvinism is built on similar shifting and situational sands. Rooted in a claim of superiority based in performance skills by some Afro-descended Brazilians, diasporic chauvinism is a discourse of authority and authorship enacted by multiple actors positioning themselves as "diasporic," whether they are descendants of European colonizers or Europeans themselves (de Sá 2024). Furthermore, as Weitzberg (2017, 118) notes, those defending Black African culture against Eurocentric ideas of African cultural inferiority have done so by enacting a kind of Black African nationalist politics, "but, in doing so, [they have] sometimes devalued the 'culture' of people deemed to be foreign to the nation." Chauvinism, in other words, is not just a diasporic problem. It can, however, complexly and at times even paradoxically reproduce colonial logics of anti–African Blackness.

18 In this respect, diasporic chauvinism is one distinct manifestation of Thomas and Campt's (2008) "diasporic hegemonies," or the reproduction of inequalities in diasporic communities. The diasporic imaginary of Africa as a site of desire can not only obscure the complexity of African contexts. It can also privilege the diasporic experience in ways that ulti-

mately undermine the inclusion of contemporary African subjects. Further, as chauvinism is most often synonymous with an extreme expression of nationalism, I employ this term specifically to signal how the first term, *diasporic*, reveals an inherent multiplicity of different cultural traditions that are then consolidated into a national identity by a process represented by the second term, *chauvinism*. Diasporic chauvinism thus describes a type of interaction during a moment of diasporic collaboration or historical reckoning or repair that, in turn, creates a hierarchy of ownership and expertise that reinforces white privilege and white visibility in African contexts.

19   The berimbau, found throughout West Central Africa, is believed to have been introduced relatively recently in the trajectory of capoeira's history (Alexandre 1974; Diaz et al. 2021). So despite the specifics of its African origins, its origin in capoeira does not trace a continuous line from Africa to the Brazilian present. Berimbau-like instruments are also found in Guam and the Philippines. Further, the berimbau as we know it in capoeira today is likely derived from a sixteenth-century version of the mvet of Bantu and Fang regions such as Gabon. As scholars of diaspora have argued, what is discursively and materially "African" is often better preserved in the diaspora out of necessity to maintain a connection to homeland (Scott 1991). Meanwhile, African continental cultural production moves on with innovation.

20   I recorded fifty-four in-depth conversations, the majority of which were with capoeiristas residing in Dakar. Some names are pseudonyms.

Chapter 1. Whose Diaspora?

1   The event used to be called La Nuit des Arts Martiaux (The Night of Martial Arts). Sensei Lô revamped the program in 2014 and gave the event its current name.

2   Five African heads of state are graduates of UCAD.

3   *Lenços* (silk scarves) were later replaced by the *cordas* (belts) common in capoeira schools today. Whereas the *lenços* often used colors associated with Bantu cosmologies, the *cordas* most often represented the colors of the Brazilian flag, showing a shift from Central West African cosmology to Brazilian nationalism.

4   The "semantic body" of prominent Afro-Brazilian capoeiristas is not limited to representing Brazilianness and Brazilian Blackness. These Brazilian figures are also working to perform their own centrality and "Afro"-authenticity that was shaped in large part by the success of reggae and Rastafarian music and aesthetics in Brazil in the 1970s and '80s (Crook 1993).

5   A jihadist movement was ramping up attacks in West Africa in 2016. The cover of *Jeune Afrique* featured a photo of the Monument de la Renaissance, with a corresponding article speculating that Dakar might be the next target. Since the attack on a popular hotel in Ouagadougou

in 2016, Gendarmerie checkpoints have popped up across the city. Elite spaces such as the Radisson Blu on the Corniche also ramped up security, and I was questioned (perhaps playfully) for several minutes when I tried to take my berimbau with me when I went to meet friends for drinks at the Radisson poolside lounge.

6 Interestingly, "Les Amazones" also happened to be a nickname given to Senegalese female trash workers in Dakar for their "strength and fearless dedication to their new jobs" (Fredericks 2018, 78).

Chapter 2. Whiteness, Blackness, and Bushness

Parts of this chapter were published in Celina de Sá, "The Obscuring Effect: Whiteness in the Celebration of Black Performance in Senegal," in *The Anthropology of White Supremacy*, edited by Aisha Beliso-De Jesús, Jemima Pierre, and Junaid Rana (Princeton, NJ: Princeton University Press, 2025).

1 TEDx Talks, "A capoeira sem preconçeito: Mestre Moraes at TEDX-Pelourinho," video, posted November 11, 2011, https://www.youtube.com /watch?v=PSNJNk8At6o.

2 The term *racecraft* was first coined in the context of the United States (Fields and Fields 2012).

3 Ana Paula Höfling mentions that what goes on between *capoeira regional* and *capoeira angola* reflects the broader debates in Brazil around binaries of folklore and modernity. The two figures credited with establishing of each of these genres, Mestre Bimba (*regional*) and Mestre Pastinha (*angola*), are unfairly pitted against each other, as they have more in common than is often portrayed (Höfling 2019).

4 Seeking to villainize white Brazilian capoeiristas, or white capoeiristas in general, is not my goal. It also is not intellectually productive. I am also not suggesting that white Brazilians and white Europeans are equally positioned in the context of West Africa or in general. Instead, I seek to name the multifaceted ways that whiteness necessarily operates in the space of Black performance to shed light on its problematic effects.

5 This reenactment is a popular trend among capoeira schools everywhere.

6 I use the Wolof spelling here. The French spelling is *toubab*.

7 The historian Idrissa Bâ's scholarship on early modern West Africa demonstrates how categories of personhood in the region relate to racial and religious schemas from the transatlantic slave trade, and from competing European, Maghreb, and Sahelian empires (e.g., Bâ 2006). In personal correspondence, he shared that *ñak* could have similar origins in this period of shifting categories of unfreedom, social hierarchy, and racial typology. I have yet to find out when people first began to use the term in a derogatory sense.

8 Notably, almost all the comments on the video mocking the wrestler's French are written in Wolof. See MPROD TV, "Vous allez mourir de rire:

avec le français mbeur du lutteur Gouyegui 95 sur la saison," video, posted December 13, 2019, https://www.youtube.com/watch?v=Qz9Wrn4YjHs.

9   Abidjan, Ivory Coast, held the same title after independence until its recent eruptions of civil war. Similarly, Nigeria has been referred to as the "Black Greece" with regard to being a source of classical civilizations and art.

10   See Toubab Krewe's website, at https://www.toubabkrewe.com.

11   This incident is a stark demonstration of how race, class, and gender are key intersecting weapons of coloniality. For further commentary, see Dieng 2021; Gueye 2021. Graffiti across Dakar stating "No to Rape" bears witness to the use of Adji Sarr as a political weapon when she accused President Macky Sall's strongest political opponent, Ousmane Sonko, of sexual assault when she worked as his masseuse.

12   There is no comprehensive study of the history of the term. There are, however, similar designations to *ñak*, such as *makafoutes* and *makatchembe*, phrases that originated in Paris but circulated to Dakar to refer to people from the Francophone West Indies (Labrune-Badiane 2013).

13   When asked about the derogatory meaning today, she said, "Senegale mën na ñaawal lepp" (Senegalese can make everything ugly). Discussions I have had with other Senegalese about this, as well as similar terms and phrases, are a source a discomfort for many, perhaps because the existence of these "ugly" ideas is at odds with other social values, such as *teranga*, the social value of being welcoming to guests and strangers that is also the gendered responsibility of women; democracy; and generosity, which is so integral to Islamic faith.

14   I keep these critiques in mind by analyzing conferences in Senegal and the United States as an extension of my fieldwork.

Chapter 3. In Pursuit of Heritage

1   I thank Yolanda Covington-Ward for offering me this phrasing.

2   However, the Diola religion remains dominant and dates back at least to the seventeenth century (Baum 1999).

3   This comment came from Cheikh Anta Babou in a paper he gave on Muslim Africans in the Americas for Second International Colloquium on African Studies in 2021.

4   *Malandragem* is a Brazilian concept that loosely translates to a style of cleverness and trickery that in the context of capoeira is almost like a physical expression of wit or slyness.

5   The epigraph to this section is from a dear friend and supporter of Afree-capoeira, the former romantic partner of Elena, one of the female capoei-ristas in the group. Alexandre was always eager to learn about every detail of our practice. He tragically passed away before his time right before the *batizado*, which he, as a non-capoeirista, generously helped to organize.

Around the same time, a well-known dancer and artistic visionary in the Dakar cultural scene, Pape Sangone Vieira, also passed away unexpectedly. He had trained capoeira with key figures in Afreecapoeira and enjoyed incorporating capoeira aesthetics into his Afro-modern dance choreographies. Capoeiristas wore black armbands during the twentieth-anniversary event in honor of these two members of the capoeira and broader artistic community in Dakar.

Chapter 4. Spiritual Baggage

1 Hilary Jones's study of mixed-race aristocrats in nineteenth-century Senegal touches on the Catholic priest Abbe David Boilat, a prominent figure in that sociopolitical group who "admonished signares to rid their homes of gris-gris because they amounted to irrational superstition" (Jones 2013, 79). The continuity from this period to the twenty-first century shows the association of gris-gris with the uncivilized and nonrational tropes promoted by anti-African colonial logics.

2 The youth movements of Set/Setal and Y'en a Marre accompanied a moment in which hip hop not only became a popular practice but was also used by the youth as a tool to create political cohesion and resistance to marginalization (Fredericks 2014). In his study of hip hop's role in the 1988 and 2012 elections in Senegal, Michael Lambert (2002, 36) argues for the "continuity of modes of youth political engagement" that are not initiated by cultural forms such as hip hop but, rather, constitute just one iteration of a longer history of political expression. Donal Cruise O'Brien (1996) sees Y'en a Marre and Set/Setal as focused as much on self-transformation as on social reform, yet the studies of these explicitly political moments examine the collectives (protesters, students, artists), reinforcing the idea of Senegalese youth as a cohesive group that these various subgroups come to represent.

3 For a rich discussion of aesthetics, hip hop, gender, and Islam in the context of the United States, see Khabeer 2016.

4 In Diola women's wrestling, protective amulets are drawn on from Islam, Christianity, and indigenous religions (Baum 1990), an instantiation of the kind of spiritual assemblage (which might be read as "syncretism" in New World contexts) already practiced in West Africa.

5 For more on Senegalese migration and the visibility of Islam in Brazil, see Ndiaye 2020.

6 *Tuur* means "to spill" in Wolof. It is a common practice across a range of ethnic groups in which people make offerings to ancestral spirits. *Tuur* is both the act and the site itself, which might be on the side of a home or at the base of a tree. The idea behind *tuur* is that when family members pass away, they do not depart but instead begin to protect you. *Tuur* is a practice of taking care of one's familial (spirit) caretakers. *Tuur* can also

be a strategic tool to accomplish goals, avoid bad luck, heal, or address wrongdoing.

7   Privileging monotheism under a discourse of modernity and denigrating the "paganism" associated with capoeira is specific to neither Islam nor Senegal. It also has gendered implications, as was the case for a capoeira student in Abidjan, Ivory Coast. Her church leaders found her training as a capoeirista to be problematic for a proper woman and thus performed an exorcism to rid her of her "warrior spirit."

8   Compared with other Islamic societies, however, West Africa educated girls through Qur'anic schooling for centuries before Western "developed" countries did so in the twentieth century. Furthermore, women held high scholarly and pedagogical positions in Islamic scholarship and worship in West African history (S. Diouf 2013).

Chapter 5. After Tourism

1   Some of the names in this chapter are pseudonyms.

2   This event came about at the tail end of former president Yahya Jammeh's dictatorial rule in the Gambia. In July 2015, there was little sign of his imminent departure; posters celebrating President Jammeh's twenty-second year in power lined the main boulevards in the capital city, Banjul, and the police state was evident in the many checkpoints. No one knew that only a few months after the event, Jammeh would be ousted due to widespread student protests and, eventually, general elections; his opponent, Adama Barrow, was voted into office. Jammeh refused to step down initially but was ultimately forced into exile by a Senegalese military threat of invasion backed by the international community. During the event, however, there was still an atmosphere of fear about speaking openly about the president. With little recourse to express dissension about the political climate, the Gambian capoeiristas focused their energy on the performance traditions that emerged as a result of the slave trade and the pleasure of building regional and international networks through the exchange of cultural knowledge.

3   Some scholars go as far as to conclude that the "issues of slavery and the slave trade never really captured the attention of the larger public" (Bellagamba 2009).

Conclusion. Protecting the Magical Possibilities of Black Movement

Parts of this chapter were published as Celina de Sá, "Unremarkable Stakes," in "Theorizing the Contemporary," *Fieldsights*, July 31, 2019, https://culanth.org/fieldsights/unremarkable-stakes.

1   Here I am thinking particularly about anxieties about *évolués* (Africans who became Europeanized—i.e., "evolved"—through education and cultural assimilation) in colonial French West Africa under a colonial schema of purity in which there were "traditional Africans" and "civilized Europeans" (Diouf 1998; Genova 2004).

REFERENCES

Acuña, Mauricio. 2014. *A ginga da nação: Intelectuais na capoeira e capoeiristas intelectuais (1930–1969)*. São Paulo: Alameda.

Adelakun, Abimbola A. 2021. *Performing Power in Nigeria: Identity, Politics, and Pentacostalism*. Cambridge: Cambridge University Press.

Ahmed, Sara. 2006. *Queer Phenomenology: Orientations, Objects, Others.* Durham, NC: Duke University Press.

Akinbola, Bimbola. 2020. "Disbelonging and Unruly Return in the Performance Art of Wura-Natasha Ogunji." *Text and Performance Quarterly* 40 (2): 152–69.

Akyeampong, Emmanuel, and Charles Ambler. 2002. "Leisure in African History: An Introduction." *International Journal of African Historical Studies* 35 (1): 1–16.

Alexandre, Pierre. 1974. "Introduction to a Fang Oral Art Genre: Gabon and Cameroon Mvet." *Bulletin of the School of Oriental and African Studies* 37 (1): 1–7.

Allen, Jafari Sinclaire, and Ryan Cecil Jobson. 2016. "The Decolonizing Generation: (Race and) Theory in Anthropology since the Eighties." *Current Anthropology* 57 (2): 129–48.

Amos, Alcione M. 2001. "Afro-Brazilians in Togo: The Case of the Olympio Family, 1882–1945." *Cahiers d'Études Africaines* 162:293–314.

Andersson, Ruben. 2014. *Illegality, Inc.: Clandestine Migration and the Business of Bordering Europe*. Berkeley: University of California Press.

Anne, Hamidou. 2021. "Le fascisme rampant sénégalais." *Seneplus*, June 1. https://www.seneplus.com/opinions/le-fascisme-rampant-senegalais.

Appert, Catherine M. 2015. "To Make Song Without Singing: Hip Hop and Popular Music in Senegal." *New Literary History* 46:759–74.

Appert, Catherine M. 2018. *In Hip Hop Time: Music, Memory, and Social Change in Urban Senegal*. Oxford: Oxford University Press.

Apter, Andrew. 2005. *The Pan-African Nation: Oil and the Spectacle of Culture in Nigeria*. Chicago: University of Chicago Press.

Apter, Andrew. 2016. "Beyond Négritude: Black Cultural Citizenship and the Arab Question in FESTAC 77." *Journal of African Cultural Studies* 28 (3): 313–26.

Apter, Andrew. 2017. *Oduduwa's Chain: Locations of Culture in the Yoruba-Atlantic*. Chicago: University of Chicago Press.

Araujo, Ana Lucia. 2010. *Public Memory of Slavery: Victims and Perpetrators in the South Atlantic*. Amherst, MA: Cambria.

Assunção, Matthias Röhrig. 2005. *Capoeira: The History of an Afro-Brazilian Martial Art*. New York: Routledge.

Aula, Inkeri. 2017. "Translocality and Afro-Brazilian Imaginaries in Globalised Capoeira." *Suomen Antropologi* 42 (1): 67–90.

Ayobade, Dotun. 2019. "'We Were on Top of the World': Fela Kuti's Queens and the Poetics of Space." *Journal of African Cultural Studies* 31 (1): 24–39.

Bâ, Idrissa. 2006. "La problématique de la presence juive au Sahara et au Soudan d'après Jean Léon l'Africain." *Outre-Mers* 93 (350–51): 249–66.

Babou, Cheikh Anta. 2007. *Fighting the Greater Jihad: Amadu Bamba and the Founding of the Muridiyya of Senegal, 1853–1913*. Athens: Ohio University Press.

Babou, Cheikh Anta. 2013. "The Senegalese 'Social Contract' Revisited: The Muridiyya Muslim Order and State Politics in Postcolonial Senegal." In *Tolerance, Democracy, and Sufis in Senegal*, edited by Mamadou Diouf, 125–46. New York: Columbia University Press.

Babou, Cheikh Anta. 2021. *The Muridiyya on the Move: Islam, Migration, and Place Making*. Athens: Ohio University Press.

Bahi, Aghi. 2010. "Jeunes et imaginaire de la modernité à Abidjan." *Cadernos de Estudos Africanos* 18–19:56–67.

Balandier, Georges. 1948. "Femmes 'possédées' et leurs chants." *Présence Africaine* 5:749–54.

Baller, Susann. 2007. "Transforming Urban Landscapes: Soccer Fields as Sites of Urban Sociability in the Agglomeration of Dakar." *African Identities* 5 (2): 217–30.

Barry, Boubacar. 1997. *Senegambia and the Atlantic Slave Trade*. Cambridge: Cambridge University Press.

Baum, Robert M. 1990. "The Emergence of a Diola Christianity." *Africa: Journal of the International African Institute* 60 (3): 370–98.

Baum, Robert M. 1999. *Shrines of the Slave Trade: Diola Religion and Society in Precolonial Senegambia*. Oxford: Oxford University Press.

Baumann, Martin. 2001. "Global Buddhism: Developmental Periods, Regional Histories, and a New Analytical Perspective." *Journal of Global Buddhism* 2:1–43.

Bellagamba, Alice. 2009. "Back to the Land of Roots: African American Tourism and the Cultural Heritage of the River Gambia." *Cahiers d'Études Africaines* 193–94 (1–2): 453–76.

Bennett, Herman L. 2018. *African Kings and Black Slaves: Sovereignty and Dispossession in the Early Modern Atlantic*. Philadelphia: University of Pennsylvania Press.

Berg, Ulla. 2015. *Mobile Selves: Race, Migration, and Belonging in Peru and the U.S.* New York: New York University Press.

Berlant, Lauren. 2011. *Cruel Optimism*. Durham, NC: Duke University Press.

Besnier, Niko, and Susan Brownell. 2012. "Sport, Modernity, and the Body." *Annual Review of Anthropology* 41 (1): 443–59.

Bhabha, Homi K. 1994. *The Location of Culture*. London: Routledge.

Biaya, Tshikala K., and Steven Rendall. 2000. "'Crushing the Pistachio': Eroticism in Senegal and the Art of Ousmane Ndiaye Dago." *Public Culture* 12 (3): 707–20.

Biruk, Cal. 2018. *Cooking Data: Culture and Politics in an African Research World.* Durham, NC: Duke University Press.

Bissell, William Cunningham. 2005. "Engaging Colonial Nostalgia." *Cultural Anthropology* 20 (2): 215–48.

Bocquier, Philippe. 1992. "L'insertion et la mobilité professionnelles à Dakar." PhD diss., Université Paris V.

Boulègue, Jean. 1989. *Les Luso-Africains de Sénégambie, XVIè–XIXè siècles.* Lisbon: Instituto de Investigação Científica Tropical.

Bourdieu, Pierre. 1984. *Distinction: A Social Critique of the Judgement of Taste.* Cambridge, MA: Harvard University Press.

Bourdieu, Pierre. 1993. *The Field of Cultural Production.* New York: Columbia University Press.

Brand, Dionne. 2011. *A Map to the Door of No Return.* Toronto: Vintage Canada.

Brown, Jacqueline Nassy. 2005. *Dropping Anchor, Setting Sail: Geographies of Race in Black Liverpool.* Princeton, NJ: Princeton University Press.

Buggenhagen, Beth. 2012. *Muslim Families in Global Senegal: Money Takes Care of Shame.* Bloomington: Indiana University Press.

Calvet, Louis-Jean. 2010. *Histoire du Français en Afrique: Une langue en copropriété?* Paris: Ecriture.

Campt, Tina. 2002. "The Crowded Space of Diaspora: Intercultural Address and the Tensions of Diasporic Relation." *Radical History Review* 83 (1): 94–113.

Campt, Tina. 2005. *Other Germans: Black Germans and the Politics of Race, Gender, and Memory in the Third Reich.* Ann Arbor: University of Michigan Press.

Capoeira, Nestor. 1995. *The Little Capoeira Book.* Berkeley, CA: Blue Snake.

Carter, Youssef. 2021. "Fisibilillah: Labor as Learning on the Sufi Path." *Religions* 12 (1): 1–18.

Castaldi, Francesca. 2006. *Choreographies of African Identities: Négritude, Dance, and the National Ballet of Senegal.* Urbana: University of Illinois Press.

Castillo, Lisa Earl. 2016. "Mapping the Nineteenth-Century Brazilian Returnee Movement: Demographics, Life Stories and the Question of Slavery." *Atlantic Studies* 13 (1): 25–52.

Castor, N. Fadeke. 2017. *Spiritual Citizenship: Transnational Pathways from Black Power to Ifá in Trinidad.* Durham, NC: Duke University Press.

Certeau, Michel de. 1984. *The Practice of Everyday Life.* Berkeley: University of California Press.

Cesarino, Letícia. 2017. "Anthropology and the South-South Encounter: On 'Culture' in Brazil-Africa Relations." *American Anthropologist* 119 (2): 333–41.

Chalfin, Brenda. 2010. *Neoliberal Frontiers: An Ethnography of Sovereignty in West Africa.* Chicago: University of Chicago Press.

Chevé, Dominique, and Cheikh Tidiane Wane. 2018. "Ce que lutter veut eire? Lamb, bëre et monde de vie au Sénégal." *Corps* 1 (6): 11–26.

Chigumadzi, Panashe. 2020. "Why I'm No Longer Talking to Nigerians About Race." *Africa Is a Country* (blog), April 7. https://africasacountry.com/2019/04/why-im-no-longer-talking-to-nigerians-about-race.

Chrisman, Laura. 2003. *Postcolonial Contraventions: Cultural Readings of Race, Imperialism and Transnationalism*. Manchester, UK: Manchester University Press.

Clarke, Kamari Maxine. 2004. *Mapping Yorùbá Networks: Power and Agency in the Making of Transnational Communities*. Durham, NC: Duke University Press.

Clifford, James. 1997. *Routes: Travel and Translation in the Late Twentieth Century*. Cambridge, MA: Harvard University Press.

Cohen, Adrienne J. 2021. *Infinite Repertoire: On Dance and Urban Possibility in Postsocialist Guinea*. Chicago: Chicago University Press.

Collins, John F. 2015. *Revolt of the Saints: Memory and Redemption in the Twilight of Brazilian Racial Democracy*. Durham, NC: Duke University Press.

Collis-Buthelezi, Victoria J. 2016. "Under the Aegis of Empire: Cape Town, Victorianism, and Early-Twentieth-Century Black Thought." *Callaloo* 39 (1): 115–32.

Collomb, Henri, and H. Ayats. 1962. "Les migrations au Sénégal: Étude psychopathologique." *Cahiers d'Études Africaines* 2 (8): 570–97.

Coly, Ayo A. 2019. *Postcolonial Hauntologies: African Women's Discourses of the Female Body*. Lincoln: University of Nebraska Press.

Conklin, Alice. 1997. *A Mission to Civilize: The Republican Idea of Empire in France and West Africa, 1895–1930*. Stanford, CA: Stanford University Press.

Covington-Ward, Yolanda. 2015. *Gesture and Power: Religion, Nationalism, and Everyday Performance in Congo*. Durham, NC: Duke University Press.

Covington-Ward, Yolanda. 2021. "Introduction: Embodiment and Relationality in Religions of Africa and Its Diasporas." In *Embodying Black Religions in Africa and Its Diasporas*, edited by Yolanda Covington-Ward and Jeanette S. Jouili, 1–19. Durham, NC: Duke University Press.

Cox, Aimee. 2015. *Shapeshifters: Black Girls and the Choreography of Citizenship*. Durham, NC: Duke University Press.

Crook, Larry N. 1993. "Black Consciousness, Samba Reggae, and the Re-Africanization of Bahian Carnival Music in Brazil." *World of Music* 35 (2): 90–108.

Crowder, Michael. 1962. *Senegal—a Study in French Assimilation Policy*. Oxford: Oxford University Press.

Dang, Christine Thu Nhi. 2013. "Pilgrimage Through Poetry: Sung Journeys Within the Murid Spiritual Diaspora." *Islamic Africa* 4 (1): 69–101.

Daniel, Yvonne. 2005. *Dancing Wisdom: Embodied Knowledge in Haitian Vodou, Cuban Yoruba, and Bahian Candomblé*. Chicago: University of Illinois Press.

Daniel, Yvonne. 2011. *Caribbean and Atlantic Diaspora Dance: Igniting Citizenship*. Urbana: University of Illinois Press.

Dávila, Jerry. 2010. *Hotel Trópico: Brazil and the Challenge of African Decolonization, 1950–1980*. Durham, NC: Duke University Press.

Davis, Olga Idriss. 1997. "The Door of No Return: Reclaiming the Past Through the Rhetoric of Pilgrimage." *Western Journal of Black Studies* 21 (3): 156–61.

Dayan, Joan. 1995. *Haiti, History, and the Gods*. Berkeley: University of California Press.

de Brito, Diolino Pereira. 2017. *A Capoeira de Braços para o Ar: Estudo da Capoeira Gospel no ABC/SP.* London: Novas Edições Acadêmicas.

de Campos Rosario, Claudio, Neil Stephens, and Sara Delamont. 2010. "'I'm Your Teacher, I'm Brazilian!': Authenticity and Authority in European Capoeira." *Sport, Education and Society* 15 (1): 103–20.

Delamont, Sara, and Neil Stephens. 2008. "Up on the Roof: The Embodied Habitus of Diasporic Capoeira." *Cultural Sociology* 2 (1): 57–74.

Delamont, Sara, and Neil Stephens. 2010. "*Roda Boa, Roda Boa*: Legitimate Peripheral Participation in Diasporic *Capoeira.*" *Teaching and Teacher Education* 26:113–18.

Delamont, Sara, Neil Stephens, and Claudio Campos. 2017. *Embodying Brazil: An Ethnography of Diasporic Capoeira.* London: Routledge.

Delavignette, Robert. 1950. *Freedom and Authority in French West Africa.* London: International African Institute.

De León, Jason. 2015. *The Land of Open Graves: Living and Dying on the Migrant Trail.* Berkeley: University of California Press.

Deliss, Clémentine. 2014. "Brothers in Arms: Laboratoire AGIT'art and Tenq in Dakar in the 1990s." *Afterall* 36:4–19.

de Sá, Celina. 2019. "Unremarkable Stakes." In "Theorizing the Contemporary," *Fieldsights,* July 31. https://culanth.org/fieldsights/unremarkable-stakes.

de Sá, Celina. 2023. "Playing with Origins: Racial Self-Making and Embodying History in Togolese Capoeira." *Transforming Anthropology* 31 (2): 100–12.

de Sá, Celina. 2025. "The Obscuring Effect: Whiteness in the Celebration of Black Performance in Senegal." In *The Anthropology of White Supremacy,* edited by Aisha Beliso-De Jesús, Jemima Pierre, and Junaid Rana, 83–94. Princeton, NJ: Princeton University Press.

Desai, Gaurav. 2001. *Subject to Colonialism: African Self-Fashioning and the Colonial Library.* Durham, NC: Duke University Press.

Desch-Obi, T. J. 2008. *Fighting for Honor: The History of African Martial Art Traditions in the Atlantic World.* Columbia: University of South Carolina Press.

Desch-Obi, T. J. 2012. "The *Jogo de Capoeira* and the Fallacy of 'Creole' Cultural Forms." *African and Black Diaspora: An International Journal* 5 (2): 211–28.

Dettmar, Kevin J. H. 2014. "There Must Be Some Misunderstanding: Unintelligible Rock Lyrics Can Teach Us What We Think." *Chronicle of Higher Education* 60 (27): B13–B14.

Diawara, Manthia. 1998. *In Search of Africa.* Cambridge, MA: Harvard University Press.

Diaz, Juan Diego, Mattias Röhrig Assunção, and Gregory Beyer. 2021. "Arching over the Atlantic: Exploring Links Between Brazilian and Angolan Musical Bows." *Ethnomusicology* 65 (2): 286–323.

Dieng, Rama Salla. 2021. "Take the Soul from Everyone, and the Liberty of All." *Africa Is a Country* (blog), March 9. https://africasacountry.com/2021/03/take-the-soul-from-everyone-and-the-liberty-of-all.

Diop, Maï. 2008. "Pagnes . . . Panos . . . Les étoffes magnétiques des Mandjak." Au-senegal.com, March 7. https://www.au-senegal.com/pagnes-panos -les-etoffes-magnetiques-des-mandjak,1622.html.

Diouf, Fabienne Ngone. 2017. "Urban Wolof Loanword Phonology." PhD diss. Indiana University, Bloomington.

Diouf, Mamadou. 1996. "Urban Youth and Senegalese Politics: Dakar 1988– 1994." *Public Culture* 8:225–49.

Diouf, Mamadou. 1998. "The French Colonial Policy of Assimilation and the Civility of the Originaires of the Four Communes (Senegal): A Nineteenth Century Globalization Project." *Development and Change* 29 (4): 671–96.

Diouf, Mamadou, ed. 2013. *Tolerance, Democracy, and Sufis in Senegal.* New York: Columbia University Press.

Diouf, Mamadou, and Donal Cruise O'Brien. 2002. "La réussite politique du contrat social sénégalais." In *La construction de l'État au Sénégal,* edited by Donal Cruise O'Brien, Momar-Coumba Diop, and Mamadou Diouf, 9–15. Paris: Karthala.

Diouf, Sylviane A. 2013. *Servants of Allah: African Muslims Enslaved in the Americas.* New York: New York University Press.

Downey, Greg. 2005. *Learning Capoeira: Lessons in Cunning from an Afro-Brazilian Art.* Oxford: Oxford University Press.

Downey, Greg, Monica Dalidowicz, and Paul Mason. 2015. "Apprenticeship as Method: Embodied Learning in the Ethnographic Practice." *Qualitative Research* 15 (2): 183–200.

Drake, St. Clair. 1993. "Diaspora Studies and Pan-Africanism." In *Global Dimensions of the African Diaspora,* edited by Joseph Harris, 451–512. Washington, DC: Howard University Press.

Drewal, Margaret. 1992. *Yoruba Ritual: Performers, Play, Agency.* Bloomington: Indiana University Press.

Ebron, Paulla. 1999. "Tourists as Pilgrims: Commercial Fashioning of Transatlantic Politics." *American Ethnologist* 26 (4): 910–32.

Ebron, Paulla. 2002. *Performing Africa.* Princeton, NJ: Princeton University Press.

Edwards, Brent Hayes. 2003. *The Practice of Diaspora: Literature, Translation, and the Rise of Black Internationalism.* Cambridge, MA: Harvard University Press.

Ekotto, Frieda. 2011. *Race and Sex Across the French Atlantic: The Color of Black in Literary, Philosophical, and Theater Discourse.* Lanham, MD: Lexington.

Ekotto, Frieda. 2020. "A Reflection on Gender and Sexuality as Transnational Archive of African Modernity." In *Routledge Handbook of Minority Discourses in African Literature,* edited by Tanure Ojaide and Joyce Ashuntantang, 185–94. London: Routledge.

Essien, Kwame. 2016. *Brazilian-African Diaspora in Ghana: The Tabom, Slavery, Dissonance of Memory, Identity, and Locating Home.* East Lansing: Michigan State University Press.

Evans, Martin. 2007. "'The Suffering Is Too Great': Urban Internally Displaced Persons in the Casamance Conflict, Senegal." *Journal of Refugee Studies* 20 (1): 60–85.

Falcão, Richard M. 2014. "Youth Appropriation of the Body: Youth Appropriation of ICTS—Senegalese Youth at the Crossroads Between Coosan (Tradition) and Dund Toubab (The Life of the Whites)." In *Fifth European Conference on African Studies*, 828–58. Lisbon: Centro de Estudos Internacionnais do Instituto Universiatário de Lisboa.

Faria, Caroline V., and Jennifer L. Fluri. 2022. "Allure and the Spatialities of Nationalism, War and Development: Towards a Geography of Beauty." *Geography Compass* 16 (9): 1–16.

Faye, Ousseynou, and Ibrahima Thioub. 2003. "Les marginaux de l'état à Dakar." *Mouvement Social* (204): 93–108.

Feld, Steven. 2012. *Jazz Cosmopolitanism in Accra: Five Musical Years in Ghana.* Durham, NC: Duke University Press.

Ferguson, James. 1990. *The Anti-Politics Machine: 'Development,' Depoliticization, and Bureaucratic Power in Lesotho.* Cambridge: Cambridge University Press.

Ferguson, James. 2006. *Global Shadows: Africa in the Neoliberal World Order.* Durham, NC: Duke University Press.

Ferguson, James, and Akhil Gupta. 1997. "Introduction." In *Culture, Power, Place: Explorations in Critical Anthropology*, edited by Akhil Gupta and James Ferguson, 1–51. Durham, NC: Duke University Press.

Ferreira, Roquinaldo. 2012. *Cross-Cultural Exchange in the Atlantic World: Angola and Brazil During the Era of the Slave Trade.* New York: Cambridge University Press.

Fields, Barbara Jeanne. 1990. "Slavery, Race and Ideology in the United States of America." *New Left Review* 1 (181): 95–118.

Fields, Karen E., and Barbara J. Fields. 2012. *Racecraft: The Soul of Inequality in American Life.* London: Verso.

Fredericks, Rosalind. 2014. "'The Old Man Is Dead': Hip Hop and the Arts of Citizenship of Senegalese Youth." *Antipode* 46 (1): 130–48.

Fredericks, Rosalind. 2018. *Garbage Citizenship: Vital Infrastructures of Labor in Dakar, Senegal.* Durham, NC: Duke University Press.

Gable, Eric. 2006. "The Funeral and Modernity in Manjaco." *Cultural Anthropology* 21 (3): 385–415.

Garuba, Harry. 2008. "Race in Africa: Four Epigraphs and a Commentary." PMLA 123 (5): 1640–48.

Gellar, Sheldon. 2005. *Democracy in Senegal: Tocquevillian Analytics in Africa.* New York: Palgrave Macmillan.

Genova, James E. 2004. *Colonial Ambivalence, Cultural Authenticity, and the Limitations of Mimicry in French-Ruled West Africa, 1914–1956.* New York: Peter Lang.

Gibson, Annie. 2014. "Rediscovering *lo Cubano* Through Capoeira in Cuba." *Postcolonialist* 2 (1): 1–10.

Gikandi, Simon. 2010. "Foreword." In *Hard Work, Hard Times: Global Volatility and African Subjectivities*, edited by Anne-Maria Makhulu, Beth A. Buggenhagen, Stephen Jackson, and Simon Gikandi, xi–xvi. Berkeley: University of California Press.

Gilroy, Paul. 1993. *The Black Atlantic: Modernity and Double Consciousness*. Cambridge, MA: Harvard University Press.

Gordon, Edmund T. 1997. "Anthropology and Liberation." In *Decolonizing Anthropology: Moving Further Toward an Anthropology for Liberation*, 2nd ed., edited by Faye Harrison, 150–69. Arlington, VA: American Anthropological Association.

Graden, Dale T. 1996. "An Act 'Even of Public Security': Slave Resistance, Social Tensions, and the End of the International Slave Trade to Brazil, 1835–1856." *Hispanic American Historical Review* 76 (2): 249–82.

Granada, Daniel. 2020. "Compreender o Brasil através da capoeira: Capoeira, 'raça' e 'nação' no Brasil." In *Cultura, Política e Sociedade: Estudos Sobre a Capoeira na Contemporaneidade*, edited by Celso De Brito and Daniel Granada, 7–21. Teresina, Brazil: Editora da Universidade Federal do Piauí.

Griffith, Lauren Miller. 2016. *In Search of Legitimacy: How Outsiders Become Part of an Afro-Brazilian Tradition*. New York: Berghahn.

Griffith, Lauren Miller. 2020. *Graceful Resistance: How Capoeiristas Use Their Art for Activism and Community Engagement*. Champaign: University of Illinois Press.

Gueye, Marame. 2013. "Urban Guerrilla Poetry: The Movement *Y'en a Marre* and the Socio-Political Influences of Hip Hop in Senegal." *Journal of Pan African Studies* 6 (3): 22–42.

Gueye, Marame. 2021. "Opinion: In Senegal, Women's Bodies Have Become a Political Battleground." *Washington Post*, March 19.

Hall, Stuart. 1990. "Cultural Identity and Diaspora." In *Identity: Community, Culture, Difference*, edited by Jonathan Rutherford, 222–37. London: Lawrence and Wishart.

Hanchard, Michael. 1999a. "Afro-Modernity: Temporality, Politics, and the African Diaspora." *Public Culture* 11 (1): 245–68.

Hanchard, Michael, ed. 1999b. *Racial Politics in Contemporary Brazil*. Durham, NC: Duke University Press.

Hann, Mark, Dominique Chevé, and Cheikh T. Wane. 2021. "'Tying Your Ngemb': Negotiating Identity in Senegalese Wrestling." *Ethnography* 22 (3): 396–410.

Hannaford, Dinah. 2017. *Marriage Without Borders: Transnational Spouses in Neoliberal Senegal*. Philadelphia: University of Pennsylvania Press.

Harney, Elizabeth. 2004. *In Senghor's Shadow: Art, Politics, and the Avant-Garde in Senegal, 1960–1995*. Durham, NC: Duke University Press.

Hartman, Saidiya. 2006. *Lose Your Mother: A Journey Along the Atlantic Slave Route*. New York: Farrar, Straus and Giroux.

Hartman, Saidiya. 2008. "Venus in Two Acts." *Small Axe* 12 (2): 1–14.

Hendrickson, Hildi. 1996. "Introduction." In *Clothing and Difference: Embodied Identities in Colonial and Post-Colonial Africa*, edited by Hildi Hendrickson, 1–16. Durham, NC: Duke University Press.

Hesse, Barnor. 2007. "Racialized Modernity: An Analytics of White Mythologies." *Ethnic and Racial Studies* 30 (4): 643–63.

Heywood, Linda M. 2017. *Njinga of Angola: Africa's Warrior Queen.* Cambridge, MA: Harvard University Press.

Heywood, Linda M., and John K. Thornton. 2007. *Central Africans, Atlantic Creoles, and the Foundation of the Americas, 1585–1660.* Cambridge: Cambridge University Press.

Höfling, Ana Paula. 2019. *Staging Brazil: Choreographies of Capoeira.* Middletown, CT: Wesleyan University Press.

Holsey, Bayo. 2008. *Routes of Remembrance: Refashioning the Slave Trade in Ghana.* Chicago: University of Chicago Press.

Hoyez, Anne-Cécile. 2007. "'The 'World of Yoga': The Production and Reproduction of Therapeutic Landscapes." *Social Science and Medicine* 65:112–24.

Humphrey, Ashley R. 2020. "Take Me Brown Girl! A Study of the Subjugation and Liberation of Black Women in Capoeira Song." PhD diss., University of Pittsburgh.

Hurston, Zora Neale. 2018. *Barracoon: The Story of the Last "Black Cargo."* Edited by Deborah G. Plant. New York: Amistad.

Idowu, E. Bọlaji. 1973. *African Traditional Religion: A Definition.* Ossining, NY: Orbis.

Ivaska, Andrew. 2011. *Cultured States: Youth, Gender, and Modern Style in 1960s Dar es Salaam.* Durham, NC: Duke University Press.

Izzo, Justin. 2019. *Experiments with Empire: Anthropology and Fiction in the French Atlantic.* Durham, NC: Duke University Press.

Jackson, John L., Jr. 2005. *Real Black: Adventures in Racial Sincerity.* Chicago: University of Chicago Press.

Jackson, John L., Jr. 2013. *Thin Description: Ethnography and the African Hebrew Israelites of Jerusalem.* Cambridge, MA: Harvard University Press.

Jaji, Tsitsi Ella. 2014. *Africa in Stereo: Modernism, Music, and Pan-African Solidarity.* Oxford: Oxford University Press.

Johnson, Marian Ashby. 1994. "Gold Jewelry of the Wolof and the Tukulor of Senegal." *African Arts* 27 (1): 36–49, 94–95.

Johnson, Paul Christopher. 2007. *Diaspora Conversions: Black Carib Religion and the Recovery of Africa.* Berkeley: University of California Press.

Jones, Hilary. 2013. *The Métis of Senegal: Urban Life and Politics in French West Africa.* Bloomington: Indiana University Press.

Joseph, Janelle. 2008. "'Going to Brazil': Transnational and Corporeal Movements of a Canadian-Brazilian Martial Arts Community." *Global Networks* 8 (2): 194–213.

Joseph, Janelle. 2012. "The Practice of Capoeira: Diasporic Black Culture in Canada." *Ethnic and Racial Studies* 35 (6): 1078–95.

Kambon, Ọbádélé. 2018. "Afrikan=Black Combat Forms Hidden in Plain Sight: Engolo/Capoeira, Knocking-and-Kicking and Asafo Flag Dancing." *Africology* 12 (4): 327–63.

Kastner, Kristin. 2024. "Born to Shine: Fashionable Practices of Refining and Wearing Textiles in Dakar." In *Fashioning the Afropolis: Histories, Materialities, and Aesthetic Practices*, edited by Kerstin Pinther, Kristin Kastner, and Basile Ndjio, 91–106. New York: Bloomsbury.

Keller, Kathleen. 2018. *Colonial Suspects: Suspicion, Imperial Rule, and Colonial Society in Interwar French West Africa*. Lincoln: University of Nebraska Press.

Kelley, Robin D. G. 2012. *Africa Speaks, America Answers: Modern Jazz in Revolutionary Times*. Cambridge, MA: Harvard University Press.

Khabeer, Su'ad Abdul. 2016. *Muslim Cool: Race, Religion, and Hip Hop in the United States*. New York: NYU Press.

Khabeer, Su'ad Abdul, Yvonne Chireau, and Paul Christopher Johnson. 2014. "Mapping Africana Religions: Transnationalism, Globalization, and Diaspora." *Journal of Africana Religions* 2 (1): 128–39.

Kondo, Dorinne. 2018. *Worldmaking: Race, Performance, and the Work of Creativity*. Durham, NC: Duke University Press.

Kringelbach, Hélène Neveu. 2013. *Dance Circles: Movement, Morality and Self-Fashioning in Urban Senegal*. Oxford: Berghahn.

Kringelbach, Hélène Neveu. 2014. "Choreographic Performance, Generations and the Art of Life in Post-Colonial Dakar." *Africa* 84 (1): 36–54.

Labrune-Badiane, Céline. 2013. "Voyages vers un 'continent imaginaire': Antillais au Sénégal (1960–1970)." *Outre-mers* 100 (378–79): 137–49.

Lambert, Michael C. 2002. *Longing for Exile: Migration and the Making of a Translocal Community in Senegal, West Africa*. Portsmouth, NH: Heinemann.

Lecocq, Baz. 2005. "The Bellah Question: Slave Emancipation, Race, and Social Categories in Late Twentieth-Century Northern Mali." *Canadian Journal of African Studies/Revue Canadienne d'Études Africaines* 39 (1): 42–68.

Lewis, J. Lowell. 1992. *Ring of Liberation: Deceptive Discourse in Brazilian Capoeira*. Chicago: University of Chicago Press.

Lipiäinen, Tatjana. 2015. "Cultural Creolisation and Playfulness: An Example of Capoeira Angola in Russia." *Journal of Intercultural Studies* 36 (6): 676–92.

Livermon, Xavier. 2014. "'Si-Ghetto Fabulous' ('We Are Ghetto Fabulous'): Kwaito Musical Performance and Consumption in Post-Apartheid South Africa." *Black Music Research Journal* 34 (2): 285–303.

Livermon, Xavier. 2020. *Kwaito Bodies: Remastering Space and Subjectivity in Post-Apartheid South Africa*. Durham, NC: Duke University Press.

Lombard, Louisa. 2016. *State of Rebellion: Violence and Intervention in the Central African Republic*. London: Zed.

Lowe, Lisa. 2015. *The Intimacies of Four Continents*. Durham, NC: Duke University Press.

Ly, Aliou. 2014. "Promise and Betrayal: Women Fighters and National Liberation in Guinea Bissau." *Feminist Africa* 19:24–42.

Maciel, Alice, Andrea DiP, and Mariama Correia. 2021. "Capoeiristas from One of Brazil's Biggest Groups Denounce Their Masters for Sexual Crimes." *Agência Pública*, July 1. https://apublica.org/2021/07/capoeiristas-from -one-of-brazils-biggest-groups-denounce-their-masters-for-sexual-crimes.

Maddox, Callie Batts. 2015. "Studying at the Source: Ashtanga Yoga Tourism and the Search for Authenticity in Mysore, India." *Journal of Tourism and Cultural Change* 13 (4): 330–43.

Majumdar, Boria. 2002. "Kolkata Colonized: Soccer in a Subcontinental 'Brazilian Colony.'" *Soccer and Society* 3 (2): 70–86.

Manning, Susan. 2004. *Modern Dance, Negro Dance: Race in Motion*. Minneapolis: University of Minnesota Press.

Marcus, George. 1995. "Ethnography in/of the World System: The Emergence of Multi-Sited Ethnography." *Annual Review of Anthropology* 24 (1): 95–117.

Matlon, Jordanna C. 2022. *A Man Among Other Men: The Crisis of Black Masculinity in Racial Capitalism*. Ithaca, NY: Cornell University Press.

Matory, J. Lorand. 1999. "The English Professors of Brazil: On the Diasporic Roots of the Yoruba Nation." *Comparative Studies in Society and History* 41 (1): 72–103.

Matory, J. Lorand. 2005. *Black Atlantic Religion: Tradition, Transnationalism, and Matriarchy in the Afro-Brazilian Candomblé*. Princeton, NJ: Princeton University Press.

M'Baye, Babacar. 2019. "Afropolitan Sexual and Gender Identities in Colonial Senegal." *Humanities* 8 (166): 1–16.

Mbembe, Achille. 2001. *On the Postcolony*. Berkeley: University of California Press.

McLaughlin, Fiona. 1995. "Haalpulaar Identity as a Response to Wolofization." *African Languages and Cultures* 8 (2): 153–68.

Melly, Caroline. 2017. *Bottleneck: Moving, Building and Belonging in an African City*. Chicago: University of Chicago Press.

Mercier, Paul. 1960. "Political Life in the Urban Centers of Senegal: A Study of a Period of Transition." *Political Research, Organization and Design* 3 (10): 3–20.

Mignolo, Walter D. 2012. *Local Histories / Global Designs: Coloniality, Subaltern Knowledges, and Border Thinking*. Princeton, NJ: Princeton University Press.

Mkhize, Khwezi. 2017. "The Violence of Belonging." *Black Scholar* 47 (2): 22–34.

Monteiro, Nicole M., and Diana J. Wall. 2011. "African Dance as Healing Modality Throughout the Diaspora: The Use of Ritual and Movement to Work Through Trauma." *Journal of Pan African Studies* 4 (6): 234–52.

Morales-Libove, Jessica. 2005. "Dancing a Fine Line: Gender, Sexuality and Morality at Women's *Tours* in Dakar, Senegal." PhD diss., Rutgers University, New Brunswick, NJ.

Mudimbe, V. Y. 1988. *The Invention of Africa: Gnosis, Philosophy, and the Order of Knowledge*. Bloomington: Indiana University Press.

Mueller, Rachel. 2013. "The Spirits Are My Neighbors: Women and the Rab Cult in Dakar, Senegal." Anthropology Honors Projects, Macalester College, Saint Paul, MN. https://digitalcommons.macalester.edu/anth_honors/18.

Ndiaye, A. Raphaël. 1986. *La place de la femme dans les rites au Sénégal.* Dakar: Nouvelles Éditions Africaines.

Ndiaye, Gana. 2020. "Mobility and Cultural Citizenship: The Making of a Senegalese Diaspora in Multiethnic Brazil." In *Migration and Stereotypes in Performance and Culture,* edited by Yana Meerzon, David Dean, and Daniel McNeil, 157–77. Cham, Switzerland: Springer International.

Ndlovu-Gatsheni, Sabelo J. 2013. *Coloniality of Power in Postcolonial Africa: Myths of Decolonization.* Dakar: Council for the Development of Social Science Research in Africa.

Ngom, Fallou. 2003. "The Social Status of Arabic, French, and English in the Senegalese Speech Community." *Language Variation and Change* 15:351–68.

Ngom, Fallou. 2012. "Popular Culture in Senegal: Blending the Secular and the Religious." In *Music, Performance and African Identities,* edited by Toyin Falola and Tyler Fleming, 97–124. New York, NY: Routledge.

Nogueira, Sidnei. 2020. *Intolerância religiosa.* São Paulo: Feminismos Plurais.

Nyamnjoh, Francis. 2006. *Insiders and Outsiders: Citizenship and Xenophobia in Contemporary Southern Africa.* Dakar: Council for the Development of Social Science Research in Africa.

O'Brien, Donal B. Cruise. 1996. "A Lost Generation? Youth Identity and State Decay in West Africa." In *Postcolonial Identities in Africa,* edited by Richard Werbner and Terence Ranger, 55–74. London: Zed.

O'Brien, Donal B. Cruise. 1998. "The Shadow-Politics of Wolofisation." *Journal of Modern African Studies* 36 (1): 25–46.

O'Brien, Rita Cruise. 1972. *White Society in Black Africa: The French of Senegal.* Evanston, IL: Northwestern University Press.

Ochoa, Marcia. 2014. *Queen for a Day: Transformistas, Beauty Queens, and the Performance of Femininity in Venezuela.* Durham, NC: Duke University Press.

Ochonu, Moses E. 2019. "Looking for Race: Pigmented Pasts and Colonial Mentality in 'Non Racial' Africa." In *Relating Worlds of Racism: Dehumanisation, Belonging, and the Normativity of European Whiteness,* edited by Philomena Essed, Karen Farquharson, Kathryn Pillay, and Elisa Joy White, 3–37. Cham, Switzerland: Palgrave Macmillan.

Ogunnaike, Oludamini. 2013. "Performing Realization: The Sufi Music Videos of the Taalibe Baye of Dakar." *African Arts* 51 (3): 26–39.

Ogunnaike, Oludamini. 2020. *Deep Knowledge: Ways of Knowing in Sufism and Ifa, Two West African Intellectual Traditions.* University Park: Penn State University Press.

Oliveira, Josivaldo Pires de, and Luiz Augusto Pinheiro Leal. 2009. *Capoeira, identidade e gênero: Ensaios sobre a história social da capoeira no Brasil.* Bahia, Brazil: Editora da Universidade Federal da Bahia.

Osemeka, Irene N. 2011. "The Public Sphere, Women and the Casamance Peace Process." *Historia Actual Online* 9 (25): 57–65.

Parla, Ayşe. 2019. *Precarious Hope: Migration and the Limits of Belonging in Turkey.* Stanford, CA: Stanford University Press.

Peano, Irene. 2007. "Wrestling Masculinities: Metaphors of Purity and Met-
onymical Bodies in Senegalese Arenas." *Cambridge Journal of Anthropology* 27 (2): 36–56.

Petrocelli, Rachel M. 2024. *Transactional Culture in Colonial Dakar: 1902–44.*
Rochester, NY: University of Rochester Press.

Pierre, Jemima. 2004. "Black Immigrants in the United States and the 'Cultural
Narratives' of Ethnicity." *Identities* 11 (2): 141–70.

Pierre, Jemima. 2008. "'I Like Your Colour!' Skin Bleaching and Geographies of
Race in Urban Ghana." *Feminist Review* 90:9–29.

Pierre, Jemima. 2012. *The Predicament of Blackness: Postcolonial Ghana and the
Politics of Race.* Chicago: University of Chicago Press.

Pierre, Jemima. 2020. "Slavery, Anthropological Knowledge, and the Racialization of Africans." *Current Anthropology* 61 (S22): S220–31.

Piot, Charles. 2010. *Nostalgia for the Future: West Africa After the Cold War.*
Chicago: University of Chicago Press.

Pires, Antônio Liberac Cardoso Simões. 2017. "'Around the World' with Women of
Capoeira: Gender and Black Culture in Brazil, 1850–1920." In *Black Women
of Brazil in Slavery and Post-Emancipation*, edited by Giovana Xavier, Flávio
Gomes, and Juliana Barreto Farias. Brooklyn, NY: Diasporic Africa.

Quashie, Hélène. 2015. "La 'blanchité' au miroir de l'africanité: Migrations et
constructions sociales urbaines d'une assignation identitaire peu explorée
(Dakar)." *Cahiers d'Études Africaines* 4 (220): 761–86.

Quayson, Ato. 2014. *Oxford Street, Accra: City Life and the Itineraries of Transnationalism.* Durham, NC: Duke University Press.

Quijano, Aníbal. 2007. "Coloniality and Modernity/Rationality." *Cultural Studies* 21 (2–3): 168–78.

Rahman, Samiha. 2021. "Black Muslim Brilliance: Confronting Antiblackness
and Islamophobia Through Transnational Education Migration." *Curricu-
lum Inquiry* 51 (1): 57–74.

Rarey, Matthew. 2023. *Insignificant Things: Amulets and the Art of Survival in the
Early Black Atlantic.* Durham, NC: Duke University Press.

Ray, Carina. 2015. *Crossing the Color Line: Race, Sex, and the Contested Politics of
Colonialism in Ghana.* Athens: Ohio University Press.

Redmond, Shana L. 2014. *Anthem: Social Movements and the Sound of Solidarity
in the African Diaspora.* New York: New York University Press.

Reis, Letícia Vidor de Sousa. 1997. *O mundo de pernas para o ar: A capoeira no
Brasil.* São Paulo: Publisher Brasil.

Repinecz, Jonathon. 2020. "Senegalese Wrestling Between Nostalgia and Neoliberalism." *African Studies Review* 63 (4): 906–26.

Robitaille, Laurence. 2007. "Les jeux de la capoeira avec l'identité brésilienne."
Revue Canadienne des Études Latino-Américaines et Caraïbes 32 (63): 213–35.

Robitaille, Laurence. 2014. "Promoting Capoeira, Branding Brazil: A Focus on
the Semantic Body." *Black Music Research Journal* 34 (2): 229–54.

Roland, L. Kaifa. 2011. *Cuban Color in Tourism and La Lucha: An Ethnography of
Racial Meanings.* Oxford: Oxford University Press.

Rosa, Cristina. 2012. "Playing, Fighting, and Dancing: Unpacking the Significance of *Ginga* Within the Practice of Capoeira Angola." *TDR: The Drama
Review* 56 (3): 141–66.

Rosa, Cristina. 2015. *Brazilian Bodies and Their Choreographies of Identification:
Swing Nation*. New York: Palgrave Macmillan.

Rosa, Jonathan, and Vanessa Díaz. 2019. "Raciontologies: Rethinking Anthropological Accounts of Institutional Racism and Enactments of White
Supremacy in the United States." *American Anthropologist* 122 (1):
120–32.

Rosenthal, Joshua M. 2007. "Recent Scholarly and Popular Works on Capoeira."
Latin American Research Review 42 (2): 262–72.

Rosenthal, Joshua M. 2009. "Capoeira and Globalization." In *Imagining Global-
ization: Language, Identities, and Boundaries*, edited by Ho Hon Leung,
Matthew Hendley, Robert W. Compton, and Brian D. Haley, 145–63. New
York: Palgrave Macmillan.

Samson, Fabienne. 2016. "L'implantation de l'Église Universelle du Royaume de
Dieu au Sénégal." In *Néo-pentecôtismes*, edited by Jesús García Ruiz and
Patrick Michel, 11–24. Paris: Centre Maurice Halbwachs.

Sarr, Felwine. 2020. *Afrotopia*. Minneapolis: University of Minnesota Press.

Savishinsky, Neil J. 1994. "Rastafari in the Promised Land: The Spread of a
Jamaican Socioreligious Movement Among the Youth of West Africa."
African Studies Review 37 (3): 19–50.

Sawyer, Lena. 2006. "Racialization, Gender, and the Negotiation of Power in Stock-
holm's African Dance Courses." In *Globalization and Race: Transformations
in the Cultural Production of Blackness*, edited by Kamari Maxine Clarke and
Deborah A. Thomas, 316–34. Durham, NC: Duke University Press.

Scott, David. 1991. "That Event, This Memory: Notes on the Anthropology of
African Diasporas in the New World." *Diaspora* 1 (3): 261–84.

Scott, David. 2004. *Conscripts of Modernity: The Tragedy of Colonial Enlightenment*. Durham, NC: Duke University Press.

Seck, Ibrahima. 2014. *Bouki Fait Gombo: A History of the Slave Community of
Habitation Haydel (Whitney Plantation) Louisiana, 1750–1860*. New Orleans: University of New Orleans Press.

Semley, Lorelle. 2017. *To Be Free and French: Citizenship in France's Atlantic
Empire*. Cambridge: Cambridge University Press.

Shain, Richard M. 2018. *Roots in Reverse: Senegalese Afro-Cuban Music and Tropical Cosmopolitanism*. Middletown, CT: Wesleyan University Press.

Shange, Savannah. 2019. *Progressive Dystopia: Abolition, Antiblackness, and
Schooling in San Francisco*. Durham, NC: Duke University Press.

Shankar, Shalini. 2019. "Nothing Sells like Whiteness: Race, Ontology, and
American Advertising." *American Anthropologist* 122 (1): 112–19.

Sharpe, Christina. 2016. *In the Wake: On Blackness and Being*. Durham, NC:
Duke University Press.

Shaw, Rosalind. 1990. "The Invention of 'African Traditional Religion.'" *Religion*
20 (4): 339–53.

Simpson, Audra. 2014. *Mohawk Interruptus: Political Life Across the Borders of Settler States*. Durham, NC: Duke University Press.

Smith, Christen A. 2016a. *Afro-Paradise: Blackness, Violence, and Performance in Brazil*. Urbana: University of Illinois Press.

Smith, Christen A. 2016b. "Towards a Black Feminist Model of Black Atlantic Liberation: Remembering Beatriz Nascimento." *Meridians* 14 (2): 71–87.

Soares, Carlos Eugênio Líbano. 2001. *A capoeira escrava e outras tradições rebeldes no Rio de Janeiro (1808–1850)*. Campinas, Brazil: Editora Unicamp.

Stevenson, Lisa. 2014. *Life Beside Itself: Imagining Care in the Canadian Arctic*. Oakland: University of California Press.

Stewart, Kathleen. 2007. *Ordinary Affects*. Durham, NC: Duke University Press.

Strongman, Roberto. 2019. *Queering Black Atlantic Religions: Transcorporeality in Candomblé, Santería, and Vodou*. Durham, NC: Duke University Press.

Swanson, Amy. 2019. "Ambiguous Masculinities: Gender and Sexual Transgression in Contemporary Dance Works by Senegalese Men." *Dance Research Journal* 51 (3): 47–65.

Sweet, James H. 2004. *Recreating Africa: Culture, Kinship, and Religion in the African-Portuguese World, 1441–1770*. Chapel Hill: University of North Carolina Press.

Sweet, James H. 2011. *Domingos Álvares, African Healing, and the Intellectual History of the Atlantic World*. Chapel Hill: University of North Carolina Press.

Sylla, Assane. (1978) 1994. *La Philosophie morale des Wolof*. Dakar: IFAN.

Táíwò, Olúfẹ́mi O. 2022. *Reconsidering Reparations*. Oxford: Oxford University Press.

Talmon-Chvaicer, Maya. 2008. *The Hidden History of Capoeira: A Collision of Cultures in the Brazilian Battle Dance*. Austin: University of Texas Press.

Tandia, Aboubakr. 2013. "When Civil Wars Hibernate in Borderlands: The Challenges of the Casamance's 'Forgotten Civil War' to Cross-Border Peace and Security." In *Violence on the Margins: States, Conflict, and Borderlands*, edited by Benedikt Korf and Timothy Raeymaekers, 219–46. New York: Palgrave Macmillan.

Taylor, Diana. 2003. *Archive and Repertoire: Performing Cultural Memory in the Americas*. Durham, NC: Duke University Press.

Taylor, Gerard. 2005. *Capoeira: The Jogo de Angola from Luanda to Cyberspace, Volume 1*. Berkeley: North Atlantic.

Thioub, Ibrahima, Momar-Coumba Diop, and Catherine Boone. 1998. "Economic Liberalization in Senegal: Shifting Politics of Indigenous Business Interests." *African Studies Review* 41 (2): 63–89.

Thomas, Deborah A. 2011. *Exceptional Violence: Embodied Citizenship in Transnational Jamaica*. Durham, NC: Duke University Press.

Thomas, Deborah A. 2016. "Time and the Otherwise: Plantations, Garrisons and Being Human in the Caribbean." *Anthropological Theory* 16 (2–3): 177–200.

Thomas, Deborah A., and Tina Campt. 2008. "Gendering Diaspora: Transnational Feminism, Diaspora and Its Hegemonies." *Feminist Review* 90:1–8.

Thomas, Deborah A., and Kamari Clarke, eds. 2006. *Globalization and Race: Transformations in the Cultural Production of Blackness.* Durham, NC: Duke University Press.

Thomas, Deborah A., and M. Kamari Clarke. 2013. "Globalization and Race: Structures of Inequality, New Sovereignties, and Citizenship in a Neoliberal Era." *Annual Review of Anthropology* 42:305–25.

Thomas-Johnson, Amandla. 2021. "Senegal: Anti-French Sentiment on the Rise as Protests Continue." *Al Jazeera*, March 12. https://www.aljazeera.com/news/2021/3/12/senegal-anti-french-sentiments-on-the-rise-amid-ongoing-protests.

Ticktin, Miriam I. 2011. *Casualties of Care: Immigration and the Politics of Humanitarianism in France.* Berkeley: University of California Press.

Tillet, Salamishah. 2009. "In the Shadow of the Castle: (Trans)Nationalism, African American Tourism, and Gorée Island." *Research in African Literatures* 40 (4): 122–41.

Trouillot, Michel-Rolph. 1995. *Silencing the Past: Power and the Production of History.* Boston: Beacon.

Trouillot, Michel-Rolph. 2003. *Global Transformations: Anthropology and the Modern World.* New York: Palgrave Macmillan.

Turner, Victor. 1988. *The Anthropology of Performance.* New York: PAJ Publications.

Valente-Quinn, Brian. 2021. *Senegalese Stagecraft: Decolonizing Theater-Making in Francophone Africa.* Evanston: Northwestern University Press.

Varela, Sergio González. 2017. *Power in Practice: The Pragmatic Anthropology of Afro-Brazilian Capoeira.* New York: Berghahn.

Vieira, Luiz Renato. 1995. *O jogo da capoeira: Corpo e cultura popular no Brasil.* Rio de Janeiro: Sprint.

Vieyra, Paulin Soumanou, dir. 1981. *Birago Diop, Conteur.* Documentary. Les Films PSV—Présence Africaine. 21 mins.

Villalón, Leonardo A. 1995. *Islamic Society and State Power in Senegal: Disciples and Citizens in Fatick.* Cambridge: Cambridge University Press.

Viotti da Costa, Emilia. 1985. *The Brazilian Empire: Myths and Histories.* Chicago: University of Chicago Press.

Wade, Peter. 2004. "Images of Latin American *Mestizaje* and the Politics of Comparison." *Bulletin of Latin American Research* 23 (3): 355–66.

Wainaina, Binyavanga. 2012. *One Day I Will Write About This Place.* Minneapolis: Graywolf.

Ware, Rudolph T. 2014. *The Walking Qur'an: Islamic Education, Embodied Knowledge, and History in West Africa.* Chapel Hill: University of North Carolina Press.

Weitzberg, Keren. 2017. *We Do Not Have Borders: Greater Somalia and the Predicaments of Belonging in Kenya.* Athens: Ohio University Press.

Werner, Jean-François. 2006. "How Women Are Using Television to Domesti-
    cate Globalization: A Case Study on the Reception and Consumption of
    Telenovelas in Senegal." *Visual Anthropology* 19:443–72.

Wesolowski, Katya. 2007. "Hard Play: Capoeira and the Politics of Inequality in
    Rio de Janeiro." PhD diss., Columbia University, New York.

Wesolowski, Katya. 2020. "Imagining Brazil in Africa: Capoeira's Transatlantic
    Roots and Routes." *Journal of Latin American and Caribbean Anthropol-
    ogy* 25 (3): 453–72.

Wetherell, James. 1860. *Brazil: Stray Notes from Bahia; Being Extracts from Let-
    ters, &c., During a Residence of Fifteen Years. By the Late James Wetherell*,
    edited by William Hadfield. Liverpool, UK: Webb and Hunt.

Wilder, Gary. 2005. *The French Imperial Nation-State: Negritude and Colonial
    Humanism Between the Two World Wars*. Chicago: University of Chicago
    Press.

Williams, Bianca. 2018. *The Pursuit of Happiness: Black Women, Diasporic
    Dreams, and the Politics of Emotional Transnationalism*. Durham, NC:
    Duke University Press.

Williams, Erica. 2013. *Sex Tourism in Bahia: Ambiguous Entanglements*. Cham-
    paign: University of Illinois Press.

Wright, Handel Kashope. 2016. "Stuart Hall's Relevance for the Study of African
    Blackness." *International Journal of Cultural Studies* 19 (1): 85–99.

Wright, Michelle M. 2015. *Physics of Blackness: Beyond the Middle Passage Episte-
    mology*. Minneapolis: University of Minnesota Press.

Wynter, Sylvia. 2003. "Unsettling the Coloniality of Being/Power/Truth/
    Freedom: Towards the Human, After Man, Its Overrepresentation—An
    Argument." CR: *New Centennial Review* 3 (3): 257–337.

Yamba, C. Bawa. 1990. *Permanent Pilgrims: The Role of Pilgrimage in the Lives of
    West African Muslims in Sudan*. Washington, DC: Smithsonian Institution
    Press.

Zeleza, Paul Tiyambe. 2005. "Rewriting the African Diaspora: Beyond the Black
    Atlantic." *African Affairs* 104 (414): 35–68.

Zempleni, A. 1969. "La therapie traditionnelle des troubles mentaux chez les
    Wolof et les Lebous (Senegal): Principes." *Social Science and Medicine* 3
    (2): 191–205.

INDEX

Note: Page numbers in italics indicate illustrations.

spiritual aspects of, 147–48, 159. *See also* diasporic chauvinism

Coly, Ayo, 59, 61, 159, 222

commodification of culture, 192

compartmentalization, 153, 164, 168, 178

coosaan, 61

cordas, 122, 133–39, 142, 235n3

corpo fechado, 167, 179

corval, 164

Cotonou, Benin, 8, 232n4

Coumba (capoeirista), 65

Covington-Ward, Yolanda, 52, 237n1

creolization paradigm, 16, 60, 233n9

critical race studies, 17

Crowder, Michael, 113–14

Cuban capoeira, 17, 233nn13–14

Dakar, Senegal: coloniality and, 9–10; Gorée Island, 1–3, 39, 41, 89, 129; House of Slaves, 2–3, 52–53, 214; Ouakam neighborhood, 53; as Paris of Africa, 110; populous neighborhoods, 102; postcolonial, 6; significance of, 7; UCAD in, 51, 235n2; World Festival of Negro Arts in, xi. *See also* Senegal; West African regionalism

dancing, xi, 59, 60–61, 62, 64

Daniel Sorano Theater, 35

Dard, Jean, 78

democracy, 94, 237n13

de Sá, Celina, 137

de Sá, Ronaldo, xii, xiii, *xiv*

Desai, Gaurav, 129

Desch-Obi, T. J., 13, 167, 233n9

Dettmar, Kevin, 129

diaspora: Chrisman on, 106; Clifford on, 35; definition of, 41, 187, 233n11; diasporic misrecognition, 62; enslavement and, 40–41; inclusive, 205–6; Livermon and, 15; regionalism and, 218; rethinking, 192; scholarship on, 19; in West African networks, 185–86

diaspora without displacement: concept of, 10; defending, 102–5; female capoeiristas and, 11–12; forgetting in relation to, 179; gender and, 54; nature of, 18–19, 218; performed, 88; roots tours in relation to, 187

diasporic chauvinism: Boa Vida and, 88, 90; capoeira tourism and, 183, 191; concept of, 20–23; definition of, 187; diasporic hegemonies in relation to, 234n18; expertise and, 201–3; nature of, 234n17; pilgrimage

as, 187; white privilege and, 186. *See also* coloniality of Black performance

diasporic return: of capoeira, 5, 14; commodification of, 192; complexities of, 200–201; of hip hop, 155–58; nature of, xi–xii; reshaping, 18–20; roots tours and, 187; white people and, 81. *See also* pilgrimage, roots tourism

Diawara, Manthia, 105

Didier (capoeirista), 126–27

Dieudonné (capoeirista), 126, 141, 146

Diola group, 112, 150, 237n1, 238n4

Diop, Birago, 77

Dior, Lat, 6

Diouf, Mamadou, 150, 166, 168, 174

Doffu Maam Bamba Yi, 155–56, 157

Dof Ndeye, 157

Door of Return, 44–45

Downey, Greg, 134

dund tubaab, 61

Dutch capoeirista, 204

Edwards, Brent Hayes, 19, 209

Eid al-Adha, 145

Ekotto, Frieda, 194

Elena (capoeirista), 1, 60, 65–67, 71, 89, 142

encontro, 24, 53

Enock (capoeirista), 25–26

eroticism, 59

ethnography, 14–15, 199, 220

évolués, 240n1

exile, 4, 18

experts and expertise: diasporic chauvinism and, 21–22, 187, 201–3; inclusive diaspora and, 205–6; pilgrimage and, 190–91; proximity to, 215; white, 92–93, 203–8

Falcão, Ricardo, 153

Fang people, 24, 235n19

Fassassi, Mamadou, 25, 47–48

Faye, Ousseynou, 111

fecc, 59, 60–61

Feld, Steven, 21

female capoeiristas. *See* women

femininity, 57, 58

feminist politics, 67–68

Ferelaha (capoeirista), 97, 98–99

FESMAN. *See* First World Festival of Negro Arts

FESTAC (World Black and African Festival of Arts and Culture), xi

fetishism, 150

First World Festival of Negro Arts
(FESMAN), xi, 5, 35–36, 38, 39, 82, *83*
Floyd, George, 115
foreign nationals, 95–98
forgetting, 146, 147, 149, 179
Four Communes, 110, 112
français mbër, 106–7
Franco/Luso capoeiristas, 119
freedom, 16, 26, 72–73, 147, 148, 170–71
French capoeiristas, 190–91, 206–7
French language, 106–7

Gable, Eric, 121
Gabrielle (capoeirista), 2, 89
Gambia, the. *See* Capoeira Association of
  the Gambia
Garuba, Harry, 171
Gavião (capoeirista), 1
gender: ambiguity and, 54, 62; Black
  performance and, 93; Capoeira girls and
  guys, 57–58, 60; coloniality and, 56–57,
  61–63, 64; diaspora without displacement
  and, 54; passive sexism, 65; perceptions
  of, 59–63; performing, 45; racial self-
  making and, 54–55. *See also* masculinity;
  women
Gery (capoeirista), 64, 73
Ghana, 81
Ghanaba, 21
Gibson, Annie, 233n13
Gikandi, Simon, 218
ginga, 56, 57
global capoeira, 15–18, 35–36, 41, 44, 48–49,
  71–76. *See also* Brazilian capoeira; West
  African capoeira
Global South alliances, 188
goor-jigeen, 62
Gorée Island, 1–3, 39, 41, 53, *89*, 129
Granada, Daniel, 55
Griffith, Lauren, 92, 190
gris-gris, 162, 163, 164, 167, 176, 238n1. See
  also *bolsas de mandinga*
Gueye, Mareme, 156, 157
Guinea-Bissau: braiders, 137, 140; crafts-
  people, 119–20; Dieudonné and, 126;
  Guinea-Conakry capoeira, 44; Manjaco
  textile expertise, 135–39; Marianne and,
  133; migration from, 124; *reality* in, 121–22

Hall, Stuart, 209
Hannaford, Dinah, 111

haram, 159, 160
Hartman, Saidiya, 198
hauntologies, 79
heritage: belonging in relation to, 120–21;
  commodification of, 192; misrecognitions of, 127, 132; objects in relation to,
  141–42; objects linked to, 118; reclaiming,
  129; religion and spirituality, 146; searching for, 119, 121–22, 141; significance of,
  142–44
Heywood, Linda, 57
hip hop, 58–59, 115, 154–58
history and symbolism, 65–68
Höfling, Ana Paula, 160, 236n3
homophobia, 64
homosexuality, 62, 63, 64
House of Slaves, 2–3, 52–53, 214
Humphrey, Ashley, 57, 99

Ibrahim (capoeirista), xiii, 221, 222
Iemanja, 69, 161
improvisation, 24, 26–27
indigenous spiritual practices: ambiguity
  and, 174; Diouf on, 168; Islam and, 158;
  ndëpp, 172–73, 175–77, 178; stigmatization of, 147–48; *Vodun*, 150, 173. *See also*
  religion and spirituality
innovation, 23
International Day for the Abolition of
  Slavery, 182–83, 193
International Organization for Migration
  (IOM), 70
Islam: African, 152; bodily performance and,
  79; in Brazil, 165; in capoeira, 167; coloniality and, 167–68; Eid al-Adha, 145; historical aspects of, 149; *Islam noir*, 158–59;
  Islamophobia, 61; Maggal pilgrimage, 181;
  Mâle Revolt, 166; moderate, 93–94; "Mahommedans," 165; Muridiyya, 127, 231n2;
  in Senegal, 81; Sufi brotherhoods and, 147.
  See also Muslim capoeiristas; Muslims;
  religion and spirituality
Ivory Coast, 49, 50, 110, 231n4, 237n9

Jacqueline (capoeirista), 175–77, 178
Jammeh, Yahya, 239n2
Jeune Afrique, 63, 235n5
Jones, Hilary, 238n1
Josselin (capoeirista), 74, 188–89, 194,
  200, 207
Juruna, Mestre, 78–79, 88

Morales-Libove, Jessica, 178
morengue, 25
Murid disciples, 127
Muridiyya, 231n2
music: berimbaus, 24–25, 69, 117, 119, 127,
    130–31, 214, 235n19; hip hop, 58–59, 115,
    155–58; Lamine and, 150–51; materiality
    of, 126–32, 134; on pilgrimage, 210–11;
    reggae, 235n4. *See also* songs and singing
Muslim capoeiristas: anxieties of, 148,
    152, 179; Apollo, 171–72, 173; Blackness
    and, 30; coloniality in relation to, 147;
    gender and, 62, 63; Islamicizing capoeira,
    170–71; Lamine, 145–46, 150–51; Muslim
    audiences, 79; significance of, 147. *See also*
    religion and spirituality
Muslims: Baye Fall, 127, 155, 156, 163; Maggal
    pilgrimage, 181; *mandingas* and, 163;
    Muslim audiences, 79; socioreligious
    movements, 168. *See also* Islam; religion
    and spirituality; Wolof people
mvet, 24, 235n19

Nagôcentrismo, 179, 233n10
ñak, 86, 97, 100, 112–13, 236n7, 237n12
Nasser (capoeirista), 24
National Association of Martial Arts of
    Senegal (L'anams), 33–35
ndëpp, 172–73, 175–77, 178
Ndiaye, Moctar. *See* Moctar (Contra Mestre)
neocolonialism, 74
Neo-Pentecostal movements, 175
New Yorker, 110
Nukunu, 8, 48

objects, everyday: belts, 133–39; capoeira
    music and, 126–32; heritage linked to, 118;
    instruments, 127; religious aspects of, 168;
    repurposing, 120, 121–22; significance of,
    142–44
O'Brien, Donald Cruise, 6, 238n2
O'Brien, Rita Cruise, 107–8
Ochonu, Moses, 99–100
Ogun Eru, 8, 47, 48, 232n4
Oliveira, Josivaldo Pires de, 161
Only the Strong, 6, 34, 38, 47
orixá, 161
Osemeka, Irene, 94
Oulimata (capoeirista), 11–12, 63
Ousmane (capoeirista), 90, 108
Owlavé Capoeira, 231n4

Palmarin festival, 69
Pan-Africanism, 35
Pangool, 174
Parana ué, 3
Paranauê, 60
Parisian Africa, 110
Pastinha, Vicente Ferreira. *See* Mestre
    Pastinha
patriarchy, 61
patua. See *bolsas de mandinga*
Peano, Irene, 59, 93
Pereira, Carmen, 125
Pierre, Jemima, 81, 106, 107
pilgrimage, roots tourism: African Ameri-
    can, 194–95, 200; Capoeira Association
    of the Gambia and, 193–99; coloniality
    of, 22; cultural exchange and, 192, 193,
    200–201; diasporic chauvinism and, 187,
    201–3; as diasporic return, xii; disappoint-
    ment with, 208–9; in Gambia, 193–99; to
    Maggal, 181; nature and purpose of, 184,
    186, 188–89; problem of, 188–92
plantation hauntologies, 85
play, 26–27, 231n1
pluralism, 94
populous neighborhoods, 102
Portuguese empire, 55, 56
Portuguese Inquisition, 168
Portuguese language, 123
postcolonial urban studies, 19
Profesora Amazonas, 20
Propheta (capoeirista), xiii, xiv
Pulaar people, 44

quartiers populaire, 102
Quashie, Hélène, 108
queda de rins, 34, 66
Queen Nzinga, 56–57
queer Afropolitanism, 64
queer capoeiristas, 57
queer diaspora, 62
Quilombo do Palmares, 166

rab, 157, 173, 177
race: in Africa, 107; Afrophobia, 99–100;
    and the coloniality of Black performance,
    79–82; critical race studies, 17; depolit-
    icizing, 106; *racecraft*, 81, 236n2; racial
    binary making, 13; racial democracy, 4;
    racial hierarchies, 8; racialized discourse,
    79–81, 85–86; racial self-making, 41,